Dear
What
What a journey!
Thanks for being my cousin!
God Bless You,

Todd

Psalm 91

A *Boy* FROM WOLLOCHET

N. TODD RIGGS

WESTBOW
PRESS®
A DIVISION OF THOMAS NELSON
& ZONDERVAN

Copyright © 2017 N. Todd Riggs.

All rights reserved. No part of this book may be used or reproduced by any means, graphic, electronic, or mechanical, including photocopying, recording, taping or by any information storage retrieval system without the written permission of the author except in the case of brief quotations embodied in critical articles and reviews.

This book is a work of non-fiction. Unless otherwise noted, the author and the publisher make no explicit guarantees as to the accuracy of the information contained in this book and in some cases, names of people and places have been altered to protect their privacy.

WestBow Press books may be ordered through booksellers or by contacting:

WestBow Press
A Division of Thomas Nelson & Zondervan
1663 Liberty Drive
Bloomington, IN 47403
www.westbowpress.com
1 (866) 928-1240

Because of the dynamic nature of the Internet, any web addresses or links contained in this book may have changed since publication and may no longer be valid. The views expressed in this work are solely those of the author and do not necessarily reflect the views of the publisher, and the publisher hereby disclaims any responsibility for them.

Any people depicted in stock imagery provided by Thinkstock are models, and such images are being used for illustrative purposes only. Certain stock imagery © Thinkstock.

Unless otherwise indicated, all scripture quotations are from *The Holy Bible, English Standard Version (ESV)*. Copyright 2001 by Crossway Bibles, a division of Good News Publishers. Used by permission. All rights reserved.

Scripture quotations marked NASB are taken from the *New American Standard Bible*, Copyright 1960, 1962, 1963, 1968, 1971, 1972, 1973, 1975, 1977, 1995 by The Lockman Foundation. Used by permission.

Scripture quotations marked TLB are taken from *The Living Bible* copyright 1971. Used by permission of Tyndale House Publishers, Inc., Carol Stream, Illinois 60188. All rights reserved.

Scripture quotations marked NIV are taken from the *Holy Bible, New International Version. NIV.* Copyright 1973, 1978, 1984 by International Bible Society. Used by permission of Zondervan. All rights reserved.

ISBN: 978-1-5127-7909-7 (sc)
ISBN: 978-1-5127-7910-3 (hc)
ISBN: 978-1-5127-7908-0 (e)

Library of Congress Control Number: 2017904157

Print information available on the last page.

WestBow Press rev. date: 03/30/2017

"Todd's honesty, openness and transparency offer a glimpse into the formation of a young boy into the man he is today. His descriptive story-telling style, inspiring quotes and song lyrics, portray God's unending love, faithfulness, grace, mercy, provision, protection, and pursuit of a love-relationship characteristic of our Heavenly Father's heart for each one of us. Todd provides us with some deeply profound and insightful spiritual lessons which are applicable to each of our lives. My friendship with Todd spans over three decades—several of our common experiences are chronicled in this account, and the story continues, inspiring me to follow the words of the Apostle Paul in I Corinthians 13:13, '...Trust steadily in God, hope unswervingly, love extravagantly. And the best of these is love' (The Message)."

Dr. Kevin R. Hoffman, DMin., LICSW (retired), LCDC-II, ICADC
Certified Pastoral Counselor & Fellow (AAPC)

President
Three Oaks Center, Inc.
Centerville, OH

Pastoral Care Ministry
Vineyard Church, Beavercreek, OH

"Wow, a powerful, riveting, soul searching read. I very much enjoyed reading it."

Spencer Johnson, M.D.
Medical Care Services
New Brighton, MN 55112

"Tender, transparent, vulnerable and uplifting.

In his powerful book, Todd invites us into his personal journey of redemption and restoration.

I have known Todd as a friend and professional colleague for 25+ years. As we worked together as co-therapists for 7 years at Minnesota Psychological Resources, I saw a man whose heart was tender toward the broken in spirit, who longed to lift those weighed down by the heavy burdens of life—with a special tenderness toward the young people he counseled so effectively, as well as those whose childhoods had left them crushed, hopeless, ashamed and feeling powerless.

While I had some glimpses into his life journey in those years, this book has opened my eyes to the way that God has used Todd's own history of brokenness and loneliness, enabling him to be able to enter in such a restorative way into the brokenness and pain of his clients, and to pave the way for them to experience the hope, redemption and restoration that he, himself found through the power of the Holy Spirit.

A story of hope and healing. Broken things made new. A wonderful read!"

Mary L Lakner, MA, LP
Licensed Psychologist
Hope Counseling and Education
Wyoming, MN 55092

In *A Boy from Wollochet* Todd provides a genuine candid look at his life through his own eyes. He brings into focus the world in which he grew up, his life within his family of origin, the transformation into his life of faith, and his eventual emergence as a husband and a Christian Clinical Social Worker. Drawing from his personal experiences Todd details his genesis from insecurity and anxiousness in childhood to an adult life of self-acceptance and peace through faith. This literary collage pieces together in a very eclectic manner a collection of true-life experiences that influenced and shaped Todd's development as he worked to find the significant needs he longed for. Todd personally invites the reader to "follow me as God pursued me and as I pursued Him" and successfully reveals that he has been and continues to be a work in progress and that the potter continues to have his hands on the clay. I have enjoyed knowing Todd since 1993. He is a highly respected mental health professional, and valued colleague & friend. Thank you, Todd, for having the courage to allow us to know you and learn from you and your journey!

David Mellberg, Ph.D., L.P.
Minnesota Psychological Resources
Plymouth, Minnesota

Thank you, Todd, for the courage to share the story of your upbringing on Puget Sound in this most candid narrative. Your descriptive words bring to life childhood adrenaline rushes from snow and water skiing, contrasted with the relative serenity of salmon fishing, as you portray significant experiences and relationships that influenced you. Your writing also offers a painful chronology of how a seemingly charmed life filled with epic outdoor experiences and well-known social partying parents did not spare you from painful emotional symptoms, such as inner emptiness and anger, and other challenges and problems. The enormous impact of your mother is so evident, and how your heart was being prepared for inviting God to enter in and change the course you were on. Your memoir is ultimately a powerful testament of personal recovery and redemption by an attentive loving God, that periodically revealed His presence along the way.

Dr. Dave Olson, Licensed Psychologist
New Day Counseling Clinic
Edina, MN

"Please allow yourself time as you read Todd Riggs' life story. The painfully honest story of his life is both entertaining and healing. As the mountains he hiked were high, the valleys he walked were deep. Frequent water skiing on Wollochet Bay near Seattle, hiking and snow skiing on Mount Rainier with his fellow boy scouts brought thrills and popularity with his peers. The beer drinking with his friends learned from his dad brought momentary relief from gnawing emptiness that shadowed his life. His beloved mother's painful death by cancer and rejection by his alcoholic father heightened the emptiness and pain of his life. Though he learned a lot through confirmation in his Lutheran church, it was through a Young Life leader's Bible study that the Lord used to lead him to whisper to Jesus, "Lord I surrender... I've done the church thing...but I want a relationship with you...I ask for your forgiveness of my many sins. My life is yours." That was the beginning of a path that led Todd to his life-long calling of bringing healing to people as a Christian licensed clinical social worker in Minnesota. Thank you, Todd for your real and healing story."

Pastor Don Richman
Founding Director, East European Missions Network (EEMN)

"Someone has said, 'There is nothing we can do to make God love us more. There is nothing we can do to make God love us less.' Todd Riggs' life story tells how he marvelously learned this to be true. He had a privileged childhood, though challenging in numerous ways. As a teenager he was introduced to Jesus and began the adventure of learning that becoming a beloved child of the heavenly Father through Jesus is the greatest privilege of all and the greatest gift ever."

Arlie Rue
Former Dean of Students
Lutheran Bible Institute
Issaquah, Washington

This book is dedicated to my wonderful wife, Cheryl,
and our two adult children, Joshua and Alyssa.

CONTENTS

Map of the Pacific Northwest xv
Acknowledgments xvii
Introduction xix

Chapter 1	The Early Years	1
Chapter 2	Alpental	13
Chapter 3	My Introduction to Wollochet Bay	22
Chapter 4	Peninsula High School	44
Chapter 5	Early Memories Living on the Bay	68
Chapter 6	Camp Hahobas	91
Chapter 7	The Storm Clouds Gather	111
Chapter 8	My Journal	124
Chapter 9	O Death, Where Is Your Sting?	139
Chapter 10	Leaving Home	152
Chapter 11	The Summer at Alpental	168
Chapter 12	A New Beginning	175
Chapter 13	Another Visit from an Old Adversary	195
Chapter 14	The Tales of Generations Gone By	212
Chapter 15	Comfort Zones	220
Chapter 16	The Royal Law of Love	232
Chapter 17	The Things That I've Learned	244

Epilogue 255
Notes 257

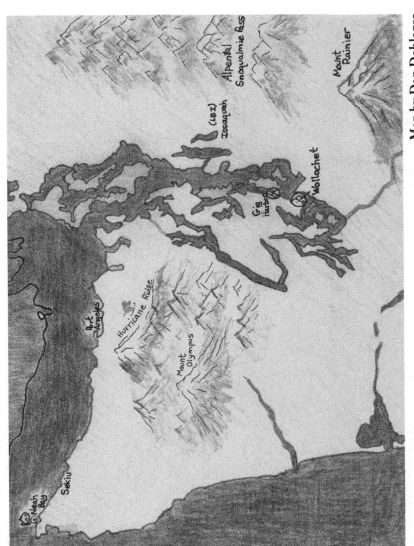

Map by Dan Dahlager

ACKNOWLEDGMENTS

Thank you to everyone who encouraged me to write out my faith journey and gave me the courage to put it on paper. It's been an incredible journey.

To my childhood friends Eric, Dave, Bret, and Mike. Thanks for allowing me to tell our stories of our early years. Our friendships back then helped saved my life.

Thank you, Candace J. Anderson for giving me permission to use your photo of Wollochet Bay on the cover of my book. I am so blessed to have grown up on the bay.

I want to express my gratitude to everyone in our faith missional community known as 'Legacy'. All of you were able to stand with me and pray for me through this project. I am in your debt.

I want to thank everyone in the Minneapolis Band of Brothers, including Steve, Jeff, Nick, Dan, Tim, Greg, Aaron, and Matt who have brought be so much encouragement and support over the years. Thank you for allowing me to be your pastor and friend.

I am so grateful for my personal editors, Sandy Dahlager and Barbara (Babs) North, for working so hard in the editing of the manuscript. The countless hours of your work of reading and editing this manuscript are only known in heaven. Thank you for your ongoing encouragement as you walked me through the editing process. You were so patient with me!

Thank you, Dan Dahlager for drawing the map of the Pacific Northwest. The map provides a compass that helps the reader understand the 'lay of the land' of my story. Thank you for your heart to serve.

I am so grateful for the personal mentors that the Lord has put in my path through the years. Thank you, Larry Wright, Judy Rossiter, Dean Neal, and David Small who served in the ministry of 'Young Life' and for showing me who Jesus is. To Pastor Edward Roe, Pastor Elden Pickering, Don Fladland, Arlie Rue, Bob and Helen Whipple, Hal Pruess, Pastor Bob Johnson, Don Pursel, Pastor Don Richman, and so many others who came alongside me and who spoke into me. Your friendships are priceless to me.

I want to say thank you to all of my friends who lived on Wollochet Bay and grew up with me. It was a special time and a special place. All of you hold a special place in my heart.

To my lovely wife, Cheryl, you are the love of my life. You have been my cheerleader for over 35 years. You have been on the journey with me through thick and thin, through the valleys and the mountain tops. I thank God for you every day. I love you!

INTRODUCTION

Storytelling. I've come to the conclusion that it's an art. Some of us can write and the words flow like a stream. For others, it's a crafted process. For me, I have come to the realization that it's both.

Thank you for joining me on this creative journey. I've wanted to share my story for a long time. You are going to hear about a boy who had an 'extraordinary childhood', so said my father before he passed away in 2000. So why am I doing this? Maybe one reason is to simply derive great pleasure and satisfaction from recalling meaningful events and to celebrate what the Lord has done in my life. I also see it as an opportunity for personal growth, a chance to reflect and seek perspective, greater self-acceptance, and insight into who I am. Additionally, it gives me the opportunity to tell of the influences that have molded and shaped me into the person that I am. Many of those aspects have been intimate and too painful to share.

Yet, I have taught my clients in therapy that identifying and dealing with difficult, and sometimes painful, past events through telling their own stories helps with the ability to practice distress tolerance, emotional regulation, and breaking harmful cycles of behavior in their lives. I don't know what I am ready to share, or even if I'm ready to share. I have had to deal with several battles in my life. Most of them have been private. I have known depression and anxiety since my adolescence. You are about to read a story that describes a relationship between a boy, his past, and his parents. You will read about addiction, loss, and redemption. My story is all about hope and forgiveness.

Six months ago, the Lord started to stir my spirit to put my faith journey on paper. As he began this process, I found that I was getting more and more anxious. The more the promptings came, the more nervous I was. Then the Lord spoke to a woman named Pam, who walks in the prophetic and who is part of our church missional community. One night, the Lord gave her a prophetic word for me. It was what I needed, it was a burden released, and a green light was turned on. She was instructed to share it with me:

> I saw a man up on a high moor. Yes, moor was Papa's word—I had to look up the spelling. You were wearing a long, dark, gray overcoat. The sky was dark and stormy, and it was raining. The moor was high, next to the sea, and the wind was blowing sea spray. You were kneeling down in a fetal position, head tucked into your chest with your hands over your head, hiding from the storm and the elements.
>
> Papa said that this is how you see yourself right now, Todd. You feel exposed and vulnerable, open to the elements. But this feeling, this picture, is not a true picture. I asked Papa, "How do you see him right now then, Papa?" And I saw nothing. Yet, right away the word *hidden* came to my mind. I saw that you saw nothing because you were hidden in his hands.
>
> Next, Papa revealed even more saying that you feel vulnerable and exposed because he is moving you into new places, places you never pictured yourself going. You are having dreams you never thought would be your dreams. But he has dreams for you and is revealing them to you now. He continues disclosing more and saying that you are still in his hands, covered, hidden, safe. He calls you his loving, loyal son. He reminds you that you are not exposed and vulnerable, but you are in a place of discomfort because it is a new place,

a learning place, a deeper place. But he admonishes you to never fear—he has you covered. Stay in that hidden place; do not fight the discomfort or give in to the fear of exposure and vulnerability. He is your sure protection, as always.

So, with that said, thank you for letting me share my story with you and more importantly, thanks for listening. Let me introduce you to a boy who was raised in the Pacific Northwest and had a childhood that was filled with experiences best characterized as extraordinary. This is my story. In the following pages, I will share my childhood memories of living on Puget Sound, specifically Wollochet Bay, with parents who were both professional ice skaters. They skated all over the world and were in relationships with many people who were in show business. My story is about coming of age and encountering God and faith. *A Boy From Wollochet* is my personal story of what happens when a young boy encounters the living God. Through each and every encounter that is penned in these pages, I invite you to follow me as God pursued me and as I pursued him. Looking back through all of the great triumphs and also the deep tragedies, I can say with full assurance that God is faithful and that he is so good. He is a good Father. His love is fierce and is the most powerful force in the universe. My story is really a love affair between a boy and his Lord and what happened when he experienced the miraculous. Let me introduce you to a boy who fell in love with the man named Jesus of Nazareth, after being saved from the clutches of death.

1

THE EARLY YEARS

"Before I formed you in the womb I knew you,
and before you were born I consecrated you;"
                                    (Jeremiah 1:5 ESV)

It was a simple time, as my thoughts are filled with many memories from those many years ago. My parents and I lived on Leona Lane in Lakewood, which was a southern suburb of Tacoma. We didn't live far from my grandmother and my aunt and uncle. My parents were in transition as my mother had recently retired from the ice show, and my father continued to skate. It was a simple time for us. We lived in the house on Leona Lane for almost three years. During that time our next-door neighbors had two boys. The oldest was always getting into trouble. His name was Hurkie. One time my dad chased Hurkie down as the kid rode away on my bike. I think he had stolen my bike from my dad. I don't remember the specific situation, other than this defiant kid got on the bike after being confronted by my dad. The kid took off and started to ride away. My dad, who was in top shape as a professional ice skater, took off and ran after him. It was not long before my dad caught up with him and threw him off the bike. My dad grabbed the kid by the scruff of the neck and marched him back to our next-door neighbor. My dad was very angry and Hurkie knew it. After that little incident, the kid never crossed my dad again. I knew that my dad had a temper. Once when I was having a little temper tantrum out in the back yard, he looked at me and took the outdoor hose and hosed me down with water until I calmed down.

Another incident I looked back on with fear was my dad taking me out on a night-time walk. We were walking on a very dark path behind our house near the end of our property. My dad stopped walking and said to me, "I'll be right back." He left me all alone in the dark, in the woods. I was scared to death. I started to panic as I looked around in the darkness. Minutes went by; they seemed like hours. Moments before the tears came, he returned.

When I was five years old, I was about a block away from my home with my friend, and we were making a fort in the wooded area near my house. We were walking in this thick, wooded area with tall shrubs and trees. We were going to build a wooded fort that was going to be on ground level tucked away, so no one could see us. I innocently stepped into a small hole, and immediately I saw an army of bees swarming everywhere on me—in my hair, in my ears, on my face, on my arms and stinging me. Little did I know that I had stepped into a yellow jackets nest, and I was being attacked by the hive. I ran home screaming and crying, "Mom, Mom, help me." I was crying uncontrollably and trying to run home. The hive followed us to my house doorstep. I was terrified. My mom grabbed me with bees still stinging me and brought me into the bathroom. She pulled off all my clothes, and placed me in the bathtub and started the shower. She then shut the bathroom door so that the bees couldn't get in. She also got stung a couple of times. Then she took a bottle of calamine lotion that was in the bathroom and began to rub my entire body with the lotion. My parents counted more than twenty-eight bee stings over my tiny body. Being attacked by a beehive is just one of many traumatic encounters in my childhood. To this day, I can't be in the same room with a bee without going into a panic.

When I was around four years old, I woke up in the middle of the night when I was aware of a large dark presence in my room. It moved back and forth around me and also over me like a large piece of fabric. I was terrified, and the colors of blue and white on the fabric passed around me when I was in my bed. It was years later when I found out the color of blue represents God, royalty, riches, or service to God and godly living. The color white represents righteousness, wisdom, holiness, or dedication to God.

On the other hand, life was not all traumatic on Leona Lane. My mom and I had a lot of time together. We spent a lot of time in the yard on our swing. I helped her in the kitchen. While she was cleaning the house and doing laundry, I was in the living room with my toys. We had a close bond during my formative years in spite of her working part time at KJR radio station after leaving *Holiday on Ice*.

My sister was born when I was five years old. She was born with a cleft lip which doctors operated on shortly after birth. Immediately, doctors put casts on both of her hands so that she wouldn't pick and poke at her face. I felt so sorry for her, but her room was off-limits to me. When she was out of her room, she still had casts on both of her hands. I can still see her as I looked down into her crib when my mom lifted me up for a better view of my sister. A sadness developed in my heart for her. She cried often because of her pain and discomfort. I had a desire at that early age to take care of my sister. I was going to be her protector.

Periodically, my parents joked with me about an incident which could have started a crime career for me. I heard my mom tell my dad that we needed a loaf of bread. That afternoon, I got on my little blue bike, rode it down to the Lakewood IGA grocery store, went into the store, picked up a loaf of bread, and rode out of the store without stopping to pay for the bread. I got home and my mom didn't know whether to be mad or laugh at my crime. She and I went back directly to the store, and she made me have a little talk with the manager. The store manager had a hard time keeping a smirk off his face when he talked to me about my serious crime. He told me that what I had done was wrong. I guess five-year-olds don't know better.

While living on Leona Lane, I attended school within walking distance from our home. On my first day of kindergarten, my aunt, uncle, and cousins from Minneapolis came out to visit. I had the honor of having my oldest cousin Jamie walk me to school that first day. Even today, Jamie and I talk about that day and how my mother walked with us that morning in 1963. I don't remember any of the conversations, but everyone was excited for me.

That memorable year, Seattle hosted the World's Fair. That was that first time I saw the Seattle Space Needle and the Science Center. My aunt Karen from Indianapolis was visiting us at the time of the fair, so we all drove to downtown Seattle and walked around the Space Needle and the surrounding buildings. To me, everything was so big and the Space Needle was so tall. I stood at the base of the Needle and stared at the top. I was filled with a sense of wonder. I felt very small that day. Still it was an extraordinary experience for a five-year-old.

When I was about four or five years old, my dad was still skating for *Holiday on Ice* and the ice show came to town. I went with him to the huge ice arena in Seattle before the show. That day, my dad and I walked together down the long stairs into the dressing room. He opened the door, and the face of a well-known TV clown greeted me. I looked up into his face, and he looked down at me and said, "Well, hello there, Todd! It's nice to meet you!" I was staring into the face of J. P. Patches, Seattle's most famous children's clown and icon. I was speechless. He had a hat on his head. His red nose and lips, along with his white face was a dead giveaway. He wore a red suit coat and sported a red and white polka-dotted tie. Large pins and buttons covered the entire front of his suit coat. He was larger than life. I remember his kindness to me. I had his full attention, and he was focused on me.[1]

Sitting in the stands that night, I watched my dad and his skating partner, Larry Ham, skate their routine in front of thousands of people in the indoor coliseum in Seattle. My dad and Larry skated around for at least ten minutes. My dad always wore a black sailor's outfit. His partner, Larry, was dressed as a large woman. Their skating was amazing to watch with their flips, arches, and other synchronized maneuvers. The large crowd was laughing hysterically as they were skating together as clowns. I watched both of them throw pies into the faces of those in the crowd. I later realized that they were plants. Then during the intermission, J. P. Patches came out onto the ice. He had no skates on, and this local clown hero of many children did his routine and the crowd went wild. I had two thoughts back then. One, my dad was making all these people laugh and very happy, and I was watching him skate as only an athlete can skate. I was so proud of him. My second thought was that I had just had a personal meeting with J. P. Patches. It was a great night in my young world. Over fifty years later, I am writing about it with a warm heart.

My dad's skating career was, to say the least, awesome. Growing up, I would often ask him about his professional skating days. He would always respond with, "Todd, I got paid a lot of money back then for fifteen minutes of skating on the ice." Both he and his partner Larry had Jaguar automobiles. My dad told me once that between shows they had raced their Jaguars in Montana. They would speed well over 140 miles per hour and then proceed to have Roman-candle fights between each car. They would race each other and the Roman-candle fights were a way to distract each other while driving at high speeds to ensure that one of them would win. I was told that on one occasion, they both flew off the road and ended up in the middle of a cattle pasture. The rancher was in the field when they both drove off the road from the fights with the fireworks. When their Jaguars came to a stop, they both looked up and the rancher looked at both of them, and said, "My, my, those are two fine cats that you both have there." During the time my father skated, he obtained his flying license and his own plane. When working shows in the United States, he would fly from show to show. On international tours, both of my skating parents collected things and later displayed them in our home. These treasures included everything from Peruvian animal furs to a shrunken head from South America. One wall in our home proudly displayed photos of many who skated with them in the different shows. My favorite picture was a black and white photo of two famous skating clowns known around the world as Frick and Frack. Along with collecting many treasures, my dad enjoyed model trains. He had a train set that he and I would set up in my bedroom. We would spend hours and hours setting up the track. My dad then taught me the skills of how to run a train set. I was thrilled that smoke came out of the locomotive. However, the train was extremely finicky. Periodically, electrical issues would pop up, along with the metal trains derailing from time to time. I learned early on that working with electrical trains required an enormous amount of patience. Little did I know that this was a lesson for life. My dad also had an interest in ham radio and photography, which included setting up a dark room in our basement. Whatever he had an interest in, he would pursue. Perhaps he learned this from not having a father figure growing up. He didn't hear the word no very often.

Dad also pursued many occupational opportunities after he left the ice show. He joined ROTC. For a brief time he helped his former skating partner start Larry's Drive In, located on Sixth Avenue in Tacoma. I sometimes sat in one of the booths watching my dad and Larry cook. My father eventually worked in Tacoma at IBM as a computer programmer, and I often went to work with him when he went into the office on the weekends. There, I visited the computer room with the large reel to reel tapes going back and forth feeding the monster computers.

When I was in the first grade, our family moved from Leona Lane to Hilltop Lane, still in Lakewood, but now only about a 300-yard walk from our small, cape cod house to Gravelly Lake. Shortly after we moved, my dad bought a small, fourteen-foot, red, runabout, ski boat with a 35-horse Evinrude outboard motor on the back. During the summer months, we would spend most of our days down on the dock swimming. One day my dad promised me that if I got up on water skis, he would take me out to McDonald's for a meal. I decided to give it a try, and one summer afternoon I got up from a dock start on two skis. I was amazed at myself. I was only around seven years old. We visited McDonald's the next day and ordered a meal.

My dad and I spent a lot of time fishing on the lake. One specific location was on the other side of the lake, about fifty yards off shore in front of an old, rustic cabin. On this lake I fell in love with the water. I was warned that in parts of the lake, officials could never find the bottom. In the mind of a six-year-old, it left a deep impression of mystery and respect for water, which has stayed with me to this day.

Living in Lakewood in the 1960s also brought its own realism. The country was in the height of the Vietnam War. Not far from where I lived were the military bases Fort Lewis Army Base and McCord Air Force Base. Large airplanes in training flew over the area and loud booms and artillery going off were a constant part of playing in the neighborhood.

I spent most of my elementary school years at this house in Lakewood. Some significant milestones occurred during this time. The first one was starting speech therapy because of my lisp and stutter. I went to speech therapy for several months at Mary Bridge Children's Hospital in Tacoma. This was a big issue because my father also stuttered, but more severe than I did. His stutter always got a lot worse when he was drinking. From my own clinical and personal experience, stuttering affects friends and families of the person who stutters. Likewise, family and friends' reactions and feelings about the stuttering can have a powerful impact on the person who stutters. As a result, my speech issues in childhood had a huge influence on my own self-concept. Clinicians refer to self-concept as to how a person sees themselves. My speech issues as a child became the doorway to a great deal of negativity in my own thoughts, and a self-perception that was tied to how I viewed my body in space and time, my self-esteem, and my identity.

According to Franklin Silverman's seminal book, *Stuttering and Other Fluency Disorders*, he shows that children who stutter may not be as outgoing as they normally would be if they didn't stutter. Children who stutter may avoid talking in many situations for fear of getting laughed at or misunderstood. They also are unwilling to express anger in an open way. Many children who stutter may experience depression and guilt.[2] As a young boy, I had a great deal of anxiety about speaking, and as I grew out of childhood, a feeling inside persisted that speaking something out loud was out of my control.

Another issue that is part of my journey is that I was born with chronic asthma. I spent some time as an infant in an oxygen tent. I have vivid memories of my mother sleeping at the end of my bed making sure that I was breathing at night. I also slept with a humidifier on. In the late 1950s, physicians would give tetracycline to infants who had severe and chronic asthma to help with breathing. What they didn't know was that one of the side effects of the medicine was blackened teeth. This left me with was an intention to not smile. I hated all the comments. In childhood, kids can be very cruel.

The third health issue that I had to deal with was that I had bald spots. I had three or four of them on my scalp. They were the size of quarters. I was given different medicines and eventually was given shots in my scalp to help the hair grow back. Everyone had crew cuts in those days, so I was often asked about them and teased.

One of the more difficult things that happened to me while we lived at the house on Gravelly Lake was an experience that left me sexually traumatized. The event left me reeling with deep feelings of confusion, guilt, and shame for many years. It left an imprint on my soul that would later become one of the places where God revealed himself to me as my Strong Deliverer.

While we lived on Gravelly Lake, my dad started the ski patrol at Crystal Mountain Ski Resort. During the winter months, we drove up to Crystal Mountain almost every weekend, and my family would sleep in the bunks in the ski patrol room in the lodge. The lodging was free, and we had free passes to ski. I have such vivid memories of these weekend experiences. I learned to snow ski by the age of five. One weekend, before the snow fell, my dad and I were on the mountain while he tested the new radios for the ski patrol. We had a day of walking around the mountain, covering about five miles while testing the radios. By the time I was eight or nine years old, I experienced my first ski race, which was on Crystal Mountain. Those days hold a special place in my heart.

My other vivid memories are from the days when my dad and I were part of YMCA's Indian Guides. We had weekly meetings where we met with several other young boys and their fathers. This program provided structured opportunities for fellowship, camping, and community-building activities. I have fond memories being with my dad during these years.

One memory on Hilltop Lane that I remember was one summer day, when all of us neighborhood kids were playing together in our back yards. One of the kid's mom pulled up with her car and shouted to all of us, "Let's go kids!" I asked everyone as they were jumping into the car, "Where are you all going?" One of the kids replied, "She's taking us to the Lakewood Racquetball Club to go swimming." The mother who was driving looked at me and said, "You're not invited". I watched as she drove away with all of my friends, up to the main road on Hilltop Lane, and turn left on Nyanza Road.

I was devastated. I came home that day and told my mother what had happened. She was livid and immediately was on the phone with the other moms in the neighborhood. Feelings of rejection had made a way into my childhood soul that day. I didn't know what to do with it until years later when I surrendered my life to the One who truly understood.

When I lived on Gravelly Lake, I went to Tyee Park Elementary

School, but I don't have a lot of fond memories of this school. I had a hard time focusing and a harder time concentrating. I was frequently sent out to the hall as a result of being put on time outs by the teachers. While I was in the second grade in 1965, the Seattle Tacoma area experienced a 6.5 earthquake. All the students were in the classroom when all of a sudden the room started to shake violently. Our teacher, Mrs. Tallman, screamed, "Earthquake! Everybody, right now, get under your desks!" Not me, I ran outside and looked out at the playground. What I saw still sends chills down my spine. The playground looked like the ocean with waves. There were small waves of dirt running the length of the field. The waves were around a foot high. The ground shook, became like water, and rolled across the playground. I don't remember hiding under my desk, but I will always remember what I saw that day. Greg Lange writes more about the disaster:

> On the morning of April 29, 1965, at 8:29 a.m. Pacific Daylight Saving Time, an earthquake registering 6.5 magnitude occurs in Western Washington centered between Seattle and Tacoma. This is the fourth strongest documented earthquake in the Puget Sound region since 1850. Other strong earthquakes occurred in 1872 (estimated at 7.3 or 7.4 magnitude), 1949 (7.1), and 2001 (6.8). In 1965, three people are killed by falling debris, one on South King Street in Seattle's Pioneer Square and two at Fisher Flouring Mills on Seattle's Harbor Island. Four elderly women die from heart failure attributed to the earthquake. They live in Seattle, Tacoma, Olympia, and Port Townsend.
>
> The ground shook for about 45 seconds and was felt over a 190,000-square mile area including all of Washington state, northwest Oregon, southwest corner of British Columbia, north Idaho panhandle. The quake's epicenter was located near Des Moines, Washington, at 47 degrees, 24 minutes North Latitude and 122 degrees, 24 minutes West Longitude. Total damage is estimated at $12,500,000

(approximately $65,000,000 in 1999), most of it in Seattle. In Olympia, the State Capitol Building was temporarily closed and government departments move to nearby motels while buildings are being repaired.[3]

I came home from school that day, and my mother and I talked about what we did when the ground began to rumble. She told me that when the shaking started, she looked out into the back yard and saw the swing back and forth by itself. She was terrified. The Pacific Northwest came together after the quake and worked together to rebuild.

Another memory of third grade is Mrs. Quiggly, our teacher. She was a combination of an army drill sergeant and a dictator. Because of my focus and concentration issues, I had the opinion that she was a mean-spirited lady. I remember the poem that I made up about her at the time:

> Mrs. Quiggly is a dope,
> And she makes us mope,
> If you are in her class,
> You will never pass,
> If you are in Mrs. Quiggly's class.

I have only two memories of her as my teacher in third grade. Once, she tied me to my desk in the classroom. The second memory was when she had me stand at the front of the class with my nose to the blackboard, with my hands extended out in a horizontal position for an extended period of time. Apparently, I was being punished. As I look back, my days in school at Tyee Park were miserable. I hated school. The good memories were experiencing the weekends at Crystal Mountain and living on Gravelly Lake with my family.

While we lived on Gravelly Lake, our neighbors, Jim and Wendy Griffin, lived about three doors down from us. Jim had a brother, Ted, who was known for capturing the first whale in captivity.

Namu the whale was caught in 1965. My dad and Jim Griffin were friends from childhood.

In spite of Griffin's celebrity, Jim and Wendy's children were a regular part of the neighborhood gang of kids that lived on the block on Hilltop. We played together, boated, and swam together. Because of Namu's capture, the Griffins had the cast of the TV show, *Flipper*, visit their home and beach on the lake. Sitting on our dock, I watched the young cast ski and swim. It was a big day for a seven-year-old. Hollywood came to our lake.

While living on the lake, Jim Griffin and his business partner, Bob Mickelson, purchased land near Snoqualmie Summit and created Alpental Ski Resort. They asked my father to be the general manager of the new resort. At their invitation, my dad took a leave of absence from IBM as a computer programmer and took the position to manage the resort. I was ten years old. It was 1968 and our lives were about to change.

2

ALPENTAL

"For I, the Lord your God, hold your right hand; it is I
who say to you,
'Fear not, I am the one who helps you.'"
(Isaiah 41:13 ESV)

When my dad was offered the position as general manager, our lives changed. We were embarking on a new adventure as a family. We were about to be introduced to Denny Mountain on Snoqualmie Pass. My memories of this new grand adventure are priceless to me. The best memories include being with my dad and watching the ski lifts being built into Denny Mountain. One day, my dad and I climbed into a small helicopter at the base of the mountain where the new lodge was being built. My dad made sure that I was in the front seat next to the pilot. As the helicopter climbed, I looked down at my tennis shoes and saw through glass beneath me. The helicopter continued and flew up Chair 1. Looking through the glass bottom, I saw the trees below and the crews working to set the large poles for the chair lifts. We flew to the mountain top that day. I hung on to my seat for dear life. As I watched through the glass bottom, the top of Denny Mountain suddenly appeared. My dad and I got out of the helicopter and walked around the top of Chair 2. The view was breathtaking as I slowly spun around in a 360-degree circle and looked at the mountain ranges that surrounded us. I remember thinking that I was close to heaven, and I was with my dad.

During the early years of Alpental, I became friends with a girl whose father was a new ski instructor at the new resort. She and I became good friends. She would come down to Lakewood and spend the weekends with me on Gravelly Lake, or I would spend a summer weekend at her home in North Bend. We were very close and we also were going through the beginnings of our adolescences together. During the winters, she and I would spend the weekends together on the slopes. We would spend the entire day skiing, and ski raced together at Alpental. Often in the spring, we would head up Chair 2 and bring food and drinks with us. She and I would find a place up the ski run known as The Ridge and sit in the snow and sun, talking to those who were riding the chair up to the top of the mountain. During the summer, with my parents' knowledge, she and I would sleep in the pull-out bed in our living room. We were the same age. I was ten or eleven years old at the time. She was a girl and it was simply very awkward for me. She was my first crush. She and I would swim in the lake during the summer. I remember that there was some sexual tension between us. My parents didn't really care about the sleeping arrangements. I think that they thought this was 'cute.' I have fond memories of her to this day. In my mid-teens, we unfortunately grew apart. She wasn't coming up to the mountain as often and I was busy bringing my friends from home up to the mountain on the weekends to ski.

Saturday mornings were also special in those days at Alpental. My dad and I woke at 0-dark-hundred and headed up to the top of Denny Mountain to ski with the avalanche ski patrol crew who were setting dynamite in all the runs in the upper area. We would watch the explosions, along with the slides and avalanches they caused. Often, we had the opportunity to ski untouched powder before the public got to ski the runs. As a boy, I had the chance to become friends with the young men on the ski patrol who were trained in avalanche and public safety. These young men taught me how to ski powder, and to have respect for the powder snow and the mountains.

Going to the top of the mountain in the early weekend mornings was common growing up on the summit at Alpental. On the weekends, we lived on the second floor of the main lodge in a small apartment. After the early morning avalanche patrol was done around 8:00 a.m., I would head to our second-floor apartment to eat breakfast while the general public began their day of skiing. I was usually back out on the slopes by 9:00 a.m. and skied until 5:00 p.m. After dinner in our apartment in the main lodge, it was an evening of night skiing on Saturdays until 10:00 p.m. We were back on the top of the mountain early Sunday morning with the avalanche crew, blowing up the ski runs on the top of the mountain.

The hardest part of skiing with these guys, who were essentially dynamite experts, was that they would always tease me about whether or not I could carry a case of explosives up both chair lifts by myself. This always made me nervous, as I was only a ten- or eleven-year-old being asked to carry thirty-pound cases of explosives up two chair lifts. My dad was always with me and provided the oversight.

The humorous thing was that I always knew that these guys were partying the night before, and all of them were experiencing hangovers from the previous evening. I would smile and laugh with my dad as the loud guns would explode and go off as they were aimed at the cornices. The blasting crew were attempting to hit as many large cornices as possible so they would fall below onto the ski run, triggering a controlled avalanche before the general public skied them. As the forest service ranger would yell, "Fire in the hole," all of us would plug our ears before the explosion came. The guys would bend over and moan and groan holding their heads and remind each other of their drinking exploits from the evening before. Most of the blasting crew generally operated on fewer than four hours of sleep on the weekend.

During the winter months, our family was up on the mountain every weekend. We became close friends with those who lived on the summit. They became our extended family. The 'mountain crew', as they were referred to, were truly a group of misfits and ragamuffins that worked hard and played hard. They were all in their early to mid-twenties. They were young mountain people that embraced their culture and were fiercely loyal to one another and to us. Most of them worked at the ski resort full time on the pro patrol. They also were highly skilled in avalanche control and rescue.

Alpental Ski Lodge – 1969

With dad's position, our family was always able to cut into the head of the ski lines. More ski time for us! As the resort was gaining the reputation for being one of the most difficult resorts to ski, well-known international skiers would come and visit. Folks like Jean-Claude Killy, who was a triple Olympic Gold Medalist in 1968, the 1964 Olympic Silver Medalist and world champion Billy the Kidd, and freestyle skiing pioneer Wayne Wong were often seen on the slopes at Alpental. Such races as the Rainier Cup and the Winter Olympic Trials brought more famous people and exciting skiing as well. One crowd pleaser was a young man who would kite ski from Chair 2 off the lip of the five-thousand-foot Denny Mountain. He skied off the ledge and flew his attached kite to land near the lodge at the bottom of the mountain.

After a day of spring skiing, I would join my family sitting on the outside second-floor balcony and enjoy watching the spring skiers coming down off the mountain. When spring began bringing warmer weather, my mom, sister, and I would drive up to the ski resort on Friday afternoon. We would arrive at our apartment and have dinner together. Sometimes my mother would have Spanish rice and pork chops already prepared and ready to bake when we left our home that afternoon. Then, I was usually able to begin night skiing each and every Friday night by 6:00 p.m.

During these weekends, there was always a lot of drinking and partying. I was exposed to this environment at a very early age. It was a normal part of our lives and continued through my late adolescence. The parties on the second floor of the Alpental Ski Lodge are infamous. At night, my friends and I would go up to the third-floor outdoor balcony and do flips into the snow below. No way was it possible to get hurt, as we always landed in eight- to ten-feet of powder below us. All the adults were too busy with the music, dancing, drinking and partying. One night, after being awoken from a deep sleep to yelling and music, I walked out of our second-floor apartment and saw things on the dance floor that children weren't meant to see. My parents saw me staring at the scene and quickly redirected me back to bed. It was a sign of the times.

Another casualty of the party days was a big, expensive snowcat. My dad drove it off the fifteen-foot bank of one of the parking lots in the back. He had drank too much and almost flipped the tracker rig onto its back. What happened that night was never mentioned or brought up again.

My Spiritual Encounter on the Cliff

"I'm not afraid of death, I just don't want to be there when it happens."
– Woody Allen

> "The value of life is revealed when it confronts death from close quarters."
> – Apoorve Dubey

> "Death is swallowed up in victory." "O death, where is your victory?
> O death, where is your sting?"
> (1 Corinthians 15: 54b-55 ESV)

For the next seven years, I would spend the winters with my family on the summit at Alpental Ski Resort. After my dad's tenure as general manager, he went back to working at IBM. He joined the weekend volunteer ski patrol, which he started. This allowed us to have season passes every winter. I have many fond memories of the summit.

One of the cold mornings when I was about ten years old, I woke up to around ten inches of new snow. My dad and I headed up Chair 2. The plan was to get to the top of the mountain and start to ski down the run called International. We were going to stay high on the ridge, traverse across into the back bowls into the back country, and ski some untouched powder. This run at the time was known as the steepest ski run in the Pacific Northwest. We headed down the top of the slope. The top part of the hill was the steepest. We headed to our left and stayed high on the ridge cutting a new trail, and then we came across a small trail on top of the cliff. My dad went first, and then he looked back at me and hollered, "Keep skiing across this little trail, and do not stop at all." That was a warning. He probably thought I would catch an edge and start sliding.

He started off onto the trail and I followed. I stayed in his tracks and then accidentally caught the edge of my skis, which caused me to fall and begin to slide. I tried to stop the sliding, but I kept moving toward the ledge. It happened so fast, I didn't have time to think about the danger. As my dad watched, I slid off the ledge and fell ten stories off the cliff. I remember free falling and hitting several ledges before getting to the bottom. Every time I hit a rock ledge, it knocked the wind out of me. When it was all over, I was at the bottom and simply laid still in the snow. I just put my hands on my head and I realized that my chest hurt. My dad quickly skied down to me, threw off his skis, and fell to his knees in the deep powder. He hugged me and held me close to his chest while he cried. As I shut my eyes, he spoke to me quietly through his tears, "I'm really glad you're okay."

As the general manager of the resort, my dad always carried a radio with him. He called out on the radio for those on the ski patrol who were close to us to come to our location. With my dad beside me, they carried me off the mountain and I was brought to the hospital. I had bruised ribs and a concussion. I realized later, and as I was falling off the cliff in the free fall, that something caught me and slowed my fall. As I was in the free fall, I knew that I wasn't alone. There was a presence, and as I watched the brown and grey rock fly by me, something was very close to me. The fall itself was surreal, and I realized that the fall actually slowed down. It felt like something had caught me.

Six years later, in the spring of 1974, I had an encounter with Jesus at a high school Young Life meeting. I was immediately reminded that it was the Lord who saved me that day on the mountain. It was an extremely powerful encounter with God. I will never forget it. A month later, a ski instructor from the resort accidentally went off the same cliff I did and fell to his death. From time to time, I still struggle with survivor's guilt. Why did I live and the other man die? Did I live for some purpose that I was supposed to fulfill? What if I mess up? What if I missed it? After my fall, a young man on the ski patrol at Alpental sketched a picture of the event for me. I've kept it ever since and when I look at it, I am often reminded of the grace of God in my life. As a further reminder, the name of the ski bowl that I fell into was changed to 'Todd's Folly' for a short time.

The artist's drawing of me falling off the cliff.

Almost every day I think about what happened that morning on that ridge, as we were heading into the back country. I can recall the feeling of free falling and watching the grey and brown rock fly by me. I am grateful for not dying that day. Over the years I have had a lot of fear that has been attached to what happened that day. I also have a great deal of sadness for the death of the man who fell off the cliff shortly after I did; I never knew his name. I have felt guilty for surviving. When my dad finally got to me, I will always remember his affection for me. As a father with two adult children, I can't imagine how he felt when he saw me go off the ledge. As I think back and remember that day, that experience was the only time in my life when we simply held each other. Time stood still for me. To this day, I know that something caught me during the fall. I remember being in the presence of such a powerful peace that was a present-moment reality. Over the years I have had to come to terms with my guilt about surviving. It was a very emotional day in my world. It was embedded deep into my memory that there was this peace I felt as I fell, and that I knew it then, that something or someone caught me. I still have night terrors and panic episodes from that day. Hardly a day goes by when I don't think about those memories.

While in my clinical training as a Licensed Independent Clinical Social Worker, I came to the realization that I had the symptoms of Post-Traumatic Stress Disorder (PTSD).

Unfortunately, I don't remember any kind of debriefing with my parents regarding this very traumatic event. As a ten-year-old, I had no one to talk to about it. My parents and I briefly talked about an earthquake that took place two years earlier, but not this experience. We also didn't talk about the attack of bees. Early on, I knew that I had to let go of the resentment that I felt towards my parents for not talking to me about the trauma. I needed to talk about it, but didn't know how.

3

MY INTRODUCTION TO WOLLOCHET BAY

> "He makes me lie down in green pastures.
> He leads me beside still waters."
> (Psalm 23:2 ESV)

Living in Lakewood on Gravelly Lake was filled with great memories. What I didn't know was that my parents were growing discontent with living in Lakewood. They were becoming increasingly tired of the socialites and upper-class folks living in Lakewood at the time. I do remember the huge homes on the water. After leaving the ice show, my dad worked for IBM as a senior programmer and despised being asked the question, "So what do you do?" My dad told me once that he finally got fed up with keeping up with the Joneses and started telling people at dinner parties that he worked on a garbage truck. I think that he got tired of the status, the wealth, and the cultural narcissism within the upper class of Lakewood.

Still, on Saturday mornings, my dad and I would head out to his old childhood hangout, the Lakewood Ice Arena. We would get out on the ice, and he would skate with me, teaching me and having fun. Then we would go into the small cafe and rest up with a small cup of hot chocolate. After, we went back out and skated some more.

On one occasion that we were skating together, I heard the following words over the loud speaker, "All right everyone. We are in for a treat today. I want everyone in the arena to clear the ice, and let our one and only hometown boy, Dave Riggs, take the ice."

My dad smiled at me and quickly led me off the ice. I watched my dad ice skate around for several minutes. The arena erupted with applause as he skated around doing his clown routine. To this day when I have hot chocolate, I find myself back in the Lakewood Ice Arena sitting in the small cafe smelling the combination of hot chocolate, wet clothing, and leather skates.

In the fall of 1969, my parents bought a small house on Wollochet Bay. I remember our family driving through Tacoma and crossing the one-mile long Narrows Bridge for the first time. I looked over the green rails of the bridge into the water below. I remember seeing the blue water, and its contrast with the clear blue sky above the bridge. It was breathtaking. We arrived at the little home nestled on the waterfront off the east side of the inner bay. Our new home was thirty minutes north from our old home on the lake. Our weekend home, on the mountain on Snoqualmie Pass, was around ninety minutes from our new home on Wollochet Bay.

"Is this really for real?" I wondered.

The house smelled of the new wood from the recently-added three bedrooms and one bathroom in the back of our house. It was a small cottage before the bedrooms were added. Best of all, the house was only fifteen yards from the water's five-foot concrete bulkhead that separated the water and our front lawn. During the first several months living on Wollochet, the tides mesmerized me. The tide was always predictable as it was always high tide in the evening, and low tide during the middle of the day. If I sat long enough on our beach, I could see the water slowly inch its way up our beach. Also, the smell of the salt water combined with the mud from the beach at low tide was all new to me. One of our neighbors told me that at low tide a person could walk across the end of Wollochet Bay, although it was extremely dangerous. The rumor was that a cow once got stuck in the mud when the tide came in, and then drowned. Needless to say, I never walked across the bay at low tide.

Our home on Wollochet Bay – view from the beach.

Our home on Wollochet Bay – view from the water.

The other side of this story was what happened on the bay almost every year in December, when the tides were always higher. A few days before Christmas each year the high tide would come over the concrete bulkhead, onto the front lawn, and into our basement where everything was on six-inch blocks. The only way to enter our basement was if we walked down the steps on the deck and into the basement from the outside front door. The basement housed our washer and dryer, and it was also used for storage, but everything was on blocks. Every December, I remember eating breakfast before school and watching the salt water surround our house. We were powerless. All we could do was watch and wait for the tide to subside. Years later, I learned that there was a correlation between my grief and the tides.

Some of my best memories during the early years living on the bay were during the summer evenings, when we would bring the boat in as the sun was setting in the west. Our house always experienced the sunset in the evening. The evenings were a time to wind down if we didn't have people over. It was such a great way to end the day.

Dunbar and Old Mrs. Forsythe

In the late sixties when we moved to the bay, I would often walk around Picnic Point where we lived. I needed to explore. I walked down to the old antique store at the end of the road, and I noticed a small house across the road, up on the hill, with an older man in his large yard. I asked my dad when I got home, "Who was that old man that I saw?"

He responded with telling me, "That's old Mr. Dunbar." I found out later that he lived by himself and that no one really knew him. He was a hermit, yet he owned all the property across the road and up the hillside overlooking the bay. I made the decision that I was going to meet him. He was the symbol of an elder type. He kept to himself and never talked to anyone, so he was always shrouded with a bit of mystery. I spoke with him only one time in an encounter that was brief, but powerful. I dared myself to walk up his driveway one day as he was cutting wood. He looked up at me and asked a couple of questions. He was nice, but not inviting. Forty-five years later with great mystery and some unfinished curiosity in my heart, I am writing about him. I now know that he owned most of the land up from the bay, across the road from the old Wollochet Bay antique store. He was worth millions of dollars in acreage. His land today is filled with beautiful homes that overlook the bay and known as Dunbar Cove on Wollochet.

Another interesting person who lived just off Picnic Point, next door to the antique store at the point's entrance, was old Mrs. Forsythe. I often would walk down to the store next to her house most days to wait for the school bus. She saw me standing there and called off her very vicious dog that guarded her property. At one point, we struck up a conversation. She invited me into her home and fed me cookies. I found out after my first visit with her that she was our next-door neighbor's mother. For the next two or three years, she and I struck up a friendship. During the summer months, I would water her large vegetable garden in exchange for five or six dollars a week. She was always willing to sit down with me and talk about her eighty-year history and the pioneering days on Wollochet. She often gave me antique coins that I stored in my room. Somehow, they later disappeared. I now know that the land that she owned was mostly waterfront property on the east side of the inner bay of Wollochet. She was also worth millions of dollars, but no one would ever know it.

Our home was at the end of Picnic Point Drive, where the road stopped at a white wooden fence that blocked the road. The road continued past the fence, but the land on the other side was owned by the Catholic Order of the Dominican Sisters. They owned a large piece of land, including waterfront property which included wooded property above our house to the east and north of us. This was their private, secluded retreat center for their community, yet it was a great piece of wooded land to explore. On the north side of their property was Mrs. Forsythe's family homestead.

From time to time, I would take my friends past the fence where our property ended and walk through the overgrown road along the bay, through the Dominican Sisters' property and then up the trail to the old Forsythe homestead. The old homestead was an older, abandoned two-level home. The windows were gone and the building was all rotten wood. In an earlier day, the building was a beautiful home with a covered porch that overlooked Wollochet Bay. Along the back side of the house was a small room. As a curious eleven-year-old, I opened the door in the smaller room, and I saw a bed with an old red-haired man sleeping. He was passed out. Bottles of alcohol littered the floor. I quickly shut the door, walked down the path back to the beach road, and headed home. A couple of weeks later, I saw the same man walk through the property next to our home and walk past our home. I asked my parents, "Who is that guy? He looks drunk all the time."

My parents responded, "That's old Red. Todd, he's harmless."

I told them, "He lives up on the hill in the old house." Over the next several months, I made the decision to get up the nerve to say hi to him whenever he walked by our house in the mornings. One morning, I saw him walk by, and I said hello to him. He simply nodded, and we made eye contact. Over the next couple of years, he was often seen walking up Picnic Point to the main road. My mom and I would often make a run to Anderson's, a grocery store that was two miles down the road. When she saw old Red walking to the store for his alcohol, she often picked him up. When I stopped by to talk to old Mrs. Forsythe, Red would be at her kitchen table smoking a cigarette with a beverage in his hand. Old Red was surrounded in mystery, but I liked the old guy.

My dad taught me so much about Wollochet Bay during the first several months we were there. We had a clam and oyster bed on our beach, and when I was in fifth grade, my dad would ask me if I wanted to go to the beach before school when it was low tide. I would always say yes and ran to collect the screwdrivers, the pliers, and seafood sauce. Then we would step off the bulkhead onto the beach and feast on our own raw oysters. To this day, I love oysters on a half shell, and I will pay dearly for them. I am thankful for Oceanaire, Jax Cafe, and the Smack Shack in Minneapolis for their fresh seafood menu, including their fresh oysters on a half shell. One can take a boy away from the ocean, but not the ocean from a boy.

It was the summer in 1969. My dad and I, along with a couple of our neighbors, decided to head out one morning to the waters of the Narrows, just south of the Narrows Bridge where there was supposed to be a lingcod fishing hole. We were in my dad's fourteen-foot ski boat, looking for the fishing hole. When we got out to the Narrows, we made several passes over the so-called fishing hole. My dad and his buddies were drinking Bloody Marys and Irish coffees. Only being in the fifth or sixth grade, my mind was somewhere else. I had heard that when the Tacoma Narrows Bridge, nicknamed the Galloping Gertie Bridge, fell due to the extremely high winds in 1940, the entire bridge fell and landed on the bottom of the Narrows ocean floor. Since that time, the world's largest octopus have grown and survived using the underwater structure to protect themselves. My twelve-year-old mind imagined four hundred feet of water only a mile across from shore to shore, a small fourteen-foot boat, and the world's largest sea creatures known to man under our boat. No wonder I could not really concentrate on fishing when I had Disney's *20,000 Leagues Under the Sea* playing out in my mind. I imagined in my mind that a giant octopus was going to rise up from the waters below us and eat us. Then at the height of my anxiety and panic, my fishing pole started to bend over the end of the boat and into the water. My dad shouted at me, "Okay Todd! Hold on to your fishing pole!" I wrestled with that fish with all the life that was in me. The boat became filled with excitement and commotion as the men put down their poles and drinks and focused on helping me land this huge fish. Roughly two hours later, I landed a thirty-five-pound lingcod. It was a rite of passage when we brought it back to Wollochet that summer morning. Three great men of my childhood helped a boy land a giant of a fish. This fish tale remains with me today and will my whole life.

One weekend morning several months later, my dad and I were fishing out in the mouth of Wollochet Bay, in between the bay and Fox Island. My neighbor buddy who lived up the bay from us was also with us. We were in our small red ski boat and were trolling for salmon. I remember that something struck my fish line, and my fishing pole bent all the way into the water. The three of us were excited as I started to reel in the fish that I had caught. My dad started to drive the boat backwards in the direction of the fish. My line was on the port side of the boat. I couldn't see the fish when it came up to the surface due to the sad fact that my seat was on the starboard side of the boat. I remember seeing my friend looking over the side of the boat and was helping my dad with the line. My buddy looked back at me and all I remember was how big his eyes were. "How big is it? How big?" I asked. My dad responded as he was leaning over the side, "It's as long as the boat!" I thought, "Long as the boat? What? That's fourteen feet long! Let me see this fish!" I then heard the sound of the line being snipped. My dad had quickly cut the line. My friend sat back in his chair and looked at me with eyes as huge as saucers and exclaimed, "That thing was huge!" My dad responded, "It was too big for us. You caught a large shark Todd. I quickly cut the line so it wouldn't potentially do any damage to the boat."

Along with great moments, living on Wollochet for the next four years brought some challenges. I went to Harbor Heights Elementary School ten minutes away in Gig Harbor for fifth grade. Transitioning into a new school was difficult for me. Friends were hard to make, partly because most of the kids lived a long way from where I lived. I didn't fit in. At one point, some of the kids bullied me on the playground. I could not focus and was inattentive, so I spent a lot of time in the hall outside my classroom. I made no connections with the teacher or the students. What I remember the most in fifth grade was playing floor hockey in the gym. I don't remember learning much of anything else.

In sixth grade, I was at Artondale Elementary School on the other side of the bay. My teacher was obsessed with training rats. Yes, rats. Our class went on tour around the area, even performing a show at the Seattle Science Center. The rats in our class were trained to climb up ladders, pull on strings, and walk across cables in order to get their food. I just went with the flow. Paying attention to academics was hard. Making friends was harder. I just didn't fit in. The other thing added to my plate was that my sister was now in kindergarten, and my parents asked me to look after her at school. On one occasion, my parents asked me to talk to one of my sister's classmates. Apparently, he was teasing her. I found out who the kid was and had a nose to nose chat with him. I told him to leave my sister alone. That took care of it, and there were no further problems.

Our family was adjusting to our life on the sound. While I was struggling in the academic and social world in school, my life at home was great. Something new was always going on. A new school, a new home, a new environment along with living on the bay. Parties were constantly going on at our home or our neighbors. On Halloween night, my dad and his friends took us out for what they called, 'Trick or Drink'. All of the kids on Picnic Point would cram into our neighbor's station wagon and go door-to-door for candy; my dad and his friends would hand their empty glasses to the person at the door who filled their orders—beer, wine, or hard liquor. This tradition actually started when we lived in Lakewood. Apparently, my dad had to educate the men on the bay that this was the way to celebrate Halloween. On one occasion, my dad and his buddy Jack were driving us around the bay getting candy. They were in the front seat and the kids were in the back. Suddenly, Jack slammed on the brakes of his station wagon and stopped the car. Both my dad and Jack jumped out of the vehicle and ran after the kids who had just egged the car. By the end of the evening, things always got interesting.

I had it all on the outside. But on the inside, I was feeling more and more alienated. I began to realize that I was expected to perform to get my parents' approval. I had an internal world where I was safe, but more and more I was detaching from my outside world.

Shortly after we moved to Wollochet, my dad bought an old row boat and a ten-horse motor for me. My parents had a storage area underneath the new addition of our house and the decision was made to store it there. The boat needed a lot of work. For several months, I had the task to sand the entire boat down to the wood, taking off all the paint and rough edges. One would think that there was all this excitement and anticipation for a twelve-year-old to have his own boat with a motor. But many nights after school and many weekends, I was in the downstairs storage room under the house sanding away. When the boat was sanded down inside and out, dad and I put fiberglass strips on the bottom of the boat. Any boat on our beach would take a beating at low tide with the sharp clam and oyster beds. The bottom of my boat was protected with paint, sealant and fiberglass strips. Such great memories of this early time on the water remain with me. Whatever was going on in school, whatever was happening in my friendships, or with my growing sense of insecurity and inner loneliness, being in my own boat at that time in my childhood made it all go away. It is the same today. I was in sixth grade and Puget Sound was my back yard.

My new friend David and I would spend our days during the summer in my boat skiing and inner tubing. Dave lived right across the bay from me and we became the best of friends. Both of us would earn gas money doing chores around our neighborhoods, and then pool our money so we would have gas for the boats during the hot summer days. After filling the six-gallon gas tanks, we would be out on the bay sometimes eight to ten hours a day. By the end of the summer, my skin was dark brown, and my hair was bleached out almost white from the salt water. When it was time for dinner, we came to shore. Usually our parents would have dinner together, which often was barbequed hamburgers. Our neighbors often had potlucks, and we would all eat together. Then Dave and I would be back out on the water until dusk. I didn't have a care in the world. The waters of Puget Sound remained a place of safety and fun. Whether my dad was taking us skiing behind his boat, or I was out on my ski boat, I treasure my memories out on the saltwater of Wollochet Bay.

Christmas in Sun Valley

When I was around twelve years old our family drove to Sun Valley, Idaho for a week of Christmas festivities with our extended family from the Pacific Northwest. This included my grandmother Florence Cornell, my aunt Patti, my uncle Don, and their kids. My dad had spent part of his childhood here. For the week over Christmas in 1970, we stayed in Warm Springs, a part of Sun Valley. Everyday my whole family skied, shopped, and even skated on the outdoor ice rink. All of my cousins and I were skating and listening to the singing group the Carpenters while our parents were watching us skate and sipping hot buttered rum. My parents even got on the ice and performed some of their routines from *Holiday on Ice*. It was a magical time for all of us. My parents rarely were on the ice together, and watching my dad perform the cantilever again always amazed me. My memories and feelings of this week I can't even put into words. I'm trying, really! What I remember is the skiing, my family laughing, and my cousins Nicole and Leslie coming back from the little grocery store in Ketchum, Idaho so excited because they saw actor Gregory Peck in line buying groceries. They came back to our condo and they were talking so fast that they had to stop and take an occasional breath. As I recall, they both fought over who saw him first. That night I remember watching all the skiers in the torchlight parade ski down Baldy Mountain in the dark. I remember watching and thinking that it was like ballet. They skied down in a glow as a slow rhythm. The contrast between the dark sky, the white snow, and the red, yellow glow from the torches they all carried made it magical. I was excited when Santa rode down Main Street in Sun Valley with reindeer pulling his sleigh full of gifts for the children. After seeing Santa, we all walked through the Sun Valley Lodge. The lodge had so much grandeur. I remember the high ceilings and the dark wood walls. The rock fireplace stood out as the centerpiece of the main lobby. It was so open and majestic. If only the walls could talk.

It was snowing that Christmas Eve. One morning my dad made breakfast. He made steak and eggs. I never had that before. I remember Bob Mickelson, our family friend, who was a wealthy entrepreneur and the partial owner of Alpental Ski Resort, had joined us one evening. In front of our entire family, he looked at my dad, rose, and gave a toast, "David, you have arrived." I will never forget that week. It was glorious. Little did I know that this was the calm before the storm that shortly was to hit our family.

It was a relief to finally get into middle school. Goodman Middle School was located in Gig Harbor, as was my fifth-grade school. I don't remember any nervousness during my first day. Instead, I was looking forward to the new schedule of six or seven classes a day. It was a relief to know that I wasn't going to be bored in one class all day long, so I looked forward to the variety and all the changes that middle school brought. My teachers still reported in my parent conferences that I was an underachiever who had a difficult time with concentration and focus.

What I now know, as someone who holds both a master's degree and a license in clinical social work and who also specializes in working with adolescents, is that three things are necessary for good performance in school: ability, good work methods, and interest. As a middle school student, I didn't have any of them.

In Josh McDowell and Bob Hostetler's book *Josh McDowell's Handbook on Counseling Youth*, they write that the studies of the personality and lifestyle factors of underachievers indicate that underachievers display some or all of the following characteristics:

> Emotional immaturity, inability to adjust, excessive fear and anxiety, low self-esteem, deep-seated feelings of hostility, resentment, negativism, perceptions of unfair treatment, and rejection of adult authority.[1]

My two years at Goodman Middle School were good years and were a lot of fun. My insecurities in academics were covered up by my life on the water and in the snow. I was passionate about the sound, boating, waterskiing, snow skiing, living in the bubble of my parents' world on the bay, and also up on the mountain summit at Alpental Ski Resort. I was in band and played the drums. My parents had purchased a drum set for me. I spent many hours at home practicing. I was the drummer in the school jazz band. Moving to the bay and attending three schools in three years forced me to begin dealing with my own sense of insecurity and alienation from my peers at school. No one really knew me at school.

My dad would sometimes have to work on Saturdays, so I would tag along with him. We drove into downtown Seattle to the Aetna Building where he worked. While he was working, I had the day to roam around downtown by myself. In the morning, I usually walked down to the waterfront and explored the shops. I also walked through all the stores on Third and Fourth Streets. I was free to explore and I always felt safe. I would watch people. I would meet back with my dad back for lunch, and we would walk into Pioneer Square. I remember the sandwiches and soups that were offered in the square. I don't remember much of our conversations, but it was special. It was a father-son-date day. It was a day of bonding.

When I was around twelve years old, I was invited to join the Boy Scouts. Scouting gave me a sense of community outside of Wollochet and offered me an incentive to work on my rank advancement at my own pace. Our troop met weekly at the Grange Hall on Fox

Island which included a group of boys who were themselves living on the Island. I already knew them in school, but Boy Scouts took our friendships to a whole new level. We went camping over the weekends on a routine basis. We were hiking on trails all around the area. We spent a lot of time on Mount Rainier where we learned to survive in snow caves, and learned snowshoeing. There were many weekend campouts on Fox Island. We learned to live outside and learned survival skills. We talked about everything. There never was any judgment regarding our friendships with one another and there was an acceptance that was the glue that held us together. We all worked on our rank advancement at our own pace. It was in Scouting where I learned something about myself. I didn't like competition. I walked in a strong fear of failure. I did everything I could do to not be put on the spot. In the competitions, we would always work as a team. As I began to rise up through tenderfoot to second class, and then first class, I was more in control. I also learned some of the basics of servant leadership. I didn't have to compete with anyone but myself. I did pretty well as I earned the rank of Eagle by the time I was fourteen years old.

We spent countless weekend campouts on Fox Island thanks to the leadership of our scoutmasters Dexter Smith and Rod Bernsten. Our many nights on Mount Rainier learning survival training, and hiking all over the Cascade and Olympic mountain ranges, taught us about being a man and learning to love the great outdoors. There were also the competitive weekend camps with other troops around the military base of Fort Lewis in Tacoma. Scouting eventually gave me a huge boost in confidence by learning how to survive in the outdoors and by earning the highest rank in Scouting. Our scout meetings were mixed with learning disciplines, working on merit badges, and rank advancement. There was also, of course, the many games of dodge ball in the basement of the building that we met in. These great memories of my scouting years warm my soul. I am greatly appreciative of the families that lived on the bay and also the mountain folks who I grew up around. By the age of twelve, I was described as confident and funny; however, on the inside, I was feeling more insecure about myself in my family. Living on Wollochet Bay and also on the mountain at Alpental was like living in a bubble for me. When I was in the bubble, things were okay. When I was outside, I felt insecure and lacked self-confidence. Because of the tetracycline that I took as a baby for my severe asthma, my teeth were black. I took great pride in the fact that I had no cavities. Yet, I was thrilled when my parents made the decision to pay for my four front teeth to be capped. They knew that I was constantly teased and made fun of because of my teeth. When we moved to Wollochet, my mouth got an upgrade. At last, I was able to smile and not follow the urge to put my hand over my mouth when I spoke. I no longer felt self-conscious or embarrassed. Also, the hair in my bald spots had grown back thanks to the shots of medicine that I had received. My lisp and stuttering were slowly going away. The exercises that the speech therapist had taught me were working.

In the sixties, as I made my way through middle school, things improved for me, but my parents' drinking and partying increased. Both my parents were edgy in many respects. They were performers and lived the life of successful skaters before we moved to the bay. My family worked hard, partied hard, and played hard. During the summer, my parents would invite the mountain crew from Alpental down to our home for weekend parties where the alcohol flowed freely. At times we would have forty to eighty people at our home. My dad would have our boat out, and we would water-ski all day long. Most of our friends would spend the night in sleeping bags covering our living room floor.

In the seventies, the calm before the storm appeared. I didn't know it then, but my darkest days were ahead. I was moving into adolescence and was an introvert living in an extrovert world where putting on the game face was the norm. To cover up my insecurities, shame, and ever growing pretense, I turned to food, porn, and alcohol for comfort. They circled their wagons and made me feel okay, that I was normal. In reality I felt like I was living in a carnival's house of mirrors. During this troubled time, I spent a weekend with one of my closest friends. We stayed at his grandmother's home on Capitol Hill in Seattle and spent two days walking around downtown Seattle. We walked into several stores and shoplifted some items. In a small neighborhood grocery store we shoplifted over two dozen porn magazines. As the cashier was helping other customers, my friend and I shoved them all into our bag and walked out of the store. That night, we spent hours at his grandmother's home looking at porn. After being home for several days, my mom found the stolen items and asked me where they came from. I lied and told her they belonged to my friend. This was just one more regret to add to the increasing pile of shame and guilt. I felt horrible about what happened that weekend, but I blew it off.

In spite of my emerging addictions and troubling feelings, life on Wollochet during the summers was wonderful. Our mountain family from the summit came down to Wollochet Bay on the weekends and partied with us. Fun was all around me. One of the things that I have learned from living in a highly functional alcoholic home was that fun always prevailed. Because of the personalities of my parents, the fun times were meant to over shadow the pain in our family. Yet, I was experiencing an increasing sense of a deep inner emptiness and a heart ache that I couldn't explain. Our Alpental relationships became close to our family. The mountain people were men and women of a rough breed that was passionate and loyal. Many times after the alcohol was flowing, I heard their personal stories. They were all addicts or alcoholics. They all had hard lives. One evening, I remember listening to one of them talk about flying helicopters in Vietnam. He had a few beers in him as he told the stories of flying the choppers down into enemy cross fire. He would hold the chopper steady for a few seconds hovering close to the ground while the wounded were being loaded into the cargo bay. Then he would fly out, again in the middle of enemy fire. He told me that he did this same thing several times a day. He told me that he had lost a couple of his copilots as they flew out of the cross fire carrying their wounded. One story he recalled was when he was talking to his copilot, turned away, and then continuing with the conversation, he looked back over at his copilot to see his face blown off.

Beside alcohol and porn, another addiction began to raise its ugly head—food. As a young boy, my asthma had a huge impact on me. In middle school, I was also diagnosed with severe allergies. My doctor prescribed allergy shots at least twice a week. My mom made the decision to give me my shots on a weekly basis. To deal with the stress, I turned to food. My father had the expectation that our evening meal was to be a stress-free zone and a peaceful experience. However, so many times by dad would get frustrated with me and I didn't want to be around him. As an adolescent with an adolescent appetite, I would eat as fast as I could at the dinner table. Finally, he insisted that I chew my food ten times before I could swallow. This edict from my father was a disaster and I would be sent to my room with no supper. I became incredibly angry at my dad. As I had these continued interactions at dinner, I learned that shame was attached to food.

When I came home from school, often I grabbed some of the cookies from the cookie jar in the kitchen. Apparently, my mom thought that I was eating too many cookies. To remedy the situation, she put a lock on the cookie jar. I came home one day from school and managed to manipulate the lock off the jar. I consumed more than a few cookies. When my mom saw what I had done, she was livid. The next day when I arrived home from school, she demanded that I sit down at the kitchen table. Then she handed me a gallon of milk and a two-pound bag of chocolate cookies. With a stern glare, she said, "You aren't leaving the table until you drink the entire gallon of milk and eat the two pounds of cookies." I panicked and I pleaded with her. She was insistent. Later that night I was sick and vomited throughout the evening.

In those early days, food was comforting. I didn't have a clue about balance, structure, or satisfaction. My food intake became connected with my body image. Both were connected to shame and my feeling like a broken failure. I also felt a tremendous amount of guilt because of the choices that I was making.

In seventh grade I started attending confirmation class at our church, Peninsula Lutheran Church, in Gig Harbor. Class was held every Wednesday afternoon for three years. I now look back on these years and I can accurately say that I hated going to confirmation class. I gave the teachers a lot of grief. One afternoon our teacher got so frustrated with me that she slapped me for throwing ice at a friend in the middle of class. During the lessons, I remember climbing the bell tower and hiding out. In addition to the Wednesday afternoon classes, other obligations included the duty of being an altar boy on Sunday mornings. Confirmation was a duty.

On the other hand, today I am grateful for my mom's insistence that I attend church with her and that I complete confirmation. The confirmation classes laid a foundation for me and created a hunger for me to know God. Little did I know that his word promised it would do that very thing:

> "So shall my word be that goes out from my mouth;
> it shall not return to me empty,
> but it shall accomplish that which I purpose,
> and shall succeed in the thing for which I sent it"
> (Isaiah 55:11 ESV).

During the three years, we memorized many Bible verses and the creeds. We examined Martin Luther's Catechism and read parts of the Book of Concord. It was seed planted into my soul.

Community also developed in those three years. I began enjoying my Wednesday afternoons with a dozen of my classmates. We were all in the same boat. Isn't that what fellowship is, but being in the company of several fellows in the same ship? We were making the best of it.

During my second year of confirmation, the church called another pastor to serve in our congregation. Pastor Roe took over teaching confirmation. His family had several kids, and they became active in our youth program. The best way that I can explain our community is that when Pastor Roe came to Peninsula Lutheran Church, things became more relevant. Even though church and confirmation was the last thing on my list of priorities, I respected him, and he had an interest in me. Our youth group was beginning to have some life. Little did I know the support that this group would bring to me.

My Spiritual Encounter on Mount Rainier

The summer after eighth grade began with a summer class that toured Washington state for two weeks. The class was called 'Mobile Education'. We toured the different places around the state that were part of the state's history. We wrote papers and kept journals along the way. We slept on the floors of the school gyms where we visited. Halfway through the trip, we were touring the grounds of a grain company in eastern Washington when I was involved in an accident. I was struck and run over by a truck. My classmates were with me when the accident occurred. We had gotten out of the school bus and were walking around the grain facility. Several of us had this game while we were on the tour that whenever we walked over rail road tracks, we all agreed to jump over them together. As we walked, we came upon some train tracks which were also on the corner of the dirt road in a rural area of the facility. I was not paying attention, glanced down, and jumped over the tracks. I looked up and saw a large red truck speeding around the corner. I remember being hit by the front corner of the truck and landing on my tail. I saw the tires in front of me and I heard the sounds of "Thump-thump, thump-thump" as the truck's tires rolled over my legs. I immediately tried to stand, and fell down, I tried to stand again, and fell down again. The other students ran over to me, and several of them comforted me and said, "Todd, stay down. We're going to get help."

This event left another huge impact on me, and I think about that day often. The doctors told me that everything was crushed between my ankle and my kneecap, except my bone. I was sent home from the tour of the state, and the doctors told me that I would have to learn the word moderate when it came to my ability to walk and stand in the future. I told them that this was out of the question as I was planning on hiking the fifty-mile Wonderland Trail in thirty days with my scout troop. Doctors said no; I said yes. That summer I was determined. There was no physical therapy or rehabilitation. I joined my Boy Scout Troop 97 and hiked fifty miles around half the base of Mount Rainier known as the Wonderland Trail. The week of hiking and climbing around Rainier remains one of the highlights of my scouting days. One highlight of the fifty-mile hike around the mountain was climbing to the top of Panhandle Gap, where I could see for miles. The summit looked so close as I stood on the ridge and looked at the top of Mount Rainier that day. Blue sky surrounded me. I will never forget the still, small voice that spoke to my heart for the very first time when I was on the ridge.

"What do you see up here, Todd?"

"I see ice, glaciers, and rock. We are so close to the mountain's summit, and we are above the tree line," I responded.

"What do you see down below?" the voice asked.

I looked down into Box Canyon, and responded, "I see the blue air, the hundreds of thousands of trees, the blue and green colors of the lower canyon."

"Up on the mountain top, you can see for miles, and the view is breathtaking. But, do you see anything growing up here?" he asked.

"No, I guess not."

"Look again, down below in the lower elevations. See the growth of the trees, the water, and the blue, thick air. Always remember the blessings of the mountain tops, but also remember that things grow best in the valleys."

Little did I know that I was being prepared for what was to

happen in my immediate future. I didn't know it then, but I later realized that this was my Lord, calling to me.

Hiking around half of Mount Rainier was a spectacular seven-day experience. Hiking fifty miles around the Wonderland Trail allowed me to push through my fears and pain about walking past what I was comfortable with after the truck accident. We hiked seven to nine miles a day. I remember the talks with my buddies along the trails. I remember listening at night, trying to sleep in my tent, hearing the avalanches on the mountain above us, or fearing that the bears would get into our food.

After being struck by the truck and then hiking the Wonderland Trail with my scouting comrades around Mount Rainier, I fell back into the summer routine on Wollochet spending most of my days on the water. I had at least two concussions from my accidents. I needed to take it easy.

My parents sat me down and told me that they wanted to sell our family's little fourteen-foot ski boat to me. They set the price at $300.00. Little did I know at the time that my dad was planning on buying a new boat for the family. He had his eyes on an eighteen-foot tri-hull, open bow, inboard/outboard boat. He already had plans to install a 440-Volvo engine in his new boat.

My parents gave me a year to come up with the $300.00. I was both scared and excited. Where was I going to get the money? That kind of money was hard to earn for someone my age in 1971. I think I panicked for a short time, but my parents assured me that if I had the motivation, I would be able to pull the money together. I spent the next several months watering vegetable gardens, mowing lawns, babysitting, and raking leaves for our neighbors who lived on the bay. In the spring of 1972, before my fourteenth birthday, I was close to having the full amount needed to buy the little ski boat. My parents let all of our friends on the bay know that I was saving my money for the boat and threw another one of their parties at the house. I was in my room and several of my parents' friends stopped by and slipped me ten or twenty dollars. Most of them commented saying, "Here you go, Todd, a little something to help you with buying the boat." By the end of the night, I had the money. So, on my fourteenth birthday in 1972, my ski boat was launched across the bay. For the next five years, my friends and I skied almost every day during the summer months. We also fished for rock cod, lingcod, and salmon all over Puget Sound. I had the means and vessel to go anywhere I wanted on the sound. My parents were very strict in that every time I brought the boat out, I was expected to clean the boat with fresh water and dish soap. That way, all of the salt would be washed off the boat. I resented that, but I later was grateful as the boat stayed clean and the red color never faded.

4

PENINSULA HIGH SCHOOL

"For this light momentary affliction is preparing for us an
eternal weight of glory beyond all comparison,"
(2 Corinthians 4:17 ESV)

In the fall of 1972, I survived the first day of ninth grade. My classes were hard. My math classes were even more difficult. I have been convinced of one thing, and I have been saying this for over forty years. In my world, letters and numbers don't talk to each other. To get through my Algebra I and II classes, I resorted to drastic measures. I stole the answer book from the classroom. The next day, I passed a quiz and a test. The next day, I challenged the instructor in front of the class and proclaimed that I didn't need algebra. I told him that his class was a bunch of nonsense and a waste of my time. He responded by saying, "Todd, you need this class in algebra to help you with problem-solving skills."

I replied, "Mark my words, Mr. Wingard. Thirty years from now, I will be paying people to do my math." Almost forty-five years have passed since that fall day in Purdy, Washington. Today, I can tell you that I was right.

Shortly after I had made this big announcement in front of my entire math class, I received a little private note from my algebra teacher informing me that he knew I had taken his answer book due to the high grades that I had received on the quiz and the test that week. He then informed me that it was to my best interest that I return his math book. He also reminded me that I needed to pass his class in order to both graduate from high school, and also fulfill the requirements for a shot at getting into college. The next day I returned his math book on his desk. No further words spoken. Then, most nights I spent in my room on my bed with my dad attempting to help me with my math homework. Most of the time, the evening ended with his shouting at me and me being left in tears. It didn't help matters that my dad worked for IBM and then started his own data processing company. He prided himself on the fact that he excelled in math. I hated the subject.

I tried out for the freshman football team that year. I was excited to be on the team and to learn more about football. My coach had his favorites. I had a difficult time with his attitude. I didn't like him, and he didn't like me. After a month of his verbal abuse on the field and his ugly name calling, I dropped out. When it came to sports, it was the worst moment of my life. After that, I wanted nothing to do with team sports. I was not competitive to begin with. I was not going to place myself in a team sport environment where I was going to be possibly shamed or humiliated. I was content in applying myself in individual sports, where I learned to compete with myself. It was safer.

The beginning of the ninth grade was also the beginning of the last year of confirmation at the church. The confirmation class always had a retreat which was great fun. That year, I was drinking a lot more. Alcohol was becoming more of my routine and was slowly wrapping itself around me like a snake. I was drinking on the weekends and had a stash of beer out in the woods, buried in the ground in back of my house on the Catholic-owned Dominican Sisters' property. On our confirmation retreat, we were at a Lutheran church camp near Bremerton. Someone had brought a bottle of Everclear and Tang orange powder drink mix. For two nights, after our counselors went to bed, we drank. Needless to say, I don't remember my first communion.

On the home front, my parents were drinking daily. On my fourteenth birthday, my parents gave me a small beer mug and plenty of beer was around to fill it. My parents would buy over twenty-five cases of Lucky Lager or Rainier Beer at a time. My dad was known for his special Gig Harbor Martinis. After all, it was the early seventies, we lived on Wollochet, and we were on the party barge. Emotionally, I didn't really care for the environment and culture that our family lived in. It was the culture on Wollochet Bay in that day. In spite of it all, I have always had a spiritual hunger since falling from the cliff when I was ten years old. I knew that I had experienced an encounter with someone who broke my fall. I wanted more of what I experienced that day.

My dad had quit IBM by this time and started his own company with two other coworkers. They formed RBM, noting their last names of Riggs, Babcock, and Mishco. Their company provided consultation and services in data processing and software. In these early days, my dad often had devices set out all over on our living room floor. No one knew yet of the things that my dad was working on. One time when my dad asked me if I wanted to play chess with the computer, I looked at him and replied, "What?" He proceeded to tell me that our phone was connected to a computer in Hartford, Connecticut.

That morning, I was able to play a game of chess with a computer on the East Coast. He was also working on such things as fax machines, floppy disks, and informational transfer via our phone line. These new gadgets were not able to replace my dad, who was gone a lot on business trips out to the East Coast, so my mom held down the fort. When my dad was home, he was at work—working on his boat or working on building things out in the garage. The alcohol in our home was always present.

There was this window of time, as I look back, where it really was the best of times for us as a family, at least for all practical purposes.

My dad's business was feast or famine. When money was coming in, things were good. When he was in between contracts, we bit the bullet. The feast or famine mentality in our family was covered up by their party atmosphere both in the winter months, when we spent weekends at Alpental, and also in the spring, summer and early fall when our house was party central with our friends on the bay.

During the good and bad times, our house was party central on the bay. One summer day, our next-door neighbors threw a party where there was waterskiing, laughter, and alcohol. Our neighbor, who was having the party, ran out of beer and someone needed to make a beer run to the local store. A close friend of my dad had a motorcycle and offered to go and get it. My dad asked me to go with him and ride on the back of the motorcycle to help carry the beer, and I said yes. His intoxicated friend and I hopped on the bike and off we went. As we were heading up to Anderson's store, something happened. He turned his bike, and the next thing I knew I was under the bike. I couldn't get out from underneath it and the bike's scalding hot exhaust pipe burned into my right inner calf. My lower leg was on fire, but we drove back to the house. Everyone at the party, including my parents, immediately sobered up. They quickly applied ice to my leg. There was no medical attention given to me at the time. Both my mom and dad, who were trained in advanced emergency first aid, examined the burn and decided to wait until I could get an appointment to see my doctor. That was a bad idea. My mom took me to the doctor a couple of days later. The wounds were both second- and third-degree burns. There were blisters and parts of my leg were red and brown in color, with a lot of moist discoloration. After taking one look at my leg, my pediatrician scolded my mom in front of me for not bringing me in earlier. He said that my burns were third-degree burns, and that I should have had skin grafts. However, because it had been several days since the accident, this was not an option. My doctor sadly said that I was going to be scarred for life.

I have never blamed my parents for what happened. It was the way it was. As I was growing more into adolescence, I was becoming more and more distant, passively oppositional, and defiant. I was scared to death of my father's anger. He had a temper that was intense, and it was not to be reckoned with. My mom's anger came out through her words. She could say three words, and it would level me. I never saw my parents hug or kiss each other. My mother was the caregiver in our family. She often made attempts to try and enter into my world. She always asked a lot of questions. She would always wait up for me. After coming home from parties, she often would be lying on the sofa. After I came home, she often smelled the alcohol. She would point me to the coffee pot and then go to bed.

My father favored my younger sister in those days. She was the baby of the family and couldn't do anything wrong. On the other hand, my dad was extremely hard on me in my teen years. He had no patience with me and was distant.

My mother and I had an extremely close, but unspoken, bond. She knew that I was drinking more. On the Fourth of July, most of Wollochet Bay came to our next-door neighbor's place for the day. When they had parties, it was always a class act. This time they had hired Three Fingered Jack, the current owner of the Tides Tavern, to come and play his guitar at their party. Everyone we knew was there. To totally enjoy the day, my buddy Dave and I managed to pick up a couple cases of beer and spent the morning and early afternoon on my boat cruising around the bay and out in Puget Sound. We were kids, who were living large on my own boat and drinking ice cold beer on a warm, clear Fourth of July on Wollochet Bay. On the outside, all was good. My close friends described me as outgoing, brash, cocky, and committed to living life large. I wanted to live life on my terms. But on the inside, there was a growing turmoil and a deepening sense of shame and loneliness.

Because of my growing insecurities, I learned to never reveal my inner atmosphere. My parents were performers. They played hard and they worked hard. They were extroverts, and they were self-made individuals and lived life to the fullest. I was an introvert, masquerading as an extrovert who loved to party and have a lot of fun. My confusion was in attempting to hide who I really was and at the same time in keeping afloat my projected image. Making that even harder were my escalating addictions to alcohol, pornography, and food. They were my comforts. They numbed the pain of not knowing how to identify and express my needs for love, acceptance, and worth. I needed to feel capable and to hear that I was never going to be alone.

Adding to my insecurities were some private secrets that I was carrying around. I had stuffed many shameful secrets of the sexual trauma that I had experienced as a boy. These experiences had brought feelings of shame, guilt, and self-hatred that I carried into my adulthood. As a fourteen-year-old, I was confused about who I really was and I was searching. I learned to keep my feelings buried and to suppress these memories. Doing so made me feel more isolated and alone. What was emerging in my inner life was that I was unworthy of love, acceptance, worth or value, and I had feelings that I was incapable of doing things. I also felt a sense of being alone. I had a private world inside my thoughts. I was fearful of letting anyone in. In order for these needs to be met, I had to dance the dance, and that's when the poser was born. Brené Brown says it so well:

> We cultivate love when we allow our most vulnerable and powerful selves to be deeply seen and known, and when we honor the spiritual connection that grows from that offering with trust, respect, kindness and affection. Love is not something we give or get; it is something that we nurture and grow, a connection that can only be cultivated between two people when it exists within each one of them—we can only love others as much as we love ourselves.[1]

Shame was taking root in my soul, and I was bound and unable to free myself.

Tim Sledge, in his workbook *Making Peace with Your Past*, tells the following story:

> The Quaker philosopher Rufus Jones told about a man who had a summer cottage on the coast of Maine. He decided that he was going to start a Bible study for some children who lived on a little island close by. Having sailed to the island, he gathered the children and, thinking he would begin with something common to all of them, asked, "How many of you have ever seen the Atlantic Ocean?" He was shocked when they just sat there. None of the children said anything or raised their hands. He thought, maybe they didn't understand me. So he asked them again, "How many of you have ever seen the Atlantic Ocean?" He got the same response. The children sat there without saying anything. Then he realized that although these children lived on an island surrounded by the Atlantic Ocean and had grown up hearing its surf and seeing it expanse in all directions, not one of them knew it by name.[2]

The Day My World Came to a Full Stop

In the fall of 1972, I was a freshman at Peninsula High School. What was about to happen was going to change the course of the rest of my life to the point of leading me into ministry and calling me to serve in the mental health field. At the time, my family had its own chaos, addictions, and dysfunction, and all of my own insecurities, shame, guilt, and self-doubt consumed me. Yet, I now can look back and say that I am grateful that I had a tribe, which included my family, those who lived on the bay, and those who lived at Alpental. My friends were also there as well. I had people around me. My tribe went well beyond the four walls of our beach home on Picnic Point. It included those who lived on the inner bay of Wollochet.

This group of families who lived life together later called themselves the Wollochet Bay Punt and Canoe Club. This was the largest group of friends in my tribe. We worked hard, partied hard, and played hard. Once a year, they all traveled to the northwest tip of Washington state and stayed in the town of Sekiu. They would fish for three or four days. My parents would come back with a couple seventy-five to one-hundred-pound salmon. Some of this same group, would drive their campers up to Alpental Ski Resort for the weekend and stay with us. These families from Wollochet became friends with the others in my tribe. The others in my tribe were those who lived on the summit. When my dad had been general manager of the ski resort, we became friends with everyone who worked and lived at Alpental. As I've already mentioned, we lived there every weekend during the winter. With what was about to happen in my family, I was going to need to lean on our tribal community fairly hard.

In September of that year, my buddies and I headed out to the Washington State Fair. After a day of fun and exploring the fair, I arrived home in the late afternoon. The first thing I noticed was our driveway full of cars. I walked into the house, curious about why the house was packed full of people. Then my dad came up to me and told me the news, "Your mother met with her doctor today, and they found cancer in her lung."

Everything went into slow motion for me. I knew that she had some doctors' appointments. I knew something was going on because her ankles were all swollen. I had just learned that one of the most important people in my life had cancer. I felt afraid, angry, and numb. I was in shock. I stared around our small living room, and I remember the somber atmosphere. I was used to seeing this group of people laughing and having fun, but the word cancer had sent a hush over the house. No one was prepared, and I was not prepared emotionally or spiritually for the days that lay ahead.

Now as a pastor and a clinically trained licensed clinical social worker who specializes in adolescence and children, I now know what kids need to hear after they are told that a parent has cancer. They need to hear that many people survive cancer. They need to hear that they are not alone. They need to hear that they are not to blame. They need to hear that balance is important. By that I mean that many kids feel like their parent's cancer is always on their mind. Others try to avoid the topic all together. In the months ahead, I was going to try and have more balance. I was really worried and concerned about my mom and her cancer, and I slowly learned to stay connected with people and to continue my normal activities as an active teenager. My parents tried the best they could to keep me in the know of what was going to happen next. Having some knowledge gave me a sense of control.

For the next several months, I was acutely aware of my feelings. I was scared. I was afraid that my mom was going to die. I was afraid that my world was falling apart. I felt guilty. I felt guilty when I laughed and had fun. I felt guilty because I was healthy and my mom was sick. I felt angry. I was angry that my mom got sick. I was angry at the health care professionals. I was angry at God for letting this happen. I was angry at myself for feeling the way I did.

Therapists refer to the emotion of anger as a secondary emotion. It often covers up other feelings below the surface. I was an emerging introvert who was living with parents who didn't talk about issues. I learned early on to never show my anger and learned the art of imploding. I also felt neglected. With my mom's new cancer diagnosis, many things were going on. The family's energy was focused on her getting better. My dad's focus was helping my mom. I didn't feel necessarily left out, but much was happening that did not include me. Lastly, I felt alone. I was aware of two things. First, no one understood what I was going through. And second, my friends didn't seem to know what to say to me anymore.

In the weeks ahead, my mom's physicians made the decision to remove her lung. On one of the most memorable days of my life, I went with my parents and my sister to Allenmore Hospital in Tacoma to admit my mom the night before her surgery. I remember the car drive across the Narrows Bridge. Not a word was spoken. We all had fear in our hearts. I felt immobilized by the emotion of fear and the silence. Once we got her to her room, we said goodbye and walked down the hall toward the exit doors. I turned around before we went out and I looked at my mother. She was standing outside her hospital room door watching us leave. I remember watching her crying. It was a horrible evening at home.

After her surgery my mom came home, but her battle was far from over. She was still as incredibly sick as she had been before her surgery. She had to quit smoking. She was out of breath almost constantly. She had to continue with the chemotherapy and cobalt treatments, and their effects. This was as hard for me as for her. I couldn't handle watching her. She lived on the couch in the living room for several weeks.

Our family focused as best as we could on my mother's health. Our friends on the bay were bringing in meals on a daily basis. My mom's domestic chores were slowly passed on to my dad and me. My sister was too young to share in the domestic chores. My dad continued to work, so that left the domestic responsibilities right after her surgery to me.

Being exposed to several extremely traumatic events before the age of fourteen, I learned that all discipline was punishment to me. Trauma doesn't respond to discipline. Yet, my family followed four set rules:

1. Don't talk
2. Don't trust
3. Don't feel
4. Don't change

Therefore, I felt emotionally paralyzed. At that age, I could not separate the difference between discipline and punishment. It was always an issue of self-preservation. Because of some of my choices in the early 1970s, my parents threatened to put me in a juvenile center in Tacoma for treatment. I agree; they should have placed me in a juvenile alcohol dependency treatment facility. Of course, my going into a treatment setting would have meant that they would be forced to address their own addictive issues. So, no intervention.

There has been a lot of research written by therapists addressed to judges in juvenile courts. Listed below were some of the things that they have found. This was all part of my inner life at that point in time, and I now wished that someone would have worked with me on these issues.

1. A traumatic experience is an event that threatens someone's life, safety, or well-being.
2. Child traumatic stress can lead to Post-Traumatic Stress Disorder (PTSD).
3. Trauma impacts a child's development and health throughout his or her life.
4. Complex trauma is associated with risk of delinquency.
5. Traumatic exposure, delinquency, and school failure are related.
6. Trauma assessments can reduce misdiagnosis, promote positive outcomes, and maximize resources.
7. There are mental health treatments that are effective in helping youth who are experiencing child traumatic stress.
8. There is a compelling need for effective family involvement.
9. Youth are resilient.
10. The juvenile justice system needs to be trauma-informed at all levels.[3]

My fourteenth year was quite an extreme year in so many ways. I started high school, my mother was diagnosed with lung cancer, and I received my Eagle Scout Award in Boy Scouts. Thanks to my father, I had my own ski boat, and I was drinking alcohol on a regular basis. That previous summer, I was run over by a truck while on tour with 'Mobile Education', which included hiking fifty miles of the Wonderland Trail going halfway around Mount Rainier. Inside I was a mess, and the mess was growing.

After my mom's surgery, my father decided to cash in on his retirement funds, and my parents made the decision to buy a two level-loft condominium at Alpental. It was a great place to live on the weekends. Even though my father was no longer general manager of the resort, he was deeply involved in the resort's ski patrol and courtesy patrol. Our weekend home had two levels and was on the second and third floors of the building. The main floor had a studio floor plan with an outdoor balcony and a black wrought iron spiral staircase leading up into the second-floor loft. The second floor had four bunk beds with a railing that looked over the living room. This place was our home on winter weekends for the next several years. A heated outdoor pool and an indoor sauna sat next door. They came in handy after a full day of being on the slopes. Our weekends together as a family was a healing balm to a young man's fear, the fear that the future would really never come. This hidden message lurked into our family, but it was never recognized or acknowledged. The message was that my mother may not live through this, but we were going to live life to its fullest until the day we faced that reality. For my dad to cash out on his retirement meant that we were going to live life to the fullest in the present. Living for the moment is probably the reason why I have never learned to cope really well with the feelings of disappointment. In my world, disappointment usually leads to anger.

The 'Don't talk' rule let my fears grow internally. This imbedded rule came from my parents' culture. One simply DID NOT TALK about it. Whatever 'it' was. This fueled chaos for me as an internal processor and introvert.

I was also a very wounded teenager. Wounded teens have their own recognizable profile. My friend Jeff VanVonderen taught me to recognize these characteristics years ago in his *Breaking the Silence* seminars:

What Wounded People Look Like:
They have a shame-based identity. [low self-esteem]
They are highly performance-conscious. [They are always focused on always doing things right.]

They tend to not know themselves well. [Being out of touch so much, they don't know that they are going without.]
They have a lack of or are unaware of personal boundaries. [There is no line where you stop, and others start.]
They are unaware of feelings and/or are experts at hiding them.
They have incredible radar. [paying attention to all the non-verbals]
They feel that they don't belong.
They can't tell what normal is.
They have a hard time trusting people. [trust isn't a feeling]
They have a fear of being deserted. [abandonment]
They have a tendency to be idolatrous. [getting approval from the things they can see vs. not seeing]
They have high anxiety.
They are tired. [Abundant life is different than survival.]
They are wounded.
They see things through a shame grid.
They have negative self-talk.
They can't admit or make mistakes.
They are over responsible.
They martyr themselves. [Martyrs die young.]
They don't trust their own radar.
They act like a victim.
They set up inappropriate boundaries.
They tend to code what they can't communicate.
They suffer from stress related illness.
They can't have fun guilt-free. [Their childhood was ripped off.]
They act in ways that are contradictory.
They have an issue with gifts.
They will sabotage their success. [Feeling good feels too bad.]
They procrastinate.
They are possessive in relationships.
They have a high need to control.[4]

I was beginning to learn that in my family, children were never to share their pain or abuse outside the family. And, as an adult, I believed I must handle all of my problems myself, in isolation. I learned to distrust my heart, and trust my thoughts. After all, when someone is in a crisis, he learns to trust his thoughts over his heart responses. I learned that the best way to live was to pay attention to my thoughts and disregard what my heart was saying. I had disconnected the wiring between my head and my heart. Charles Dickens once wrote in his work *The Tale of Two Cities*, the following words:

> It was the best of times, it was the worst of times, it was the age of wisdom, it was the age of foolishness, it was the epoch of belief, it was the epoch of incredulity, it was the season of Light, it was the season of Darkness, it was the spring of hope, it was the winter of despair, we had everything before us, we had nothing before us, we were all going direct to heaven, we were all going direct the other way.[5]

I was experiencing a lot of tension between my love for my family, my inner insecurities, and inner self-hatred.

In the fall of 1974, my family was slowly moving forward after the surgery. I was invited to my first school kegger. The party was out in a wooded area somewhere in Rosedale. When I arrived in the early evening, I was surprised by the large number of my classmates there drinking beer. One of the jocks in my class saw me, greeted me, and poured me a glass of beer. "Hey Todd, glad you're here. Drink up." I put my three dollars in the cup as he poured. This experience was new. I was doing something illegal, and I was with friends. As the evening progressed, I was aware that the keg party leveled the playing field. All the different social groups at Peninsula High School were non-existent at our parties out in the woods. I felt accepted; I felt that I had worth and value and that I was not alone when I was drinking. Drinking opportunities came to me easily with parties at our condominium on the weekends, with the mountain parties in the winter, and with the parties at our beach home on Wollochet during the summer. It wasn't long before my drinking became more of an issue. Alcohol gave me confidence. It was the way of life on the bay. It was the place of acceptance and fitting in with my friends. My alcohol use also medicated my feelings about my mother's cancer, of fear, of my trauma, and of survivor guilt from my three earlier near-death encounters: the fall off the cliff, being run over by a truck, and the motorcycle accident leaving me with second- and third-degree burns on my right leg. My alcohol use also buried my painful and confusing boyhood memories of sexual trauma. I was never given the opportunity to process my traumatic experiences, and alcohol was my liquid courage.

In the early 1970s on Wollochet Bay, many neighborhood dinners and gatherings provided opportunities for many activities. When my parents invited the Alpental mountain crew down from Snoqualmie Pass for the weekend, dozens of folks would arrive to stay with us for three days. Our beach home was not large by any stretch of the imagination. My bedroom was in the back of the house, and I have no idea how I ever got any sleep when the weekend parties were hosted in our home. Several times I woke up in the morning and had to step over the dozens of sleeping bodies to get to the kitchen, start the coffee, and make breakfast for everyone. My dad taught me how to make egg soufflé, and I was able to serve everyone in the morning. When I handed people their plate of food, they always spoke kind words to me.

One morning while I was making eggs, I looked into the living room not knowing who was sleeping and who was passed out. I watched a man in his early twenties sit up in his sleeping bag, pick up a wine bottle next to him, and speak out into our living room, "The blood of Christ shed for you!" He took a small swig of wine, finished the bottle, and fell back into his pillow. I didn't know what to think or say. I just stirred the eggs on the stove. I remember whispering under my breath, "That's just wrong."

Brian

In the early years of my life on the bay and on the mountain, a young mountain man became part of my story. He was about eight years older than me. My dad had befriended him when my dad was general manager at the ski resort. He was an orphan of sorts, lost in the drug culture of the 1970s. Yet, I hung out with him nearly every weekend when we lived at the summit during the winters. Brian was on the pro patrol when he was just seventeen years old and lived on the summit when my dad took him in. He was part of the avalanche dynamite crew that I spoke of earlier and I got to be a part of the skiing in the early morning hours during the weekends when we were up on the summit.

Brian came down to our home on Wollochet Bay for the weekends several times during the summer. He was always the first to arrive and my family loved him, especially my mom. He always challenged me to ski with him behind my dad's boat, *The Rocket*, an eighteen-foot tri-hull, open bow, inboard/outboard with a 440-Volvo engine on the back of the boat. Brian's challenge was to see who could knock the other person off his slalom ski first. It was like wrestling on water skis. I always had the upper hand because I would wait until he was half in the bag and intoxicated, and then I would take him on. It didn't help matters that my dad would be throwing empty beer bottles at both of us when he was driving the boat during this duel. I was fourteen or fifteen years old at the time.

Several years later, I worked for Brian helping him build homes and chalets in the Alpental Valley during the summer before I went to Bible college. I was told by my father that Brian passed away on Snoqualmie Summit in 1996 from a drug overdose/suicide. I miss him dearly every day.

The years between 1972 and 1974 were painful. I felt like I couldn't talk to anyone about my inner life and what I was dealing with. I was painfully aware of my public side and also my private side. All of us are made of three sides—the public, the private, and the secret side. It took a great deal of energy for me to manage these three worlds that I was living in. While living on the bay, the playing and partying intensified. On the mountain at Alpental, it was the same environment. I had a hidden stash of alcohol, and once a week I would raid my parents' liquor cabinet and the refrigerator and restock my stash.

Another summer event for Wollochet families who were part of the Punt and Canoe Club included a trip up to Sekiu, Washington, for a week of fishing for salmon and halibut. Fishing most of the day, our friends would head out to sea in their boats at 3:30 a.m. in sometimes ten- to fifteen-foot swells and fished until breakfast. Then they would return to the sea after breakfast. Each family would come home with several fifty- to seventy-pound salmons each year. We would fillet them and often smoke some of the them on our deck.

During one of these trips, I stayed with my friend who lived across the bay when my parents were gone. I was probably fifteen years old. I had managed to get a large quantity of alcohol from our living room liquor cabinet and carry it up to my old tent up on the hill above my friend's house. Our plan was to stay there and party all week while my parents were gone. We partied every night. We were out on the water during the day. His parents looked after us and made sure we didn't do anything really stupid. One evening, one of the adult neighbors snuck up to our tent where we were sleeping and shook our tent, and began to growl and scream. He had every intent on scaring the daylights out of both us. His little charade worked. We thought it was a large animal.

The next day, I had several friends over to my empty house for an afternoon of skiing. A lot of alcohol was consumed that day, and I had my own ski boat running and took many people skiing. The girls who joined us took showers after the day of skiing. What I didn't know was that someone left their bikini in the shower as she changed into regular clothes. My parents came home from their trip and found the bikini on the floor of the shower. I was across the bay at Dave's house when they came home. My mom got right on the phone and called Dave's mom. When Dave's mom hung up the phone, she looked at me very seriously and told me to quickly go home. She also said, "Todd, your mom sounded angry". So, I drove my boat home and I walked into the house. My mom was furious. She started yelling at me by asking, "What did you do when we were gone? Why are there girls bathing suits in the shower?" She then walked over to the liquor cabinet and continued with the barrage of questions and asked, "We had full bottles of liquor in this cabinet when we left. Where did it go?" My mother was onto our plan. She saw that the liquor cabinet was half-empty. She asked many questions about the swimsuits in the shower. She then told me that she wanted to send me to the nearest juvenile detention center in Tacoma known as Remann Hall. I knew then that I was on thin ice.

Looking back into those years, close to forty-five years ago, I see that this incident could have been my moment of truth with my parents. However, my dad took me aside privately and laughed. He suggested that if I do that again, I should pour water in the gin and vodka bottles, so that no one would notice that so much was gone. I remember thinking, "Really, Dad, really? That's all you have to say?" I couldn't believe that he was passively cheering me on. I was in trouble, and I knew it. For the next several months, I laid low. I knew that I had crossed the line with my parents, and my mom was heartbroken. I felt a tremendous guilt for my behavior. My mom was in remission from her cancer, but the silent message in our home was that she was still sick.

Guilt and shame were my constant companions. In order to feel good about myself, I had to meet certain standards and expectations that I placed upon myself. I knew that I was making a lot of bad decisions for which I had a tremendous amount of guilt. In my mind, those bad decisions also made me a bad person. I had no idea how to separate my actions from who I was as a person. I hated playing in team sports out of fears of potentially failing my team members. I continued in Boy Scouts as an Eagle Scout, but was drinking a lot. My grades in school were average at best, and I felt that I was a disappointment to my parents. There was the public side of my life, along with the private side. The secrets that I carried in me were suppressed, and I was scared, with nowhere to go. My own expectations to perform to get people's approval were beginning to take a toll on me. My parents partied on. I was along for the ride, but my inner introvert was being ignored. I was an introvert in an extrovert family. I played the part of the oldest son and did it well. I received a lot of accolades from my family and friends for excelling in water and snow skiing, and becoming an Eagle Scout at the age of fourteen. Our friends from the mountain loved it when I learned to yodel by the time my voice changed. I was often asked to yodel a song while riding the chair up to the top of Denny Mountain. I was an extreme skier both on the water and the snow. After several attempts and several hours on the water, I learned to barefoot and trick ski behind our boat out on the bay. I never got used to people watching me ski. I didn't like the attention.

My mom continued to do life differently with only one lung. She knew that her cancer and surgery had a deep impact on our family. With the purchase of our condominium, we spent a lot of time together at the mountain. Full days of skiing, the outdoor pool with the deep snow, and the sauna were so much fun. The night life with watching my parents party kept things edgy. I am so grateful for those years. Mom was very sick, but we made 'fun' and 'play' work for us.

In high school, I was a member of the ski club. The club came to Alpental for an evening of night skiing. Alpental was my home. I was so excited to have my friends from my high school join me for a night of night skiing. I was eager to show my friends around the resort. When the bus showed up in the resort parking lot, I was so excited. I had a smile on my face during the entire evening. My friends were going to spend some time with me on my turf, and in my world. Even if it was for only one evening, I was thrilled.

I especially remember the friends that I was able to bring to the ski resort with me for the weekends. One night at the mountain, one of my buddies came up with us for the weekend. We night skied Friday evening, and all day Saturday. On Saturday night, my buddy Eric and I decided to head out to the road which had twelve-foot snow banks on each side. We decided that it would be fun to throw snow balls at the cars heading up into the Alpental Resort parking lots. We thought the cars would never have the chance to even see us from the road. We threw snow balls at cars for a short time. Some cars were hitting their brakes. Then, something unplanned occurred. A car stopped, the driver got out of the car, and started running toward us. He couldn't see us, but was planning on getting to the top of the snow bank where we were. I started running toward our condominium building. I sprinted across the snow, opened the hallway door, and ran up the stairs. I ran down the hall and ran into our condominium. I had no idea where my buddy Eric was. I immediately shut the door. My parents and their friends were inside partying. As the door shut, they all looked at me. They looked puzzled. Then there was a BANG-BANG on the door. My dad opened the door. The man that chased us had my buddy by the collar and said, "It would seem that your boys are throwing ice balls at cars." I noticed that as the man began to speak, my dad's friend Jack who lived on the bay with us stood up and started walking toward this guy. Jack was ready to take this guy on. My dad looked at Jack and told him that he would take care of it. Jack remained quiet. I was relieved. The driver eventually left the building. My dad smiled at me. My friend, well, he had some not so kind words for me, and thanked me for leaving him in the snow bank outside.

After the lung surgery, one of my mom's coping skills was found in some Tole painting and decoupage classes. She would find old pieces of furniture, paint designs on them and then shellac the furniture. After drying, she either sold them or they went into our home.

Many afternoons when I came home from school and walked into the house, my mom was sitting at the kitchen table with pieces of furniture in front of her as she painted. The kitchen table was in a small nook in front of our kitchen and had windows on three sides that looked over the bay. This special nook allowed her to focus on her paintings and enjoy the calming and beautiful view of the bay. As soon as she saw me, she would start to slowly put things away and ask me how my day went. Looking back on those four years of my high school, I think her painting was therapeutic. She was a cancer survivor, and one of the ways she processed her healing journey was that she chose to create. She sold many of her tole-painted furniture pieces at the lodge at Alpental.

I have been so blessed to come from a family of artists. Along with my mother's painting, my aunt and all of my cousins are also artists in their own right. Many years ago, my aunt Patti and uncle Don left the Pacific Northwest and moved to Carmel, California, and started an art studio now known as the White Rabbit.[6] When my cousins have the chance to get together, I remind them that I am not a painter or potter. They then remind me of the same thing that Erwin McManus speaks of in his book, *The Artisan Soul*:

> I have come to realize, after over thirty years of studying human creativity, that the great divide is not between those who are artists and those who are not, but between those who understand that they are creative and those who have become convinced that they are not. The great divide is between those who understand that their very nature is that of an artist and those who remain unaware or in denial of their artisan soul. Creativity should be an everyday experience. Creativity should be as common as breathing. We breathe, therefore we create.[7]

I look back on my mother's intentional time where she painted as a form of therapy to cope with her cancer and I agree with McManus' words:

> Fear is the shadow of creativity. When we choose to create, we bring light to our fears. The darkness does not prevail over us. The creative act is inherently an act of courage. We are born to far too many fears and far too great a darkness. It is only when we find the courage to create that we are freed from those fears and that darkness. The past will be our future until we have the courage to create a new one. To make our lives a creative act is to marry ourselves to risk and failure. True creativity does not come easily; creativity is born of risk and refined from failure.[8]

During this time, the message in our family was that any and all pain would be put on hold. What my family needed was family therapy to deal with the chaos and confront the denial of what was happening. My mom was really sick. My dad wanted to play and forget. My sister disappeared, and I wanted to medicate and try to make everyone happy. My dad was never able to talk about his pain during this time, but he made sure that our winters as a family were spent at the mountain at our family condominium. He would also invite families from Wollochet to come up and spend the weekend with us. On Friday and Saturday nights the parents would be at the Alpental Ski Lodge or over at the summit partying while others were skiing or in our pool and sauna at the condominium. I remember that my mom could only ski for a couple of hours because of her one lung, and we would often find her resting back in our mountain home by one o-clock in the afternoon.

We skied for many hours every weekend, and later I was able to join the ski patrol. By that time my dad had resigned from being general manager of Alpental, but he did volunteer on the ski patrol and started what was known as the courtesy patrol at the resort. I continued to head up to the top of the mountain with the avalanche patrol and help blow out the runs before the general public was able to ski them. This usually meant that we were done with the dynamite work by 8:30 a.m. in the mornings.

Setting the dynamite was risky and several incidents occurred when I was with my dad helping out on the avalanche crew in the early morning hours. We were always subject to being caught in slides and avalanches up on Chair 2, yet we took advantage of the ability to ski fresh, untouched powder as we watched the sun come up. On one occasion, I watched my dad try to ski away from a small avalanche on Edelweiss Bowl. I watched him be buried up to his waist. It was a close call.

On another occasion, we were skiing the run known as International which, at the time, was the steepest ski run in the Pacific Northwest. One of the avalanche crew skied down about fifty yards and set several sticks of dynamite on each side of the run to blow any potential avalanches. We were safe on the top of the run above the slide area, so we skied off the top lip of the run and positioned ourselves. We all carried beepers and skied with our ski straps loose just in case we needed to pop our skis off if we were caught in an avalanche. Craig, our dynamite expert, skied about fifty yards below us and set the dynamite charges. My dad looked at me and shouted, "Plug your ears and keep your mouth open."

Then Craig shouted our warning, "Fire in the hole!" Seconds went by, then a huge "Boom...Boom." The entire hill below us started to slide and caused an avalanche.

Several seconds went by, and several yards below me someone yelled out, "Where is Brian? Where is he? He disappeared!" It got real quiet on the upper slope of International that early morning. I started to panic thinking he was buried.

Another voice below me proclaimed, "I think he skied down before the hill blew."

I whispered, "Oh no, I hope he's ok!"

Then there were several seconds of silence. Finally, a small, muffled voice about five hundred yards below us yelled out to all of us several words that I really can't repeat. We skied down to Brian to see if he was alright. He told us that he had skied down below us on the hill. When he heard the words "Fire in the Hole!" he quickly skied over to a tree and hung on. I was surprised that Brian didn't look scared when he explained to us what had happened. There wasn't a lot more said as we huddled together and debriefed in the middle of the steep run. We all knew that we had more runs to blow, so the public could get to the top of the mountain that morning. We were all relieved and laughed it off. We found out later that the avalanche went right over him and the tree protected him from the impact.

5

EARLY MEMORIES LIVING ON THE BAY

"And the peace of God,
which surpasses all understanding,
will guard your hearts and
your minds in Christ Jesus."
(Philippians 4:7 ESV)

On hot summer days, I loved to take my boat up the bay and tie it up to the Tacoma Yacht Club dock with my buddy Dave. We then spent hours either fishing off the pilings or hoping we would be invited onto one of the huge boats that were tied up for the weekend. To fish on their dock, we had to find bait. Dave and I would look for small quarter-sized crabs on the beach by rolling over rocks where the crabs were hiding under. After getting a bucket of crabs, we would dangle our hooks five to eight feet off the pilings where the perch and sea bass were feeding. The people who owned the docked vessels were amazingly kind to us. They always wanted to talk with us and feed us. They were part of a boating culture that has stayed with me throughout my life. Here we were on a yacht club dock, just two boys wearing only cutoffs, sporting white hair bleached by the salt water and the sun, and fishing in a small saltwater bay, while talking to wealthy people with incredibly large boats. We didn't have a care in the world. We didn't wear watches. We didn't have cell phones. We were never inside. Puget Sound was our back yard. I didn't know any different. I often use these memories when I need to retreat to a peaceful place and calm my high stress.

At this point in my childhood and adolescence, I had been water and snow skiing for most of my life. I was up on skis, both on water and snow, by the time I was five years old. I was literally living on the water and with that came the opportunity to learn to slalom and get up on trick and foot skis. I eventually learned to barefoot by the time I was in my early teens.

If we weren't skiing, we were fishing. Once or twice a year, we would head out to Minter Creek Fish Hatchery when the salmon were running into the sound. I remember being in our boat fishing for salmon all morning and having hundreds of salmon jumping out of the water around our boat. But they were never biting. It was so frustrating! In the early years, I loved to fish with my dad.

One morning, when my dad and I were fishing for salmon and rock cod on the south side of Fox Island, we encountered a navy submarine. The south end of the island was at one time used for sonar testing. We were out fishing, and it was quiet. Then to the south, around two hundred yards from us, a large submarine surfaced without any warning. There was no sound, just this large black object rising to the surface. It was surreal and frightening at the same time.

One weekend, I was invited by my friend Adam to go fishing on their fishing boat for the weekend. Their fishing boat was docked in Gig Harbor. They were taking the boat up into the waters of Port Townsend for the weekend. It was a weekend that I will never forget. I was on the boat for two and a half days. The boat was after salmon. Their nets would go out, and then the crew would wait and play cribbage. Then, when the nets were full, they would reel them in. The deck of the back of the boat was knee-deep in salmon and cod. I watched with amazement as the boat crew worked to get the fish stored. This was my culture, this was my tribe. This was what it was like to be a fisherman from Gig Harbor.

One of the many benefits of living in the south part of the sound was that we saw a lot of navy vessels coming in and out of the area. The Bremerton Naval Shipyard was south of Wollochet Bay. Numerous times, my friends from the bay and I would head out in my boat to the Narrows. The Narrows is about one mile across, with depths of around four hundred feet. These navy ships would come into the sound on their way to Bremerton and would pass through the Narrows. As a boy, I would take my fourteen-foot ski boat and we would 'cruiser wake' back and forth in between the wakes of these large vessels. At times, they would throw a five- to eight-foot wake as they passed through the Narrows. I would drive the boat back and forth across the wakes of the air craft carriers and destroyers and would be air born across their wakes as they passed. As my boat was in the air, the engine would cavitate, otherwise known as to spin in high gear until it hit the salt water again. It was a lot fun.

We lived a short distance from the town of Bremerton. Bremerton is known for its large military shipyard, which was the home of an old war hero. She was mothballed in the shipyard. Her name was the USS *Missouri*. I had the honor to visit the ship on a regular basis when she was there. Every time I had the opportunity to walk on board and tour the ship, I was experiencing a piece of history. As a boy, I stood on the spot of the ship that was the site of the signing of the surrender of the Empire of Japan which ended World War II. It was always surreal for me. A very proud nation surrendered on this ship.[1]

I have a lot of memories of boats and ships. I'd like to talk about the planes. As I was growing up, I hung out a lot with several buddies of mine who lived not far from me down on Point Fosdick. Point Fosdick is on the east side of the mouth of Wollochet Bay. We would often get together to walk up through the woods on the west side of the Tacoma Narrows Airport, and into the clearing right beside the runway to watch the planes come in. We would smile and wave our hands to try to get the pilots to give us a thumbs-up as they landed and took off. The airport police were about a mile away. They would get into their cars and come after us. We were on the end of the runway and could always see when they got into their vehicles. As soon as we would see their lights on, we would make a sprint into the woods. They never found us. One time, I remember that they had helicopters...and dogs with them.

One evening, I spent the night over at one of my friends who lived on the point. It was really late in the evening and we were in our sleeping bags. My buddy looked at me and said, "Hey, let's go swimming!" I looked at him and said. "What are you talking about?" He said, "We can go down to the beach and there's a pool at my friend's house. Let's go down to his pool on the beach, and then we can come back." I said, "Okay! Let's do this!" He handed me a towel, and we walked a block down to the pool on the beach. We got there and we found that the pool was covered. We pulled back the cover just enough to slide in and swim. It was pitch black outside and there were no lights. We were both under the covered pool laughing. Then we heard the words, "Hey you two! What do you think you're doing in there?" My friend hopped out of the pool and sprinted down the beach. I hopped out as well, and began sprinting down the beach on Point Fosdick in my birthday suit. I didn't look back. I was in a dead sprint as I ran away from the guy that started to chase us. I ran for about a quarter mile and stopped. It was in the middle of the night. I had no idea where I was and I had no clothes. I slowly found my way back to my friend's house. I walked into his basement, where he was laughing hysterically. I was not amused, but I was relieved to be inside his home.

I remember during the early days in my adolescence when my dad and I would head up to Neah Bay, near Sekiu, Washington for a long weekend of fishing. We would travel up to the northwest tip of Washington and for three or four days, fish for fifty- to seventy-five-pound king salmon and two-hundred-pound halibut. We would take our boat out about three to five miles into the ocean and often find ourselves in ten- to twenty-foot swells. My dad would always hand me warm beer and Dramamine at four o' clock in the morning as we headed out to fish each morning in the large swells. It was amazing that I never got sick! Fishing in our eighteen-foot tri-hull, open bow, inboard/outboard boat in large ocean swells was at times truly terrifying. One time it took me four hours to reel in a 150-pound halibut up to our boat. You have to shoot that kind of fish with a .22 before you gaff it and bring it into the boat. It was like reeling in a refrigerator. We got it to the boat, and the fish snapped the line.

As a boy, with my little red fourteen-foot runabout ski boat, I had access to the sound. I could go anywhere I wanted to go on the water by boat. My buddy Dave and I would pack our tent and beer and sleep over on the beach on Dead Man's Island. I can remember being out of the water at dusk and witnessing the forty-foot basking sharks come up to the surface to feed at night, around the south sound, near McNeil and Anderson Islands. We skied until it was dark all summer long. This was my 'normal' at the time. This was life on Wollochet, yet there was something deep down in my inner being that yearned for more. I was being brought to a place of spiritual bankruptcy. I was empty on the inside and I knew it.

There were the haunting questions that I thought about often:

"Why am I so afraid?"
"Is Mom going to die?"
"Why is Dad always so mad at me?"
"What really happened when I fell off the cliff? There was this presence I felt."
"Why did I survive? Why did someone have to die?"
"The doctors told me that I would have to learn the word 'moderate' when it came to walking again after I was run over by the truck. Why am I walking like nothing happened?"
"The doctors told me that after the motorcycle accident, that I would be scarred for life with third-degree burns. Why are the scars fading?"

"Bees, I hate bees, why can't I just forget about what happened when I was attacked by a hive, and move on? I am such a big baby. Man up!"
"Why can't I just be comfortable in my own skin?"
"Do my mom and dad really care about me?"
"Why do I feel so alone on the inside?"
"Why can't I be grateful for the things that I have and why do I feel so empty?"
"Why can't I be okay with who I am?"

During the winter of 1974, one of the neighborhood families who lived close to us on Picnic Point invited us to their family home up on Steven's Pass for a weekend of skiing and partying. I had never been to Steven's Pass before. It was a fun weekend of two full days of skiing with our neighbors from the point, along with their kids. We partied hard in the evenings and were up early to hit the slopes the next morning. We were in their home and cottage. One particular night, the kids were in one home and all of our parents were next door in another home. There were a lot of chemicals being passed around during the evenings. I was drinking hard liquor that night. I went to the bathroom, and I became violently ill and rushed outside and proceeded to vomit blood into a snow bank. I was shocked and stunned. I went back into the guest cottage and didn't drink another drop that night. I was scared. I didn't tell anyone. Several days later, I was passing blood in the toilet. The following week, I remember going to my doctor after the party weekend. He looked me in the eye, and said, "Whatever you are putting into your body Todd, it has to stop!" This man was my only doctor up through that point in my life. For the first time, I saw a concerned look on his face as he looked at me. I didn't give it a second thought.

The partying continued. On one occasion, I was at one of my school class outdoor parties. There was always at least one keg of beer on tap at these secret school parties out in the woods. I remember that there were a lot of kids there at the party. The beer had run out, and kids started to ask for more money for the next beer run. We collected the money, and a couple of us jumped into a Volkswagen Bug to go make the purchase. I jumped into the front seat. Someone yelled out to me, "No, let me go!" I said, "Okay, fine!" I jumped out of the car, and we waited for their return. My buddy was in the back seat. They never returned. I found out later that night, that after they bought the beer, they headed back to the party. They were intoxicated. They accidently ran a stop sign and had run into another vehicle. The keg of beer was in the back seat of the Volkswagen. My buddy was seated in the back seat holding on to the keg. The person who was in the passenger front seat didn't survive. The driver was severely injured in the accident.

Several months went by and one of my close friends, the same friend who lived on Point Fosdick and who was one of my drinking buddies, talked to me at school and said that he was going to start selling drugs to our school friends. I knew that he was already smoking pot on a regular basis. He said that he had the opportunity to sell cocaine. He asked me if I wanted to join him in his little business. He made the promise that for every eighty dollars I put into the deal, I would make around three hundred dollars in profit. I really struggled and debated over this invitation. I never had smoked pot before simply out of the fear of the cancer that my mom had. I look back on those days, and I am glad that I had that fear. It was embedded deep in my heart. But cocaine, that was a different story. I knew that I would never consume that drug and put it into my body. But the thought of taking advantage of someone else's stupidity by allowing them to buy from us, put the drugs into their own bodies, and us profiting from their stupidity sounded like a good plan. They get high and we make some money. It was a win-win plan as far as I was concerned. For the next few days, I considered ways that I could cough up the eighty dollars and start making the profit.

Young Life and the Day When My New Life Began

Shortly after my private discussion with my friend, I was in the school lunch cafeteria during my lunch hour. I overheard this same friend talking to some of his buddies in between classes. I overheard him saying that he was going to an event that night. I asked him, "So, what's going on tonight?" He responded, "Yeah, it's called a Young Life meeting. Do you want to come?" I said, "Sure!" I got the name of the person's house and the time it started. I wasn't sure what I was getting into. That night, I don't remember how I got there. But I went to the meeting. I walked into this student's home, and there were around eighty kids from our school in the living room. I sat down on the floor next to my friend who had invited me. The first thing that I noticed was the excitement and joy that was in the room. There were several young adult leaders that were up front who were goofing around, and making fun of themselves. There were skits and group activities. I watched in amazement. "These are all kids from my school," I thought. Everyone is happy. There was joy in the room. There was no judgment. The main leader's name was Larry Wright. He started to call out names of those who were there that night. He said, "Okay, so right now we are going to need some volunteers. We're going to have two teams who are going to compete with each other." Then he started to call out names. "Will so-and-so come up front? Hey, so-and-so, come up front!" He rattled off several other names of the first-timers to the meeting. Then he asked, "Will Todd Riggs come up?" All of the kids around me started to shout out my name and shoved me up from my seat on the living room floor. I began to make my way to the front. Larry handed each team a long string of frozen spoons as he explained the rules. Each member had to send the string up inside their shirt and out their neck, and then pass the frozen spoons to the person in back of them. The first person who passed the entire string through each team member won. I looked at everyone and said, "Oh no, nope, I'm not going up!" I attempted to go back to the seat on the floor. Everyone stopped me, and started to chant, "Go, Go. Go!" I was fearful. The acceptance in the room overwhelmed me. As I remember, several of us did the frozen spoon race. I think as I look back on that night, our team won the race. I sat back down. Larry picked up his guitar. He led us in songs like, "The All Day Song," "One Tin Soldier," and "Have You Seen Jesus My Lord?". After the singing was done, he laid his guitar down. He picked up his Bible and shared for almost a half hour. He talked about God. He talked Adam and his sin. He talked Adam's broken relationship with God because of his own sin. He shared about the rift in the relationship between God and Adam because of Adam's sin, disobedience, and rebellion. He said that the rift and separation between God and man went on for thousands of years. Then he told us about God's plan about sending his own son Jesus to earth. He spoke of Jesus' virgin birth, life, ministry, death, and resurrection. He spoke about the fact that three days after Jesus' death, God raised him from the dead. I was intensely listening. Larry then said, "And Jesus died in our place. We should have been put to death that day, as punishment for our sin. But God sent his Son instead, to die in our place." Then he said, "And that's not all." He went on to quote the following scripture:

> "The true light, which gives light to everyone, was coming into the world. He was in the world, and the world was made through him, yet the world did not know him. He came to his own, and his own people did not receive him. But to all who did receive him, who believed in his name, he gave the right to become children of God, who were born, not of blood nor of the will of the flesh nor of the will of man, but of God. And the Word became flesh and dwelt among us, and we have seen his glory, glory as of the only Son from the Father, full of grace and truth" (John 1:9-14 ESV).

As I listened, I thought, "Wow, Jesus took my place." Larry kept on sharing and went on to say that Jesus died in my place so I wouldn't have to. This man named Jesus really loved me. He died so that I could live in heaven with him. All I had to do was turn to him, repent, and ask for his forgiveness, and follow him. Larry looked at me and said, "Jesus wants a relationship with you."

After the meeting, I don't remember the drive home. When I got home, I remember going to bed that night. I stared at the ceiling. I whispered, "Lord, I surrender. I know that I've done the church thing. That stuff is all boring. I don't know what this all means, but I want you. I want a relationship with you. I need you. I ask for your forgiveness for my many sins. My life is yours. Show me the way, and I will follow." "Jesus said to him, 'I am the way, and the truth, and the life. No one comes to the Father except through me" (John 14:6) ESV).

I wish that I could say that the waters on Wollochet Bay parted that night. Maybe I was hoping for a sign of some sort. But honestly, I simply fell asleep and for the first time in my life, peace started to fill my soul.

> When my life was empty, I tried so hard to be filled
> Smiling eyes were fading and the laughter had been stilled
> Reaching out so desperately to fill the inner need
> That we all are trying to satisfy, but none of us succeed
>
> Trying every substitute for love that I could find
> Temporary pleasures that would keep me for a time
> But when each thrill was over, my sorrow would increase
> For nothing that I tried had ever brought me lasting peace
>
> And then, You came to me, when I was ready to listen
> Dissolved the mystery, when I was ready to listen
> And I knew your name
> And I knew your face
> And I knew I belonged to...you
>
> Jesus
> Jesus
> Jesus
> Jesus[2]

The season of new beginnings was under way. In the days and weeks ahead I was aware that heaven was eager. The awareness of Jesus' presence slowly began to enter into my life. I was also becoming aware that he had been there all along. I was a new person. Jesus had taken a hurt, confused, fearful, and empty young man and gave him a new heart. I was a new person who was beginning to walk on a new road, a road paved by a passion to know God. I slowly was learning that I now had God's spiritual DNA infused into me when I surrendered my heart to him. The following months were filled with slow and steady course corrections. The first thing that I noticed was that I wasn't alone anymore. I knew in my heart that he had always been with me. He had been at my side from the beginning. I began to understand in my heart that this presence that I felt at age ten when I had slipped off the cliff in the back country of Alpental was really him. I began to know the reason why I was able to walk again after I was run over by the truck in eighth grade was because of him. That the voice that I heard on top of Pan Handle Gap on the Wonderland Trail on Mount Rainier was him. The reason why my second- and third-degree burns on my right inner leg were slowly disappearing was because of him. He was healing me. He had been there all along. He was waiting for me to respond. Once I did, I found him to be everywhere. My eyes were opened, and I remember thinking the thought, "Toto, we aren't in Kansas anymore." From the earliest of days, my spiritual life has always been filled with his encounters. Grace began before I was aware.

As I have continued to follow Jesus, the Son of God throughout my life, I have learned, and even expect, that his encounters are part of our relationship. I am open to his signs and wonders simply due to the experiences that I had as a boy. John Wimber, the founder of the Vineyard Church movement, used to say that when cold air and hot air come together, there will be thunder and lightning. His light began to drive out the darkness.

The 1956 Oscar winning movie *The Red Balloon*, which has a music score but almost no dialogue, tells of Pascal (Pascal Lamorisse), who, on his way to school one morning, discovers a large helium-filled, extremely spherical, red balloon.

As Pascal plays with his new-found toy, he realizes it has a mind and will of its own. It begins to follow him wherever he goes, and not rise, at times floating outside his bedroom window, as his mother will not allow it in their apartment.

The balloon follows Pascal through the streets of Paris, and they draw inquisitive looks from adults and the envy of other children as they wander the streets. At one point the balloon enters his classroom, causing an uproar from his classmates. The noise alerts the principal, who becomes angry with him and locks him up in his office until school is over. At another, he and the balloon encounter a little girl (Sabine Lamorisse) with a blue one that also seems to have a mind of its own, as evidenced by its act of following his.

In their wanderings around the neighborhood, Pascal and the balloon encounter a gang of bullies, who are envious of the latter, and they soon destroy his new friend through the use of slingshots.

The film ends as all the other balloons in Paris come to Pascal's aid and take him on a cluster balloon ride over the city.[3]

This was the picture that I had of the Lord after I gave my heart to him. He had followed me throughout my sixteen years and I never really knew it. After my encounter, I realized that he had been there as someone who was cloaked. I had never seen the red balloon until now. So, in the spring of 1974, I started to pursue him. I brushed off the leather-bound RSV Bible that I received when I was confirmed. I started to read it. Later, I bought a Bible version called *The Way Living Bible* and began to read it daily. Everyone in Young Life was reading this particular version. The Lord started to teach me and show me how to make better choices. I knew that I was a brand-new person on the inside and my behavior began to change ever so slowly.

Neil Anderson tells the following story:

> When I was in the Navy, we called the captain of our ship 'the Old Man'. Our Old Man was tough and crusty and nobody liked him. He used to go out drinking with all his chiefs while belittling and harassing his junior officers and making life miserable for the rest of us. He was not a good example of a naval officer. So when our Old Man got transferred to another ship, we all rejoiced. It was a great day for our ship. Then we got a new skipper – a new Old Man. The old Old Man no longer had any authority over us; he was gone – completely out of the picture. But I was trained under that Old Man. So how do you think I related to the new Old Man? At first I responded to him just like I had been conditioned to respond to the old skipper. I tiptoed around him expecting him to bite my head off. That's how I had lived for two years around my first skipper. But as I got to know the new skipper, I realized that he wasn't a crusty old tyrant like my old Old Man. He wasn't out to harass his crew; he was a good guy, really concerned about us. But I had been programmed for two years to react a certain way when I saw a captain's braids. I didn't need to react that way any longer, but it took several months to recondition myself to the new skipper.
>
> You also once served under a cruel, self-serving skipper: your old sinful self with its sinful nature. The admiral of that fleet is Satan himself, the prince of darkness. But by God's grace you have been transferred into Christ's kingdom (Colossians 1:13). You now have a new skipper: your new self that is infused with the divine nature of Jesus Christ, your new admiral. As a child of God, a saint, you are no longer under the authority of your old Old Man. He is dead, buried, gone forever.[4]

That summer, I turned sixteen years old. On my birthday, I took my driver's test and passed. Shortly after, our family flew to Minneapolis to see my mother's side of the family. I remember that

I was given a great deal of attention during that trip to the Twin Cities. My dear aunt and uncle threw a golden birthday bash for me at their house in south Minneapolis. My aunt gave me a copy of the New Testament as a birthday gift. The house was filled with family. It was a glorious evening. Later that week, my cousin took me out for the evening. He and I talked all evening. Beer was available for both of us. He drove me back to my aunt and uncle's home at the end of the evening. I walked into the house. My mom took one look at me and said, "You've been drinking." My aunt was in her kitchen, and I heard her muffled words under her breath that I will never repeat again. I was embarrassed to hear her say the words that she said, as I knew that she was a strong Christian. I knew that night my behavior had angered her and that I had broken her heart. Alcohol had its grip on my Midwest family as well, and I was reminded that night that I was going to have to fight for my sobriety.

"I can't, God can, and I'm going to let him."
– A prayer soaked in
Alcoholics Anonymous (AA) Steps 1-3

The rest of that summer I struggled with letting go of alcohol. I was sixteen years old and I was attempting to get sober. I asked Jesus for his help on a daily basis. I was continuing to attend Peninsula Lutheran Church. I threw myself into the church youth group. In the Lutheran tradition, I was baptized and confirmed. Then, a year after my confirmation, I professed my faith very openly after my encounter with Jesus that past spring. The pastor really didn't know what to do with me and my conversion. He never attempted to shut down my new born faith, but he listened and he supported me. My church youth group at Peninsula Lutheran Church was awesome. We had several retreats while I was in high school that hold a lot of memories. The negative memories of my confirmation retreat in ninth grade were overshadowed by the retreats later in high school. I was walking with Jesus. I remember one that we had at Ocean

Shores. I remember telling the entire group that I was finally at peace with myself, and that I was no longer afraid to die. It was during that summer that I became good friends with several in our youth group at church. There was a kid that began to show up a lot in my life. Our friendship started in our church youth group. We started to hang out on a regular basis. I noticed that he came to Young Life. His name was Eric. Little did he know at the time, but he began to support me. He never criticized me. He never judged me. He was a year behind me in school. His dad was one of the guidance counselors at my high school. He wanted to hang out, and more importantly he was intentional about entering into my world.

On the home front, my dad purchased a 1969 yellow Triumph Spitfire convertible. He always loved his toys. Whatever he wanted, he eventually got. I think my mom was resentful of this. He loved his cars, and he loved his boat. After he sold the little red ski boat to me when I was fourteen years old, he went ahead and bought our next boat. He purchased an eighteen-foot inboard/outboard, open bow, tri-hull ski boat. He replaced the engine with a 440-Volvo engine. He named our new family boat *The Aetna* because of the finances from his business with Aetna Insurance enabled him to buy the boat. We called it *The Rocket*.

Shortly after I received my driver's license, I asked my dad if I could go over to my friend Ruk's house and hang out. After he said yes, I pushed him for one more question. I asked him if I could take the Triumph Spitfire out for a drive. To my surprise, he said yes. I left the house and walked up to the garage, and started the engine. It was a beautiful sports car to drive. The top was down and I drove over to my friend's house and picked him up. He walked out of his house and looked at what I was driving.

"Wow Todd! How did you manage to get permission to drive this? Is this your dad's sports car?" he asked. I responded, "Yep it is. I actually learned how to drive in this tiny thing." We pulled out of his driveway, and drove around for a while. We drove around Rosedale and the different bays. We ended up driving over the Fox

Island Bridge and drove to the Fox Island Grange and parked. "This is the place where we meet for Boy Scouts," I told him. We sat in the car for a long time and talked about our friends, school, and, of course, girls. After about thirty minutes I started the car and looked at Ruk and grinned at him and I said, "I'm going to turn this thing around out on the baseball diamond." I drove off the parking lot and onto the grass. I drove the car in a fast circle on the diamond and drove back into the parking area, and then got back on the road to head back to his house. We were close to leaving the island when I looked back into the rear-view mirror. There was a police car with its lights on behind us. The police car came upon us and threw its sirens on. We pulled over and I recognized that it was the Pierce County Deputy Sheriff. The officer came up to us, and asked for both of our licenses. He then walked back to his car. Moments later, he walked back to us and told us that he wanted to talk to us. He asked us to get out of the car and walk back to his squad car. He then asked for both of us to get into the back seat. We both climbed in, and he shut both doors. I looked at the inside door panel and started to panic that we couldn't get out of the car, without the officer opening the doors from the outside. Ruk and I looked at each other and we knew that we were in trouble. The officer was talking on his radio, and after several minutes he spoke to both of us while looking at us from his rear-view mirror.

He said, "I just received a call from a resident a short time ago. The resident called in to report that a small yellow sports car was driving erratically on the dirt of the baseball field up at the Grange."

It was at this point of the conversation that I remember wetting my pants.

I replied, "Officer, we were up the road at the Grange, and I turned around on the dirt to get back on the road so that we could go home." He listened and glared at me through his rear-view mirror. He never took his eyes off me. When I had finished talking, he looked ahead out in front of his squad car and looked at the Spitfire. After what seemed like an eternity of silence, he reached his right arm and laid it out on his bench seat. I remember his green uniform and the red hair on his huge arms. He turned his face around where we could see his face. With piercing eyes that were glaring into our souls, he said a lot of words that I can't repeat, but I remember him saying to both of us, "Well you two, everyone deserves at least one break in their lives, and you have just been given yours. Now both of you, get out of my squad car!"

He then got out of his squad car, and reached back and opened the back door and let us out. We got in my dad's car and slowly drove away. We were silent all the way to my friend's house. I drove home with my tail between my legs. A lesson was learned.

I went back to school that fall. I was attempting to be sober and was very active in the ministry of Young Life. I started to attend Young Life's Bible study called 'Campaigners'. It was in this group that I learned about accountability and godly friendships. At this point, I had not fully realized what I had just come out of. I had been partying hard for at least three years. I was a mess. I had so many secrets. I had spent so much of my emotional energy hiding my true inner self from those who were close to me. I was engulfed in shame and self-loathing because of my earlier sexual trauma. I knew that God loved me unconditionally, but I couldn't love myself. I was always quiet in the Bible study. I listened, and soaked it all in. At that time, I was so hungry for more of him and I wanted to be loved.

Several months after my conversion, my dad and I were watching TV in our small annex off the living room. He walked to his bar in the living room, and took out several bottles of hard liquor. He brought the bottles over to me and said, "I've been told that you have been drinking quite a bit. Tonight, I want to see how you really handle your liquor. For the next couple of hours, we drank. We went drink for drink. Later that night, I remember watching him stumble to bed before my mom came home. Evidently, he couldn't handle his liquor. My tolerance for alcohol was higher than his.

On one Friday night, my friend Adam was having a pool party at his home on Point Fosdick. I decided to go and hang out. When I arrived, most of my classmates were there. It was warm and someone had brought a keg of beer. I stood on their patio sipping on my Tab soft drink, and watched all of my fellow school mates getting more and more inebriated. I went into the bathroom. One of my classmates who was also in the bathroom looked up and said to me, "Wow, Todd. it means a lot that you came to the party tonight. I thought that since you became a Christian, that you wouldn't come and be with us anymore. It means a lot that you are here with us." I responded, "Well you need to know that just because I'm a Christian doesn't mean that we're not friends anymore. I'm still coming to the parties, I just don't want to drink anymore." That night, I knew that my friends were watching me. They had known me in the past as a party animal who always had a beer in his hand, to someone now who gave his heart to Jesus.

On the home front, however, it was a different story. My parents' partying continued. My own alcohol sobriety took some direct hits my junior year. I had a close friend by the name of Mike. We had known each other since the ninth grade, when we had advisory together at the beginning of each day. He was deeply involved in choir and theater at our school. I remember that he had the voice of an angel. I think it was a win-win relationship for both of us. He was a new student, and I enjoyed hanging out with him. We became very close. So, during my freshman and sophomore years, he watched me spin out of control in my addictions. In my junior year, after my surrender to Jesus earlier that spring, he intentionally came alongside of me. He had a close friend named Bret. The three of us became inseparable during the school year. One afternoon, we were hanging out having lunch at the Jack in the Box fast-food restaurant. I told them that I needed their help with my sobriety. I told both of them that I didn't know how to have fun without alcohol. They both looked at me and smiled. They affirmed me and said, "That's okay, you're with us, we'll teach you how to do it." I stared at them and thought to myself, "Oh great. I'm their rehab project, and they're okay with this and I am too."

N. Todd Riggs

That next summer in 1975, it was as though someone hit the "PLAY HARD" button really hard. I had to make some decisions in some of my close relationships on the bay. My close friend Dave and I started to drift apart because of my faith, and my desire to not party anymore. He saw firsthand of my struggles with sobriety. He and I went to the outdoor summer jam concert at the outdoor University of Washington field. Bachman Turner Overdrive was headlining the show along with the J. Geils Band, and Flash Cadillac. We drove up to Seattle that day. We had a twenty-four-pack of Mickey's malt liquor in our two backpacks. We had drunk some before we were met at the concert gate by police officers. The officer looked at me and knew that I was already intoxicated. He then looked at both of us and said, "Boys, empty out both of your backpacks." We handed them to the officers, and we watched the bottles drop into the fifty-gallon drums and shatter. We walked into the outdoor arena and I looked at Dave, and mumbled, "I'm glad that they didn't arrest us." Dave responded, "Yeah, me too." Later that fall, we started to drift apart. For six years, he and I did everything together during the summer. One of my fondest memories was taking my boat out to Dead Man's Island in the sound not far from our homes on Wollochet. I think we brought a case of beer and my tent. We slept overnight on the island. Early the next morning, we both woke up to the cold water creeping into our tent. We had forgotten that the tide was coming in.

On one summer evening, my buddy Dave and I went and saw the movie *Jaws*. The day after I saw the movie, I purchased a new O' Brien slalom waterski. With the reality of living on Puget Sound, watching a shark movie was more than a reality for me. By this time, I had already been exposed to close encounters with sharks, gray whales, and the large basking sharks as a kid. Basking sharks could grow up to forty feet. My dad wanted to take me out for a test run with my new ski. We went out almost to the mouth of Wollochet Bay with me skiing with my new fiberglass Mach One. In the early days, I didn't fall very often. So my dad kept a steady eye looking forward driving our boat, never looking back at me thinking I was not going to fall. Well, near the mouth of the bay, I took a sharp cut and fell in the water. I came up and bobbed in the water watching my dad drive out into the distance of the bay. He never looked back. I waited for him to turn around and bring the boat back to me. It felt like an eternity. As I watched the boat turn from about a half mile away, the theme song from the movie started to play in my head. Duh duh...Duh duh... Right then, I experienced my first panic attack. I was about one half mile from shore. I was thinking that there was a great white shark underneath me ready to eat me for supper. I slowly took the ski off my foot, and proceeded to go into a fetal position bobbing in the water. I was watching my dad very slowly drive toward me. My dad drove up to me and with the inboard/outboard engine still running, I hopped onto the back of the motor. The propeller was still turning when I jumped into the boat on a sigh of relief. My dad responded, "What in the world is wrong with you, at least wait until I turn off the engine. Are you okay?" I looked at him in panic, "Yep, I'm fine dad, just fine." Nothing more was said. Normally, my dad would throw empty beer bottles at me from the boat when I was skiing. With what just happened, he knew I was fairly shook up.

Deep down in my heart, I didn't think my parents were happy with me. I was taking a stand for my faith and I no longer bought into the party scene and atmosphere in our home. Both my parents lashed out with a lot of criticism, reminding me that Christians don't act the way I was acting. They knew that I was struggling with alcohol. The fact was that I couldn't talk about my feelings and I couldn't trust them. The Lord was slowly changing my outward self, in the light of the choices that I was making. The Lord had touched my heart, and the transformation was working its way from the inside out.

There were several silent messages that were emerging in my family. What I started to hear were these unspoken messages:

"We were to embrace the good times, and forget the bad times."

"Anyone who sets healthy boundaries inside the family system is seen as someone who is disloyal to the family system."

"Anyone who says, 'Hey, I think that there's a problem here', is then considered the problem."

"A family is as sick as the secrets they keep."

And finally...

 "Don't talk about things,
  Don't trust anyone,
   Don't share your feelings,
    And don't ever change..."

Sometime during my junior year, my parents pulled me aside and sat me down to talk. I looked at both of them and thought that I was in some kind of trouble. My dad started talking, "Your mom went to the doctor, and she found out that she is pregnant." My response was, "Wow, that's great!" My dad interrupted me, "We were told that because of your mother having only one lung, that she would die if she were to have the baby. Your mother and I were given the choice of either she would give birth to the baby and die in childbirth, or, we can abort the baby, and your mother will live."

I went numb...

"What?" I said.

My mom looked at me and said, "I'm going to have an abortion."

Nothing more was said that day. What I remember is feeling really excited that I was going to have another younger sibling. Then feeling incredibly sad. I remember several months later, I talked to my mom once about the fact that I almost had a younger sibling. We were in the kitchen, and she turned around and looked at me with her piercing eyes and said, "You are never to speak of this again! Do you understand me?" I responded, "Yes, okay."

With the 'PLAY HARD' button being pushed in my family, and my faith growing, I often retreated on my little Yamaha motor bike that my dad had bought for me. I often would get on the bike and ride through the woods on the Dominican Sisters' property above us and over into the woods across the road. Often, I would take my little New Testament Bible and go up into the woods or sit in the field, read my Bible, and pray. It was an oasis for me. There were many times when the words of the scriptures would leap off the pages and speak to my heart. I was learning to hear the Father's voice as he spoke to my heart through the scriptures.

The Lord was gradually setting me free from my alcohol dependence. I was a junior in high school. I set my sights on walking with Jesus, no matter what the cost. I had close friends like Mike, Bret, and Eric and the rest of the Young Life club where I could talk about faith issues. My Young Life leader, Larry, would pick me up in his blue Volkswagen before the meetings. I was grateful that I had yet another tribe, who were Spirit-led and sober. They became my life link.

My parents on the other hand, became my greatest critics. I remember on one occasion, my parents grounded me from the Young Life weekly meetings for a month because I had lied to them about something. I was crushed and I hated them for the grounding. That night, I remember crying myself to sleep.

As I look back on those days, I am aware that my parents had no idea how to show unconditional love. Every ounce of love that was shown was conditional to some degree. There was always an expectation of performance attached. I wrote earlier in this writing that my family went to Sun Valley one year to celebrate Christmas. It was a Christmas filled with tremendous memories. Several months before we went, my parents had bought me a pair of brand-new K2 snow skis. They gave the skis to me as an early Christmas present. I don't remember what happened, but I did something horrible. It was horrible enough for my parents to inform me that I was not going to get the new skis, but in fact they were returning the skis as a consequence for my behavior. I was crushed. I remember telling my close friends what had happened and that my Christmas present for Sun Valley was being taken away. Well, one of my close friends told his mom. I found out years later that his mom talked to my mom about this situation, counseling my mom that it was a bad thing to give a gift and then take it away. My mom told me later that she never spoke to my friend's mom again.

During one of the summers during my high school years, my dad decided to have small pea gravel brought in on our beach on Wollochet. After all the permits were granted, several families paid for a large barge to come into the inner bay with the help of a fireboat. The fireboat used salt water and sprayed huge piles of pea gravel onto our beach at high tide. It was a big ordeal and a huge party. My dad invited most of our friends on the bay to come over to our home and witness this ocean bearing vessel, pulled by a large tug boat, come in and station itself around one hundred feet off our water bulkhead and spray all the pea gravel onto our beach. We had to put boards on our windows so that the gravel wouldn't break any glass. We all watched with amazement and the alcohol flowed freely. I invited my buddy Eric to come over to witness the event. It was something that I will never forget. My dad always did things his way, and he lived life large. During the weeks that followed, he hired a person with a small bulldozer to come at low tide to spread out the gravel on our beach. I remember that the week before he came, my friends and I would swim out to the piles of gravel at high tide, climb up, and jump off into the water. Memories were made that summer.

6

CAMP HAHOBAS

> "But you will receive power when the
> Holy Spirit has come upon you,
> and you will be my witnesses in
> Jerusalem and in all
> Judea and Samaria, and to the end of the earth."
> (Acts 1:8 ESV)

During the spring of my junior year in high school, I made the decision to apply at the Boy Scout camp known as Camp Hahobas, located in Tahuya, Washington for a summer staff position. I had just turned sixteen years old. I had been a Christian for about three months. My house was party central during the summer, and I wanted out of that culture. I applied, interviewed and I was accepted for a position at the camp. It helped that I was an Eagle Scout, and I wanted to be away from my family. So, that summer in 1975, I worked and lived for six weeks at the camp, coming home briefly on Friday nights, and staying home until Sunday mornings. My dad had bought an old, red truck with a huge engine and lots of horsepower. He let me drive the truck up past Bremerton to the camp during the week, and I drove it home on the weekends. The six weeks on staff were amazing. I taught merit badges, and I learned to work together with others on a team. There were three of us that lived together in one of the staff cabins. I shared a cabin with a kid by the name of Brian and an older kid who was from Nigeria. We would stay up at night and talk in the dark until the early morning hours. We talked about everything. One night we were talking about Christianity. To my surprise, all my roommates were Christians. We each talked about our faith and how we came to know Jesus. My roommate from Nigeria would pray each night as he laid on his stomach with his hands folded. I will never forget watching him pray. My roommate Brian eventually asked me, "Okay Todd. I know you have met Jesus. But have you ever met the Holy Spirit?" I asked, "What? Who?" "You know, the Holy Spirit," he said. "Hmm, well I don't know," I responded. Brian then began to talk about the third person of the Trinity over the course of the next several nights. "Todd, the Holy Spirit wants a relationship with you. He works closely with Jesus, and God the Father. All three are part of the Godhead. All three of them have been part of your life from the beginning. God is delighted that you asked his Son Jesus into your heart, but the Holy Spirit wants a relationship with you, too. You know that my brother Dana, is also here on staff this summer. He's in the other cabin. My brother knows the Holy Spirit. Let's ask him to come over tomorrow night and he can tell you about him. Okay?" "Okay," I said.

The next night, our cabin was up talking about faith and our relationships with Jesus. We always encouraged each other, and taught each other what the Lord was showing us. That night, Brian's brother Dana knocked on the door. He was the same age as I was. We began to talk together in our cabin about the goodness of God in our lives. Dana asked me if I wanted to know the Holy Spirit on a more personal basis. I said, "Yes, I do." He responded with saying, "The Holy Spirit loves to show himself by healing us. I was wondering Todd, do you need healing anywhere in your body?" I responded, "I don't think so, not right now." Dana looked at me and said, "I believe that God, through his Holy Spirit, wants to heal something in your body." I asked, "Really?" "Yes, God wants to heal you. Can you put your legs up together on the chair? Let me see something." I threw both of my legs up on the chair in front of me. I looked down and with several others watching, we all saw that my legs were not at an equal length. One leg was about an inch and a half longer than the other. I looked at Dana and said, "Wow, one leg is longer than the other!" I joked a little and said, "Well, I've fallen off a ten-story cliff, been run over by a truck, been in a motorcycle accident where the motorcycle landed on top of me and I couldn't get out from underneath it, and I've been attacked by a swarm of bees. This is no surprise to me." Dana looked at me and then took both of my legs and held them in his arms. As we were all watching, he began to pray for my healing. He asked the Holy Spirit to come and to lengthen my one leg to make both of my legs equal length. As we watched, my shorter leg slowly grew to the equal length of my other leg. Everyone in the cabin started saying, "Wow!" Dana then thanked the Holy Spirit for healing me. I was astounded, amazed, and grateful. I will never forget that one summer. It was the summer that I was formally introduced to the Holy Spirit. It was like déjà vu all over again. That night, his sweet presence filled our old Boy Scout cabin on the lake. I was thrilled in the encounter. I knew that I needed his power in my life to help me with my sobriety, depression, anxiety, and trauma issues. Like the red balloon, he had followed me all the days of my sixteen years, waiting for me to follow him back. That night after my encounter, I welcomed the Holy Spirit, even though he had been there all the time. I realized for the first time that I was hungry for the things of the Spirit and I was thirsty for more. As I look back on that summer, I can recall that I was at peace with myself.

When I got back from working at Camp Hahobas that summer, it was back to the same routine as usual on the bay. By this time, we were around three years out from when my mom's cancer was diagnosed. The only remnant of the illness was when my mom would lose her breath from having one lung now. I was no longer drinking, and I immersed myself in Young Life meetings and a Bible study group that was associated with the Young Life community. I had only one regret from that summer. My friendship with my close summer buddy Dave continued to drift. Once I made the decision to be sober, our time together became more and more awkward. I didn't want to drink anymore. I had enough of the party culture both on the bay and at the mountain. I still remember several evenings during that particular summer, when I would sit on my deck and wonder what Dave was up to. We still were friends, but our time together had diminished. I missed him a great deal. His family had their summer house across the bay from us. I only saw Dave for the three months of summer. In September, he and his family moved back to their home in Tacoma. The highlight from that summer was meeting up with the Connelly Water Ski Team.

Meeting the folks at Connelly Skis

My family's contact with the Connelly ski folks started with my dad's hobby of woodworking. I can remember that he made our breakfast nook dining table out of a dozen 4x4 pieces of wood that he glued together and sanded down and stained. Our table was beautiful. He also made wooden slalom water skis that were patterned off the Connelly skis. I loved to ski on the skis that he made. At one point, he contacted the Connelly ski representative in the Pacific Northwest region, Greg Horn. We wanted to buy some trick skis and some slalom skis from the ski company. My dad invited Greg to come down to Wollochet and spend the weekend skiing with us. Greg came down with his wife and introduced the Connelly skis to us. I was able to ski on brand-new, cutting-edge slalom skis and also their trick skis. Greg brought the Connelly water ski boat and its driver down for the weekend as well. I was so excited to ski on the brand-new skis. Their boat driver allowed me to drive the Connelly boat. I still have the pictures. No words could begin to describe my emotions. I was beyond excited. Greg and the rest of the Connelly team came down to ski with us several weekends during that summer of my junior year and also my senior year of high school. I learned more about skiing from the best. I already was skilled at slalom, trick skiing and barefoot before I skied with the Connelly ski team. They taught me how to excel in the sport. I also learned the science of how to drive a professional ski boat. Our days on the bay with the Connelly team was also a distraction for our family. We were all so unsure about my mother's illness and where it was going to take us. Their presence with us on the bay was a respite for my family. During the summer months, my buddy Dave and I would ski all day and often into the evening on Wollochet. One afternoon, I was practicing performing aerial 360-degree flips on my trick skis. It was low tide, which meant that we often skied into the beach that was mud and full of barnacles. I was behind the boat while Dave was driving. I came into the beach way too fast and hit the beach at low tide and slid into our beach that was an oyster bed and full of barnacles. The right side of my body hit the bed of razor-sharp barnacles and cut open the entire right side of my chest and legs. They were shallow cuts, and there was little or no pain, but there was blood everywhere. I walked up the beach, as it was low tide, and walked up the stairs to the deck. My mom came out of the side door next to the kitchen and went into a panic after seeing all the blood. She brought out towels, and I remember that it took a while to calm her down. She thought that I was bleeding to death. After I told her what had happened, she gave me the glare and turned around and went back into the house.

 Of the years that I spent growing up on the bay, there were also some tense moments that I remember. It was the summer of my fifteenth birthday. I brought my ski boat onto the beach, cleaned it up, brought out its buoy, and tied it off. I swam in and as I was walking up the beach up to our house, I noticed that several of the Catholic Sisters were also on their beach next to us. I said hi to them and waved. They knew who I was. I was excited to head over to the party that was starting at our neighbors. The parties on Picnic Point were always a great time. The entire bay would show up. Everyone would bring their own alcoholic beverages and something to pass for the dinner potluck. I managed to get cleaned up and walked over and joined my family at the get together. I was out on the front lawn and my dad walked over to me and yelled, "Your boat is sinking!" I ran over to the concrete bulkhead that was above their beach and saw the site. My heart sank. My dad continued to yell at me and told me to get out to the boat and bring it into shore. It was a very long process, but with the help of those at the party, we managed to drag the almost submerged ski boat to the shore. My dad and many of our friends detached the 35-horse engine from the back transom and we carried the engine up the beach, up the stairs that went up the concrete bulkhead, through our tiny yard, up the deck stairs, and through our entryway and living room. We placed the huge outboard in the bathtub. My dad looked at me and with a stern voice said, "Turn the cold water on. Your engine is going to get a bath in fresh water." So for the next couple of days, my boat was beached, and my engine experienced a miracle of sorts after spending several days submerged in a fresh water bathtub. Several days later we carried the heavy outboard engine down the steps and down onto the beach. We attached the engine to the back of my boat, along with putting in some new spark plugs and I turned the key. It started! I found out several days later that my dad had spoken to the Catholic Sisters next door to us about my boat sinking. He told them that I had forgotten to put the plug back in the boat after I had cleaned it up. The sisters then told my father that I wasn't to blame for the boat sinking. They told him that after I had brought the boat out to the buoy and swam to shore, I had said hi to them. Shortly after I had left and walked over to the neighborhood party, another young man walked onto the beach and slipped into the back of my boat. He then had slipped back into the water and swam to shore, walked up to his car and drove away.

After several days, my dad sat me down and told me what the Catholic Sisters had told him. They saw the whole thing. What they didn't know was that this kid had pulled the plug from my boat. He said, "They told me that it wasn't you." Then he paused and looked away and smiled. He looked at me again and said, "I'm not about to argue with a couple of Catholic Sisters. I'm sorry for blaming you." I was relieved. Over the next week, I was quiet about what had happened, but I was told through friends that a very jealous former boyfriend of a girl that I was talking to, and had an interest in, had done the deed. Nothing else came of it.

Another tense moment on the bay was when our neighbor Jack had his buddy come over with his drag boat for the weekend. I walked over to his house when the boat was there. Jack yelled at me from the drag boat and said, "Hey Todd, let's get you up on barefoot behind this thing!" I remember looking at his friend who was driving and got a little nervous when I peeked up into the front of the racing boat and saw the gas pedal on the floor of the boat. "Umm, sure. We can do this!" I remembered my inner voice said, "Don't! You will regret this!" I don't know if that was prophetic or pathetic at the time. I also remember that they both had a beer in their hands. I yelled, "Hit it!" Immediately, I was up on my slalom and they took me down the bay to the end of the inner bay, and circled. The boat was doing around forty- to forty-five-miles per hour as it headed up and circled again in front of the Tacoma Yacht Club dock. I made the decision to stay inside the wake and not make cuts due to the boat's speed. As the boat passed in front of Jack's house, I skied to the outside of the wake, and signaled that I was ready to drop my slalom ski. I nodded to Jack in the boat, and the driver punched it. I put my left foot in the water, and with my right foot, I stepped out of my ski, and as I put it in the water to begin to barefoot, something happened. It happened really fast. All I remember was that I hit the water and bounced at least six or seven times. The water felt like concrete. I shut my eyes and tried to absorb the multiple impacts before I slid across the water and came to a dead stop in the middle of the bay. After several moments, I opened my eyes and realized that the boat had already made a sharp turn and was coming right toward me. Jack was standing in the boat looking at me. He looked really concerned, and that would be the only time in our current forty-five-year friendship that I would see fear in his face. His friend drove the boat right up to me. Jack looked at me and said, "I was ready to jump in after you, Todd. We were going way too fast for you to drop your slalom ski. We turned the boat around on a dime as soon as you hit the water." The driver of the boat looked away from me and said, "When you dropped out of your ski, my speedometer said fifty-five miles per hour." I didn't ski the rest of the summer.

A year or two later, on a warm summer's night, my friend Dave and I were on my beach hanging out after a long day on the boat. We heard a lot of commotion across the bay just slightly northwest of us. We witnessed an incredibly scary site. Someone was pulling a skier behind a boat. The skier had made a sharp cut across the wake so hard that it threw both the driver and the passenger/spotter out of the boat. The skier managed to swim away from the driverless boat that was going in circles. The driver and passenger watched helplessly as the boat circled them for several minutes. I looked at Dave and said, "Let's go! We have to do something! Maybe I can drive the boat over to their boat, and one of us can jump in and stop the boat!" Dave just looked at me. My dad came down the stairs and said, "You are going nowhere." The three of us helplessly watched as the boat made circles around those in the water. It seemed like a lifetime, but the boat finally drove right into the shore slamming into the beach.

Back in those early days, we skied hard. It was known that when I slalomed with either my Connelly or O'Brien water ski, my cuts across the wake could almost stop the boat. When I dropped my shoulder, which would often touch the salt water as I made each turn, the ski handle would often break in two. There were several summers when I would go through several handles during the ski season. Then one day, my dad walked down to the beach where we were getting ready for another ski run. With a smile on his face he looked at me and said, "Okay, so I fixed the problem." He then handed me a new ski handle that he made. It was a steel bar that was in the exact shape of a handle. He continued with saying, "You're not going to be able to break this." I looked at the steel handle in shock. I replied, "Probably not, but I will most likely break my head open with it when I fall." He grinned and walked back up to the house.

My Senior Year at Peninsula High School

In September, I went back to school for my senior year. I was in a better place emotionally. I was seventeen years old, and I had been sober for less than a year. The Lord was in the process of healing my heart in the way of his speaking into my own self-hatred and shame from the things that I had experienced in my past, and my fear that my mom was still sick. I tried really hard to not think about the fact that she might die from cancer. Alcohol was no longer my friend, Jesus was. I was doing life differently. My friends who attend AA tell me an old phrase in the program:

Once alcohol is out of the 'alcoholic', you still have the 'ic'.

As a senior, I was voted in as the class vice president. I was active as a representative on student council. It was my goal to be friends with everyone in my class. It was a great year that year. It was 1976, and the bands, Paul McCartney and Wings, Wild Cherry, StarLand Vocal Band, and Children of the World had songs at the top of the charts. In the midst of that year of sobriety, fun, and great memories, way off in the distance, faintly seen to the human eye, dark storm clouds were beginning to form. I was unaware that the perfect storm was coming. I was way too busy enjoying my senior year. My parents were partying and we were all enjoying our life on the bay. We never talked about the cancer in our family openly. Three years previously, I witnessed my mom go through her cancer, and the removal of her lung, along with all the chemotherapy and cobalt treatments. I don't think anyone wanted to talk about it, including me. I didn't know the questions to ask, let alone being able to hear the answers. What I can remember, is that I had this deep fear that something was going to happen to my mom. Since the age of fourteen, I medicated that fear with alcohol. Now that I was sober, I threw myself into my Christian friends. Living on the water and at the summit at Alpental Ski Resort on the weekends in our family condominium was my life. I remember one evening, sitting on my bed in my bedroom after I had just finished my homework. I was listening to the album *An Evening with John Denver* on my record player. Something came over me that I can't explain. I knew in my heart of hearts, that something really, really bad was going to happen in my family very soon. I remember shutting my door, and weeping. I whispered to the Lord, "Jesus, help me. What is it? Is this me or is this you?" I only heard silence. I have had several powerful prophetic moments throughout my life. This experience was the most quiet, and was cloaked with the most questions, and I had no answers. I was about to learn something very important. During a test, the teacher is always quiet.

During these years, both in middle school and high school, I always went to the school dances. I had a couple of girlfriends. I enjoyed the dances at the school. There were always live cover bands. The music was always great. During my senior year, I was at one of the dances. I was sober and having a great time. We were in the school gym and I was dancing, and all of a sudden there was a huge "BANG", and a bright light. Then I felt a sharp pain in my right chest. I remember trying to get to the doors into the light. I then realized that a piece of wood from the gym floor was lodged in my lower chest. Someone on the dance floor had thrown an M-80 at my feet while I was on the dance floor. An M-80 is an explosive that urban legend says is the equivalent of a quarter stick of dynamite. I was startled and I was angry.

During this time, I was growing in the Lord. The tap root in my life with him was growing deeper and deeper. Little did I know that I was on a crash course with another encounter with him. I was going to need to have a deep tap root in order to sustain me with what was coming.

> **"The name of the LORD is a strong tower;**
> **the righteous man runs into it and is safe."**
> (Proverbs 18:10 ESV)

One afternoon, I came home from school, and threw my books onto my bed in my room. I walked out to our entry way, down the deck stairs and sat on the bulkhead on our beach. I remember that I was in a prayerful discussion with the Lord. I remember that I was at peace. I was looking out over the water, and I noticed that my dad was behind me walking down the deck stairs. I started to get uncomfortable as he walked toward me and sat down next to me on the cement bulkhead overlooking our beach. As I think back on this conversation, I remember how angry I was with him. Since my mom's illness, we did not connect very well. From my perspective, he was always irritated and frustrated with something. He was a difficult man to get close to. He was always working, and when he wasn't working, he was in a party or selfish mode. Now that I professed my faith in Christ, it seemed that I was a bother to him. So, he sat down next to me. As we both looked out over the bay, he said to me, "You know Todd, I have worked for everything that I have. I have done very well. From the world's perspective, I would be called a self-made man. I have known fame and fortune, I have all the money and possessions that I would ever want. I've made it. But, I look at you. I look at your faith, and you have something that I really want, but I could never buy it. What you have is not for sale. You have a peace in your life that I've never had." I stared into the water, and I went numb. The conversation at that point went gray to black. He got up and walked up the stairs of the deck and went into the house. I sat there staring across the bay. I was frozen, I was shocked, and for the second time in my life, I saw my dad's vulnerability. I accepted it with a joyful heart of my dad's validation of my faith. The first time was, as I mentioned earlier, after I fell off the ten-story cliff at the age of ten. That time, I saw my dad cry and he just held me in his arms in the back ski bowls of Alpental until help arrived.

In the following months of my senior year in high school, the mission organization, Youth With A Mission, known as YWAM, started a Discipleship Training School (DTS) and mission base on Tanglewood Island. The base was just outside the mouth of Wollochet Bay, off Fox Island. This missionary organization, and its influence became a huge part of my early Christian life. YWAM's early teaching pioneers were teaching in our communities. I became familiar with Loren Cunningham, Brother Andrew, John Dawson, Joy Dawson, Winkie Pratney, and Corrie Ten Boom. I was enamored and attracted by the YWAM's Slavic Training School in Oregon. I heard of stories of eighteen-year-old kids who were buying one-way tickets to Russia to serve as missionaries. They weren't planning on coming back. Later that year, a small group of young people known only as the Agape Force came into Gig Harbor. This group of young people, led by a youth pastor named Tony Salerno, became part of our Christian youth culture out on the Peninsula. This group are known for their Christian music teams known as Candle and Silverwind, and children's music known as Agapeland. I say all of this to point out that along with my youth group at Peninsula Lutheran Church, I was also blessed to have Young Life, and the ministries of YWAM and the Agape Force around me. They had a giant impact on me during my early years as a young believer. I am so grateful to have had these voices speak into me as a young man.

My relationships within the youth group at my church were growing deeply. I look back on the retreats with fond memories. A favorite youth group memory of mine was the time when our group learned mime and presented a mime drama during one of our church services. The drama that we presented was acting out the Life, Death, and Resurrection of Jesus. I was asked to play the Christ figure in the mime. It was very moving for me, so moving that we reenacted the mime play in 1997 during our medical mission in Costa Rica, and again in Guatemala in 2008.

In the early months of 1976, I was happy. I was growing as a Christian. I had strong Christian brothers and sisters around me. I was starting to make decisions about what was going to happen in the fall after graduation. There was a brand-new Safeway grocery store that opened in Gig Harbor. I applied at the store to bag groceries and I was hired. In the spring of that year, I worked as a grocery bagger after school. I remember that after working there for a short time, I was given the 'Employee of the Month' award. I was deeply involved in Young Life and my church youth group. Things at home were good. My inner circle included my church friends, along with my friends in Young Life. My parents were more and more uncomfortable with my faith. I was no longer drinking, and I had a Bible next to my bed and was reading it every day. I never pushed my faith onto my friends at school or on the bay. My church and my Young Life friends embraced me. My friendship with my friend Dave on the bay continued to drift.

As I got closer to graduation, the pace picked up a bit. I made the decision to go to Tacoma Community College part time in the fall. I was also working at Safeway part time. I wanted to work for a year after graduation. This would give me some time to really look at my academic options. That winter, I was on the ski patrol at Alpental. We continued to live at our condominium every weekend. During the week, my best friends were Mike, Bret, and Eric. They continued to be my lifeline. As I have already mentioned, the harbor had several para-church ministries, such as Young Life, YWAM, and the Agape Force, serving the youth in the area. They each had a strong voice in my life.

The big event that everyone was looking forward to was the Senior Ball. Let me tell you, it was an event. I was the senior class vice president, and that meant that I was part of all the planning and arrangements. It was an awesome experience and we had so much fun. My two buddies, Bret and Mike, and I decided to triple date for the evening. We all had a great time. The best part was that I was sober, and we all knew Jesus.

Sometime that spring, Bret and I hung out together one night. He was heading off to the naval academy and was graduating several months early. We decided to drive to the Narrows Bridge, walk down to the beach, and sit on the huge concrete foundations near the beach. I wasn't sure that I was going to see him again. That night as we watched the sun go down and then come up, we talked about our lives. We talked about our futures and predicted where we would be ten or twenty years from that day. That night we talked about our hopes and dreams. He was excited to head off into a naval career, while mine included attending a local college and begin saving some money. I think that Bret knew that I was tired, tired of not knowing if the future would really come to pass with my mom's cancer remission. I remember thanking him for his friendship. He never judged me. At times, I was socially uncomfortable, and he could draw me out onto life's dance floor. He was the extravert and the social magnet, while I was the socially awkward yet grateful introvert. That night under the Narrows Bridge was an evening and early morning that I would not forget.

The next few months were festive prior to graduation. I made the decision to take the next year off and work for a year. I was already working for the Safeway grocery store in the harbor. Things were good at home as well. My family was excited to see me graduate. I was asked to give the opening invocation at the senior class Baccalaureate Service. I was humbled to be asked. It was also a reminder that others who knew me, had witnessed the Lord's transformation in my life. Later that week, my class met offsite down on Tacoma's waterfront at one of the restaurants for a luncheon. After lunch was given, the class officers passed out the class awards. Since I was the class vice president, I helped plan and prepare for the event. I remember sitting with the other class officers, along with the faculty advisors, as the awards were handed out. I wasn't really paying attention as the names were spoken. Then I heard,

"And the class inspirational award goes to...Todd Riggs!"

I looked up, as I was still eating my food. I was stunned. The entire class had voted for me. I couldn't believe it. I walked up to the podium and smiled and everyone was clapping. It was an experience that I will never forget. I sat back down, and whispered, "Thank you Lord." Four years earlier, my classmates saw me as a young person out of control. I was known as one of the class drunks. I went to almost all the parties and the keggers. I was reminded that day that people are watching. The world is watching those who profess Jesus as their Lord and Savior. I had no idea that my classmates saw the changes in my life. I was, and still am, simply a trophy of his grace.

On June 3, 1976, I walked in the ceremony to receive my high school diploma at the University of Puget Sound field house. After the graduation ceremony, the class had an all-night party. We had a great time. I spent most of the evening with Mike and Bret, along with several hundred other classmates saying goodbye. The three of us had breakfast up on Sixth Avenue before we went home that next morning. Bret had been accepted at the United States Naval Academy and he was shipping out shortly. Mike was accepted at University of Puget Sound in Tacoma. I wanted to work and get out on my own. I was planning to attend Tacoma Community College in the fall and also work at Safeway. All was well in my world, I was working, and I was going to go to college part time and hopefully also save up some money. In the days ahead, my parents sat me down on my eighteenth birthday and handed me $1,000. They both spoke to me about going to college, and using this money to further my education. That was the plan.

My Transition Year

Over the summer after graduation, I transitioned into a full-time employment position working the third shift stocking shelves at the grocery store where I was already working part time. I loved the hours as it gave me the opportunity to work at night, sleep during the day, and also spend time on my boat waterskiing. I was spending a lot of time with Eric and his brother Brian. We both had ski boats and spent a great deal of time on the bay that summer. My buddy Dave and I were hanging out together as well. I was able to maintain my sobriety throughout that summer. I also continued to be deeply involved in the Young Life Campaigner Bible study. I continued to also be part of our church. There was a small group of us through the Campaigner Bible study that became very close. I was so grateful that we had people around us who were connected to YWAM and the Agape Force. There was a lot of spiritual growth that summer. I can still remember that in this fellowship of friends, I wanted to listen and learn. Back when I was drinking, I was often the life of the party. When we were on the bay, I was comfortable with anyone that joined me out on the water. I continued to hang out with Eric, Mike, and Dave, who knew me the best. They were standing with me. Eric was part of our Campaigner Bible study and my church youth group. During that time, Eric and I spent a lot of time together. We had similar interests and had known each other from our home church at Peninsula Lutheran Church. We water-skied a lot together. We were very close friends. There was one occasion when I was skiing behind Eric's boat near his house on the sound. We had a group of friends that were in the boat at the time. We were having a great time. I was on my slalom ski cutting back and forth across the wake. Everyone in the boat was laughing and smiling. It was a clear hot day on Puget Sound. As I was skiing and noticing everyone's smiles, I quickly became aware that their smiles turned into panic and fear. It was then when I looked to my right. As I looked, a large grey whale came up to the surface and sounded right next to me. The whale was about ten feet away from me on my right. The whale's breath blew all over my body. Everyone in the boat started laughing hysterically. I immediately filled my shorts. I pointed to the shore, and lip synced, "Get me to shore! Now! Take me to shore!" I got to the beach, and everyone in the boat was laughing about the incident. I remember that nobody got close to me the rest of the day. I never knew why until almost four decades later. Eric's brother, Brian, who was also in the boat told me that the reason that my friends stayed away from me that day was because the whale's breath and stench landed on me when the whale sounded. I smelled horrible the rest of the day. No one told me. But I still have the memory of having a close encounter with a whale while skiing on Puget Sound.

When we met as a group, I wanted to listen and learn more about the Bible and my relationship with Jesus Christ. I knew that I was deeply loved by God and those in the college-bound fellowship. But I continued to hate myself. I continued to have this deep-seated fear about the future and my family. I was insecure and felt unworthy of God's love for me.

Eric and I were asked by our pastor at our church to start a contemporary worship service that summer. We named the service Ephphatha, which in the original Greek is translated, "be opened." This word was uttered by Jesus when healing the man who was deaf and dumb (Mark 7:34 ESV).

In the fall, I was working and I decided to sign up for one class. The class was Psychology 101. I was eager and also nervous to start college. The teacher rambled on week after week about the basics of psychology that fall semester. I passed the class by the skin of my teeth. My mother was beginning to get sick again, and my head wasn't in the academic game. I also was looking for a place to rent and get out on my own for the year that I was working. My mother had a close friend whose family had a beach cottage out on Fox Island. They were hoping to rent it out over the fall and winter. I jumped at the chance and said that I was interested in renting the beach place. The monthly rent was $145. I was making six dollars per hour working forty hours per week at Safeway. I moved into the cottage that fall. The cabin sat on pilings over the water. There was a deck out on the front that went over the bulkhead. The cabin had windows from floor to ceiling in the front end. I still remember the driveway from the road that led down to the beach house on the water. It was secluded, and it was isolated. It was perfect. I slept during the day due to the fact that I worked nights. I bought a Saint Bernard puppy to keep me company. I was out of my parents' house, I was working full time, and I was living in a beach cabin by myself out on Fox Island. Everything went well, until I could no longer handle the quiet and the sense of isolation. I couldn't handle it.

After four weeks of living on my own, I came back late to my parents' home on Wollochet crying at their doorstep. I was lonely, and afraid of the environment that I had created. Even an introverted and shame-based kid can have too much solitude. It was an embarrassing time for me. I wiped my tears as my mom came to the door. I told her that I wanted to come home. I told her that I had made a mistake, and that I wasn't ready to move out. What I remember that night, was how gracious she was. She smiled and told me that I could sleep on the couch. She told me that I could move my things back in the morning. I was thrilled. Deep down inside, I knew that something was wrong. Something was not right, yet I couldn't put my finger on it. Everything in me wanted to be home. I swallowed my pride, and made the transition and moved back home. I didn't care who knew. So for the next couple of weeks, I finished up my psychology course. I signed up for a class in sociology that began after Christmas.

I was eighteen years old and had been walking with the Lord for a little over two years. I was absolutely in love with this man named Jesus. During one of my devotional times, he spoke to my heart. I was not prepared for his words to me. His intention with his Word to me was to start talking to me about my addictive tendencies that I had brought into our relationship. My identity with him was totally about my behavior. From my perspective, I had to not drink, not swear, and not get angry. I had to tithe, read my Bible every day, and pray every day. I had to go to church, and simply immerse myself in Christian activities. Jesus wanted me to surrender my addictive neurotic personality to him. One morning, he whispered these words to my heart:

> Todd, there is not one thing that you can do or not do, that can make me love you more than I already do, because I already love you to my fullest.
>
> You have struggled all your life, and have battled so hard with your spiritual walk. Your spirituality is not the issue, it never has been. It's your humanity that you struggle with. I took care of that as well. You need to bring your humanity to me.
>
> Your inner voice has told you that somehow what I did on the cross was not enough. The truth is that I purchased you with my own blood. You were bought with a price. I was slain, so that you might live. Can you simply, with the faith of a child, believe this? I took the fall for you, so that you wouldn't have to. I became like you, so that you could be like me.

When I heard his words, it was as though a little bubble had burst in my heart. There was an activation that had occurred in me that day. I didn't know then, but I do know now, that Jesus had spoken to the orphan spirit that lived inside of me. The orphan heard that he was loved. As Leif Hetland says it so eloquently:

> The orphan spirit cannot be cast out. It cannot be forced out of our systems. It can only be healed. Healing can only be found in our Father's house. We need to learn to find our way home. Father is waiting there for us. Let us come home to him and experience his love.[1]

Once I moved home, my welcome was short lived. I had lived out on Fox Island in the rented beach cabin for less than two months. After I moved back home, it wasn't long before my father started to demand that I move out. He was ruthless and incredibly shaming and demanded that I find a place soon. My father was throwing me out. I became desperate, and asked two of my friends, Jim and Steve, who were living up on Sixth Avenue, about apartment rentals. They were both a year older than me and were both attending Tacoma

Community College, living in a low-rental apartment. I talked to the building manager, filled out the application, and was accepted due to my low income. My rent was $160 per month. I moved in to my one-bedroom place along the busy Sixth Avenue. I was also glad that I had the apartment next door to Jim and Steve's apartment. I wasn't totally alone in my new living situation.

During this time living on Sixth Avenue, my friend Mitch and I made the decision to travel to Sun Valley, Idaho for a long weekend of skiing and an opportunity for evangelism. I talked to my dad and he talked to one of our old friends from the summit at Alpental. He owned a studio apartment in Sun Valley. He agreed that we could rent the place while we stayed in Sun Valley. The trip itself was an anointed trip from the get-go. Mitch and I asked the Lord for opportunities to share our faith along the way from Tacoma to the resort. We headed east out on I-90 toward Spokane. The last time I was on I-90 heading east was when I was eleven or twelve years old, heading to the Valley with my family for Christmas. We headed into eastern Washington. I was looking out the window of the Volkswagen Beetle that we were in. Mitch was driving at the time, and Abba's still small voice whispered to my heart,

> "You will be in rural Russia someday."
> I turned and looked at Mitch, and said, "Did you hear that?"
> He responded, "Hear what?"

At that time, I was pondering about the possibility of heading down to the YWAM's Slavic Training School in Oregon. It was a word that I pondered in my heart for the rest of the trip, and the years that followed. The Lord planted a seed in me that day traveling across I-90 heading into Spokane. Little did I know that his word would be fulfilled. In the spring of 1997, twenty years later, as I stepped off the train in Petrozavodsk, Russia at six o'clock in the morning while on a mission trip, the Lord brought back that word to me again.

7

THE STORM CLOUDS GATHER

> "He who dwells in the shelter of the Most High
> will abide in the shadow of the Almighty.
> I will say to the LORD, 'My refuge and my fortress,
> my God, in whom I trust.'
> For he will deliver you from the snare of the fowler
> and from the deadly pestilence.
> He will cover you with his pinions,
> and under his wings you will find refuge;
> his faithfulness is a shield and buckler.
> You will not fear the terror of the night,
> nor the arrow that flies by day,"
> (Psalm 91:1-5 ESV)

It was during the early months of 1977, when my mom had her ongoing health issues with breathing and being weak for short periods of time, that she went to her doctors a lot. I remember that her legs were swollen and she wasn't feeling well. At one point her oncologist and his team admitted her to Allenmore Hospital so that they could run some more tests. I was assuming that they were running more tests to find out why she was so weak, along with finding out why her legs were swollen. I was at home, and to this day, I don't remember where my dad or my sister were at the time.

The phone rang. I answered the phone and it was our neighbor Barb Rossi, one of my mom's best friends, on the other line.

"Todd, can you come down to Allenmore Hospital and talk to your mom? She needs you." she stated.

"Sure," I responded, "I will be right over".

I drove up the road and crossed the Narrows Bridge into Tacoma and headed toward Allenmore Hospital. I walked into the hospital room. My mom's best friends, Audrey Hemphill and Barb Rossi were standing on both sides of my mom and she was in her bed. As I stood at the foot of her bed, both of these dear ladies walked past me out of the room in silence. I sat down, and asked, "How are you?"

The next few moments have been frozen into my memory. I saw her face, and she looked into my eyes and started to cry.

"My doctors have told me that my cancer is back, and it has spread." I looked at her, and thought, "What? It has spread? What has spread?"

I asked her, "What?" I was in shock and disbelief.

Then she said, crying through her words, "My doctors have told me that I have six months to live."

I went numb. My thoughts were, "No! No!" I looked at her and said, "Mom, you can't cry, because if you do, then I'm going to start crying." I fought back the tears. My thoughts were that I couldn't cry, because I needed to be strong for her. Recalling that day, I don't remember leaving the hospital, and I don't remember the rest of the day, or the weeks that followed. My trauma brain kicked in and it took charge. Just like it did when I fell off the ten-story cliff when I was ten years old. And also when I was run over by the truck, when the motorcycle flipped and landed on top of me burning my right leg with second- and third-degree burns, and when I was stung by a swarm of bees. Up to this point in my journey, this was the darkest day of my life.

I came home to my apartment. I was crying, and I went over next door and knocked on my friend's door. Jim opened the door, and looked at me in shock.

"What happened, what's wrong, are you okay?" Jim asked. His roommate Steve stood up, and looked at me. He knew that something was wrong.

I remember saying to them, "My mom has six months to live. She's going to die." I was crying. I was out of control with sobbing.

"Oh Todd, I am so sorry," Steve responded. Jim looked at me, and said, "I think that we need to pray." They both came over near the door, and stood around me and lifted me in prayer. I don't remember their words, I don't remember anything that night after our prayer time together. Both Jim and Steve were also active in Young Life. I am so grateful for them, that they came around me that dark evening and prayed for me and my family.

The weeks that followed were a blur. I had signed a six-month lease at my apartment and I was ready to move home again. I needed to support my family. I felt very isolated. My friends had moved away, with Mike moving to California with his parents. Bret was in the Naval Academy. My friendship with Eric was my lifeline. I was still deeply connected to the Campaigner Bible study that was meeting on a weekly basis, along with my church. I can't speak enough about the power and strength of being part of a Christian fellowship. I was thrown into the depths of despair when I was told that my mother had a short time to live. It was so surreal. My college fellowship surrounded me. The leaders of the group, Larry Wright, Judy Rossiter, Dave Small, Dean Neal, and others came alongside me and kept me from falling off the edge. I am alive today because of their love for me. I am also very thankful for the Holy Spirit. During this time, the Holy Spirit was on the move in our small fellowship. That year, there were several of us who experienced personal encounters with the Holy Spirit and some of us began to move in the gifts of the Holy Spirit in fresh ways. God's Spirit became an active part of who we were when we met together. It was a time of revival and outpouring of the Holy Spirit's renewal. I found myself more and more envious of those who were experiencing the Holy Spirit in a greater way than I was. I was hungry for more, and

I wanted more of Jesus in every way. I kept asking for more. I would be at home, and I would go to my room and shut the door. I would turn off the lights and wait for God to speak. My times in his Word were always refreshing and where I always found strength.

> **"Your word is a lamp to my feet and**
> **a light to my path."**
> (Psalm 119:105 ESV)

I recall several poignant memories from January through July of that year, and yet I also remember the emotional fog. My mother was dying. I had a close college-age fellowship of believers that carried me and stood with me during this time. There were many times that the families that lived on Wollochet with us would bring over prepared dinners for my family. I was so grateful. As my mother became more sick, I took on more of the family chores. I periodically did the laundry and vacuumed the house. My sister and I usually rotated doing the dishes. My mother was in and out of chemotherapy and cobalt treatments. I can't tell you the countless times I remember her being sick and vomiting. I always remember her face after the treatments. As the weeks went on she looked more and more gaunt and thin. She was losing weight, and this frightened me. I tried to encourage and support her. We had our faith. On one occasion, after our pastor came and visited her, she looked up at me from the sofa in the living room and said, "I just can't talk to him. It's so hard." I was heartbroken. I was angry and disappointed that our family pastor couldn't connect with her. I know that he tried. But I was emotionally frozen with the thought that my mother couldn't talk about her fears about dying with our pastor.

In the weeks ahead, dinners were brought to us from those who loved us. My mother was always sick. I have memories of watching both my parents sitting at the desk in the living room next to the fireplace. My mom was attempting to teach my dad how to pay the bills. She was the one who paid the bills and kept our family afloat financially over the years. My dad made the money and my mom ran the checkbook. To see both of them sitting at the desk and my mother explaining to my dad how and when to pay the monthly bills will forever be in my memory.

My friends continued to circle around me. We met on a weekly basis out at a small cottage on the water in Rosedale. This weekly gathering saved my life on more than one occasion. They listened, they prayed, and they stormed heaven on my behalf.

There were several occasions where my dad and I would carry my mother up to the car from our house and bring her to the hospital because of her sliding into a coma or a seizure. On one occasion, my aunt told me several years later, my aunt's phone rang. She answered the phone, and there was no one on the other line. "Janet, is this you?" she asked. There was no answer. My aunt responded, "Janet, I will be right over!" My aunt hung up the phone and raced over to our home and found my mother on the floor in a coma. She was hospitalized shortly after that. This was the way it was for almost four months. There were several lapses into comas, several seizures, and several trips into Tacoma to Allenmore Hospital. It became routine, and I had lost my sense of normal. All I remember was that I was on autopilot.

I worked hard at pushing away the trauma responses that I was having. Watching my mother fight for her life in her battle with her cancer periodically brought up recurrent, involuntary, and intrusive distressing memories of my own past trauma. I also was having distressing dreams related to the trauma in my past. I was having sleep terrors at night. I was experiencing my own internal battle with depression and anxiety, but I couldn't talk about it because the focus of the family was on my mother's battle to live. Often my dad would head out to fish early in the morning on the weekends. I think it was his way to escape for a short time. As the years of high school progressed, he stopped asking me to go out with him. I generally said no to the invitation. The thought of spending three to four hours with him in the boat fishing out on the sound became terrifying. It was clear that we were drifting apart. I couldn't handle his temper and general irritability. I regret my decision to stay away from him to this day. He didn't know what to do. He was so scared, and I sensed that he couldn't talk about it. I was scared. No, let me rephrase that, I was terrified.

The domestic responsibilities in our home were mounting. My dad was attempting to work full time. I was working twenty-five hours per week at Safeway. I moved off nights working as a stocker, and took a position on days in grocery. My new hours were 8:00 a.m.—1:00 p.m., Monday through Friday. My new position allowed me to be home by 1:00 p.m.

Mom lived on the couch in our living room. As she became more sick from her treatments, and from the cancer that was progressing, my dad hired a nurse to come in for several hours during the day. He also hired a housekeeper to come twice a week for four to five hours per day to help clean.

I remember one occasion when my Volkswagen Beetle was in the shop. My mom was in the hospital. I really needed to see her. I was fearful and concerned. I made the decision to hitchhike to the hospital to see her. My dad was working, and I needed to go. I walked out to the main road on the east side of Wollochet, and stood in front of the old antique store. I stuck out my thumb, and in minutes a nice man pulled over and asked me where I was going. I told him that I needed to get across the bridge and into Tacoma. He said, "Okay". As we were heading across the Narrows Bridge, he turned to me and asked me where I needed to go. I told him that I needed to go to Allenmore Hospital. He looked at me in shock and said, "What?" Again, I said that I needed to go to Allenmore Hospital. I told him that my mom was there, had cancer, was receiving treatments, and that it wasn't going very well. I remember the car trip very well. He was incredibly polite to me. He asked a couple of questions about my mom's illness. Then it got really quiet in the car. We crossed the bridge and he headed south. I turned to him and asked him what he was doing. He looked at me and told me that he was taking me to the hospital. We drove into the hospital parking lot. I got out of his car, and turned around and thanked him. I will never forget his words when he said, "Not a problem. I hope that your mom gets better." He then drove away. Never underestimate the power and influence of a caring soul. To this day, I have believed that I was visited by an angel. The encounter that both he and I had was peaceful, compassionate, caring, and filled with Agape. I walked into the hospital shaking my head. I asked myself, "Why would this man do this?"

"Whoever is generous to the poor lends to the Lord, and he will repay him for his deed" (Proverbs 19:17 ESV).

The Final Days

"The Lord is near to the brokenhearted and saves the
crushed in spirit."
(Psalm 34:18 ESV)

"And we know that for those who love God all things work
together for good,
for those who are called according to his purpose."
(Romans 8:28 ESV)

It was June of 1977. My mom had nurses coming into our home daily. We had dinner coming into our home every night from our friends. My mom was in and out of the hospital. It became routine. There were people from out of state that started to come and visit her. There was one time when this huge yacht came into our bay on Wollochet. At the time, I didn't know the details but I knew he and his wife were friends of my parents. His boat, which was almost seventy-five feet long, was buoyed out in the middle of the bay. There was never anything spoken. But I knew that he had come to say goodbye. I don't remember being introduced. I remember his kindness. When he came into the bay, it wasn't the typical party scene as usual. It was a quiet and somber get together.

There were several families that came out to visit. In their private way, they came to say goodbye to my mom. The most impactful and memorable visit was when my aunt and uncle from Minneapolis, Dorie and Eric Williams, drove out in their camper. They stayed with us several days. Eric and my mom were siblings. It was an emotional visit. I remember that there were a lot of tears. Several months earlier, my dad had encouraged me to keep a personal journal through my mom's illness. During their visit, I asked Auntie Dorie to read the journal. After a few days, she handed it back to me crying. She simply said that it was beautiful.

During my aunt and uncle's visit with us, all of us went up to our family condominium at the mountain on Snoqualmie Pass. It was a great get away for us. The only memory of that weekend was precious Auntie Dorie pulling me aside. She told me that often God weaves a tapestry in our lives. She said that sometimes in our lives all we see is the backside of the tapestry, with all the knots and the jumble of threads and colors. All we see is the mishmash of the threads with no hint of design. She told me that when we get to heaven, we will have the honor and privilege to see the front side of the Lord's tapestry that he had woven during our lifetime. She looked at me and said, "It will be beautiful, my Todd. Just you wait!" We both stood outside in the driveway that led into our covered garage and hugged and cried together.

That afternoon, Uncle Eric had to catch a plane back to Minneapolis. My dad asked me to drive him back to our home. We arrived back at the harbor and Eric asked me to stop off at the liquor store. I knew what he wanted. My uncle was an alcoholic. He had been through treatment a couple of times. I think that the weekend with us was too much for him. He purchased a fifth of whiskey. We both came home, and I spent the evening in my room while he slept out on the couch. Later that evening, I went out to check on him. He was passed out on the couch, and the bottle was empty. He was grieving in his own way, and on his own terms. I was grieving as well, but I kept my grief to myself. I had nowhere to go with my feelings other than the Lord and my close friends. My little sister was absent, my dad was distant, and my mother was fighting for her life.

I was in a place of great need. We didn't have the time to talk about what was really happening. I found out years later that when my dad was told that my mom had six months to live, he went to my grandmother's house in Lakewood and wept as he told her and my aunt Susan. The three of us in our family were in survival mode. I had spent my early years in a house full of mirrors with the internal inner dialogs of the 'should have', 'could have', and 'ought to'. I came to the conclusion, after getting lost in that mental cul-de-sac, that this type of negativity was pointless.

As a therapist, I teach my patients that there are two things underneath their anger. Anger is known as a secondary emotion. It's actually the door that leads us into deeper emotions. Anger is similar to the tip of the iceberg. It's what we see. What's under the emotion of anger is what is at the heart of the matter. Anger always connects us to our vulnerability and feeling unprotected. Through my high school years, with my mother's diagnosis, my father's anger became more pronounced. His wife was dying. When I allow myself to look back into these dark memories, I have also learned to look through the lenses of emotional wellness. My father was a self-made man. As I have already mentioned earlier, his father had died when my dad was five years old. I think that this loss left a deep narcissistic wound in his life. It was his way or the highway most of the time. He never learned how to express empathy. He had learned to distance himself from pain. He often carried himself with a sense of entitlement. Within our extended family, the comments of "David always had to have his toys!" continue to be shared to this day at our family gatherings. If my father didn't know how to deal with the pain in his own life, including the loss of his own father, then how in the world could he have any sense of empathy towards his son's pain? With my mother being as sick as she was, what slowly began was a sense of my need to overcompensate for the lack of empathy in our home. During my four years of high school, I learned the art of caretaking.

I tell my patients that it will always be easier to take care of someone else's pain than our own. Little did I know that in the weeks ahead, I was to have an encounter with someone that would send me into a trajectory that I continue to be on.

My Encounter with the Holy Spirit

> "I will instruct you and teach you in the way you
> should go;
> I will counsel you with my eye upon you."
> (Psalm 32:8 ESV)

> "And I will ask the Father, and he will give you another
> Helper,
> to be with you forever, even the Spirit of truth,
> whom the world cannot receive,
> because it neither sees him nor knows him.
> You know him, for he dwells with you and will be in you.
> I will not leave you as orphans; I will come to you."
> (John 14:16-18 ESV)

It was a spring evening in 1977. Our college Bible study fellowship continued to meet weekly at our leader's beach cottage in Rosedale. The topic that night was on the subject of learning to have a private daily devotional time. Our leader invited us to head outside for forty-five minutes to be by ourselves with the Lord. We all left the cottage and spread out on the property. I found myself walking down to the beach that evening. When given the invitation, I always go to the beach. I walked out on the dock and sat down. I looked out over the water. The sun's light reflected off the water and made the water look like it was glowing. I closed my eyes and said, "Father, I need you to heal my mom. I need you to touch her and heal her and make her well. I'm not prepared to see her die. Please intervene in her life like you have done in mine. Please help me..."

As I remember, it was a beautiful evening. I stared at the water and waited in the silence. I heard him speak to my heart. I knew that I had heard his voice before. Then Abba whispered,

> Todd, I cannot give you what you want. Your mother will die shortly. You need to trust me, for through her passing there will be great fruit. I will be glorified in her death. I will not leave you or forsake you. You will never be alone, but you have to trust me.

All I remember was that his words burned into my heart. I just stared into the salt water and started to cry. Then his presence came over me. It was so comforting and gentle. It was like a warm bath and his Spirit filled my entire being. As I was filled, I realized and became aware that there was a new language coming from my lips. I didn't have a clue what I was saying, but I knew that it was his language. I was also aware that he was giving this new language to me. It was his gift. After what seemed like an eternity, I stood up and wiped my tears and walked back to the cottage. Everyone came back and talked about what they read about or prayed about during their time alone. I just remember being quiet. The experience that I just had was a private and holy encounter. He had spoken into my heart a very difficult word regarding my mother, but I will never forget the presence of the comforter and my encounter with him. I will never forget.

My spiritual encounters were something that I was beginning to become accustomed to. Pastor Bill Johnson writes,

> It is abnormal for a Christian not to have an appetite for the impossible. It has been written into our spiritual DNA to hunger for the impossibilities around us to bow at the name of Jesus.[1]

My hunger for the presence of the Holy Spirit was growing. I remember that I had told the Lord that I wanted everything there was to encounter about his presence. I went to several churches and different Bible studies. I went once to a Full Gospel Businessmen's meeting and hungered for the things of the Spirit.

One day, a friend and I drove to the Tacoma mall to do some shopping. I walked through the men's department and past the men's colognes. I dropped to the floor and exclaimed, "Praise God, the anointing is here!" My friend looked down at me, and begged me to get up. I told him that I was smelling the same fragrance that I had smelled at the Full Gospel Businessmen's meeting. I was convinced that it was the smell of Jesus. My friend looked at me and said, "Todd, you're smelling Brut cologne. I think that's what you smelled at the meeting, not Jesus." I was embarrassed. I may make light of this little experience now, but let me tell you something. Jesus does have a fragrance. I have smelled it before, and it's not Brut. It's the fragrance of heaven. When we get close to Jesus and walk with him, it will rub off on us. "But thanks be to God, who in Christ always leads us in triumphal procession, and through us spreads the fragrance of the knowledge of him everywhere" (2 Corinthians 2:14 ESV).

During these months, God's presence in my life was a huge thing. There are times in our spiritual journey when God hides himself and it is a season of hiddenness. Then there are other times when we see God moving everywhere, and these are known as times of manifestation. I found myself in a season of manifestation. As Graham Cooke says:

> Manifestation describes the times when you feel God's presence and his touch upon your life in a very immediate way. He is just there! Those times are wonderful and effortless. But God also brings seasons of hiddenness into your life, and although he is still very much with you, you don't feel his presence in the same way. It seems at times that God strips away all the external paraphernalia of your life and denies it to you. At those times, you have to believe that you have peace with God, because you don't feel it in your emotions. Manifestation is about experiencing all that God is doing.

> Hiddenness is about possessing the things of God through his Word by faith. During times of hiddenness, you must learn to rely on the promises that God has made to you through the Bible.[2]

I am grateful for the encounters and the prophetic words during this time. I needed them. I needed God to speak to me and he did. As my mother was getting more and more sick from the cancer and the side effects from the barrage of cobalt and chemotherapy treatments, the Father's presence increased in my life. I walked and lived in a great sense and awareness of his love for me. His love that he showered on me during this time was what held me together. During the last several months, I made the decision to keep a journal of my thoughts and feelings as I watched my mom battle cancer. I made the decision early in this writing, that I would share my journal, in its entirety, without any editing. What you are about to read are the words of a broken-hearted young man writing about his faith in God while watching cancer ravish his mother's body. It's raw and full of many moments of joy and sorrow.

8

MY JOURNAL

"Let not steadfast love and
faithfulness forsake you;
bind them around your neck;
write them on the tablet of your heart."
(Proverbs 3:3 ESV)

"Let this be recorded for a generation to come,
so that a people yet to be created may praise the Lord:"
(Psalm 102:18 ESV)

Sunday, March 20, 1977
Whoever is reading this, I pray that it will encourage and strengthen your faith in our Lord Jesus so that you can experience the glory of strength, power, and wisdom from the true living God as I have. My mother has cancer. She's had it for almost three years now. It started in her lungs. Because it spread to such a large infection, doctors took out one of her lungs thinking that this would cure it. Nothing was said for about two years after that until the doctors found the disease had spread to the other lung. Mom went through cobalt treatment which then stopped it.

This was the second time that God brought her family through the realization that she might die. I really didn't think of it as serious. I know it might sound funny thinking death is something not serious. I learned that by trusting God in the situation, we as a family would overcome it. This goes for everything and anything, God can deal with it. He can prepare your heart to trust in him in every situation and believe me, it's a great God who can do it. He really can. Just step out, he won't fail you.

The disease did indeed stop in the lung but it then reoccurred in her hip. She went through the cobalt again and stopped it. This is the first time I ever saw my mom in extreme pain, and the pain was unbearable. She was on painkillers that made her higher than a kite but helped her a great deal. This went on for about a month. The treatments that she was getting went on for about three weeks. Every day she went into the hospital. Every day she went in. Near the end of the treatments she was admitted into the hospital. This was caused by over nervousness. It was like a nervous breakdown, but not that serious. She couldn't talk or write, and she could not comprehend very much. She just had to take it easy and not keep everything inside. God asks this of us, to not keep our problems to ourselves. If there is any burden in our hearts, any problems in our lives, we take them to God. That's the best place for them. He'll honor you for that and he'll deal with them.

The doctors took a brain scan and found that the reason she couldn't write or speak and why she was exhibiting such odd behavior was that a tumor was lodged in her brain. They couldn't get to it by surgery. And they told her that she had one to six months to live.

I was the first one to know. I won't ever forget what she told me with tears in her eyes. It was like a big load fell on my chest. I walked out of the hospital and cried and cried in my car. But you know, an amazing thing happened to me there in my car. There was a confidence inside me that God was with me, and the rest of my family and I were uplifted. It was as though God reached down and helped me back on my feet again and helped me brush the dust off my pants from the stumble (Jude 1: 24-28 ESV).

Through this experience, God has shown me many things.

Through our weakness, God always shines his strength. When we are weak and full of burdens, God works to increase the faith we have by his Spirit, the very hope that is in us. Patience has been one of the things God has taught my family. We shouldn't be over anxious and try to step ahead of God. In one of the Psalms it says that we must "wait for the Lord" (Psalm 27:14 ESV), trusting him to take us through the situation. Whatever happens is for the best because God's wisdom and judgment is far greater than any human can understand. The way I feel now is that it's in God's hands.

I'm sort of caught between either rejoicing that my mother will soon live with God in heaven, and crying because I won't see her for a while. It is hard because I'll miss her.

I've always seen that even though there is a heavy crisis in the family, my walk with God still continues. It's kind of funny because I'm saying, "Lord, shouldn't we stop here until the problem is over?" But God's saying, "Trust me Todd, I know what's best. Don't hold onto the burdens you have. Give them to me and I will deal with them, but don't take your eyes off me for the world is a cold place when you do."

This reminds me of John 16:33 (NASB), "These things I have spoken to you, that in Me you may have peace. In the world you have tribulation, but take courage; I have overcome the world."

I've now brought you up-to-date. It's been about four weeks since we found out about the tumor. The pain is still there. She's lost all of her hair because of the radiation. This is kind of an ordeal for her. She's bought some wigs which look great, as though she still had her hair.

I am amazed over the love that I've seen from the other Christians that I know, and some that I even don't know. Prayer groups all over the peninsula are praying for my mom. They really care. It's really neat. It's really true when I think of the body of Christ, when one person is feeling down, the rest of the body should share with him and carry the burden also. This has happened. "Bear one another's burdens, and thereby fulfill the law of Christ" Galatians 6:2 (NASB).

March 22, 1977
God is so good, I can't believe it. We sin over and over again, and we've got the gall to ask him for things. I look back and see that I've sinned again and again, but I still ask for God's guidance and that he would heal my mother. It's like stealing from your friend and then asking him for a dollar. And you know what God says? He says that he'll give us two dollars.

The love of God is so great and so powerful. He's got an unconditional love for us. That means he loves us, and his love will never stop. No matter what, he loves us. To experience his love, believe in his Son Jesus, and he will take away the sins that you have. God wants us to know his love so much he wanted to go through the agony of death, to live and experience the desires of our bodies, and to have had the power to break the barrier of death that Satan had on us. He wanted to die himself so that we could be closer to him, instead of us trying, and not knowing him, and falling short of him. All we've got to do is to believe that God did this by sending his Son Jesus, who is God himself, and that he would take away our sins by trusting God. This is where we come to have a relationship with Jesus. I praise God for giving me life. I look back and try to see how I would feel the experience of this crisis if I was not a Christian. Oh, it would be so miserable. I thank God because it is not like that anymore since his light has come into my life.

This is mom's last day of radiation. The doctors are going to look at the tumor to see what the deal is. Yesterday, mom experienced a deep pain in her leg. The pain seems to travel up and down. She is now in the hospital for an x-ray. Pastor Roe was in yesterday. He's helped my mom a lot the past couple months. I don't know how to thank him for all of this. God knows how my heart feels about all the friends who have helped us.

There's nothing better than an answered prayer. Mom went to a doctor today to see if the cancer has been stopped by the radiation and it had. The hip and lungs were both clear of the disease. You know, God never fails in all situations. He comes through every time. Trust God and he'll do it. Praise God, for all that's left is the tumor and Lord willing, that will disappear too.

March 31, 1977
I have been with friends who have said, "Well, she is a Christian right?" I say that she's got a silent confidence. She doesn't come out and shout "Hey, I'm a Christian," but she does believe in Jesus Christ. And that's all I have to know. People have come up to me and ask if she was Spirit filled. God is spirit and is the One who fills us and he is with her. She is filled with God's Spirit. People think that if you're Spirit filled, that you're pure and holy. That's not true. I feel that I am Spirit filled. God has talked to me many times through his Spirit, but man, I am so sinful. I am dirty through and through. But God is a person who is saying, "Hey, love your neighbor." I want to strive to be clean, though we never will be clean in God's eyes without Jesus. He's the one who gives us confidence in times of travail. What I'm saying is that when you become a Christian you're given all the gifts of the Spirit. You may use them if you want. Getting it won't force you into anything. It is true that Christians seek more of the Spirit and that is given to them. But it all boils down to whether you believe in Jesus, the Son of the living God, and your sins are forgiven and you will receive eternal life.

It is good to seek the gifts of the Holy Spirit and truly you won't regret it. But it's not true that if you speak in tongues, or prophesy, which are gifts of the Spirit, that you are any better than any person who just believes in the Lord. The way I see it, we're all the body of Christ, given special gifts from God through his Spirit, but we're all working together in unity. We're all a tool for Christ. God can use us for his glory to bring the good news to the people of this world. True, Mom's got a lot to learn. But so do I and those around me.

The Corinthian church had the same trouble. They were all tied up in being Spirit filled, and moving in the gifts of the Spirit. They forgot who the Spirit is, and where it's all coming from. Our pastor gave a sermon a couple weeks ago saying that by believing in God and trusting Jesus to take away our sins, we've been given the tickets to the glorious Kingdom of God. But we, in order to know more about his kingdom, seek for more. We seek to come closer to God, asking for the gifts of the Spirit.

Mom's got the tickets into the kingdom, just like all of us who are Christians and that's all I need to know. That's all God asks of us, to believe in his Son.

April 1, 1977
One thing that has come up is that there has been a lot of crying. One thing I can't stand is to see my mom crying. It's the most depressing thing I can witness. The pain is a thing that's causing her to do this. I say, "Lord, why do you let this happen?" But you know, there's a purpose for everything. When you enter into the body of Christ, this comes to you. There's a purpose for living and a purpose for dying. There's a purpose for suffering, there's a purpose for crying. James wrote in his letter saying, "To rejoice when tested for one suffering because it brings endurance" (James 1:2-14 NASB).

April 18, 1977
To bring you up-to-date now, mom was in the hospital for about a week right after Easter because the pain in her hip was so bad. Doctors found out that another tumor has sprung up and that she would be taking cobalt for another two weeks. The good part was that we got back from the hospital and she was not feeling so much pain as before she went in. Now that it's been a couple of weeks, she's getting better every day. Today she hardly had any pain. Praise God! The cobalt treatment she's been going through seems to be making the tumor smaller.

We have learned to live day by day, taking each day as it comes. I think this could apply to all Christians. God doesn't want us to look ahead and plan things for the next year or even five years from now. God wants us to live for today and today only, as the Lord wills, because tomorrow might not come (James 4:13-15 NASB).

N. Todd Riggs

April 20, 1977

I've come to realize that God doesn't work his miracles to the extent that whatever happens comes out of the ordinary. What I'm saying is when you pray for something, the answer will just happen. To give an example, let's say you're late to a meeting and you pray, "Oh Lord, please get me to this meeting on time." Well, God is not going to keep all the lights green as you travel down Sixth Avenue in Tacoma. This could happen, yes, but also what will happen is that he'll just get you to the meeting on time. No bolt of lightning and now all the lights will be green, but it will just happen. Sometimes we think like this but the important part is that if you pray for something, you will get an answer. Matthew 7:7 (NASB) says to ask and you shall receive. This doesn't mean that the world is going to stop as he answers your prayer, but it just happens. Please don't get my words confused. The other way can happen too and this is where God is the most glorified. He could be glorified in the other way too, but that's in our hearts.

April 24, 1977

People are telling me things like "You're so happy considering what's happening with your family and especially your mom." Yes, I am a happy man. I'm full of joy because I've given my life to God. Sometimes it doesn't seem that way because I get caught up by the world's ways and my desires. That's when we see God with his arms wide open and ready to receive us.

April 25, 1977

Sometimes God waits until the right time for him to answer our prayers. The Lord knows the best time for everything. He knows us better than we know ourselves. This is why we sometimes attempt to beg to differ with him. We think we know how to run our lives when we really don't have a clue.

April 26, 1977
Mom's doing okay today. She's got her pain back though. It seems that the water has built up in her ankles. It's not the greatest thing to look at. She's also starting to lose her hearing and vision but it's barely noticeable. She would be reading the paper and it would go blurry, and I've had to repeat many things to her. I've been kind of dwelling on this today and then a Bible verse popped into my head. God does it sometimes to me. I would be very low one day and I'll be working or studying and a verse pops into my mind. It's encouraging in the way God does this. The verse was, "for we walk by faith, not by sight" (2 Corinthians 5:7 NASB). I looked it up and found references for the verse which breaks the verse down. One of the references was 2 Corinthians 4:18 which says, "while we look not at the things which are seen, but at the things which are not seen; for the things which are seen are temporal, but the things which are not seen are eternal" (2 Corinthians 4:18 NASB).

Another reference was 1 Corinthians 13:12 (NASB) which reads, "For now we see in a mirror dimly, but then face-to-face; now I know in part, but then I shall know fully just as I also have been fully known." Now for us lay people, the Living Bible says, "Now all that I know is hazy and blurred but then I will see everything clearly, just as clearly as God sees into my heart right now." For me, this really hits home.

April 30, 1977
Today mom and dad went to the mall. It's great to see her up and around. Her leg is still huge, plus she's got this pain on the tip of her spine. The doctors think it's another tumor. She's almost through with radiation, and then she starts chemotherapy in a couple of weeks.

A friend of mine, who is also a brother in the Lord, was hit on the head by a block and tackle on a fishing boat. He was unconscious for about two weeks which seems like eternity. His doctors told the family he would probably have brain damage and could be paralyzed. Well, the Lord laid on my heart to go talk to him and his parents. I went to see him in the hospital and found out that the doctors would not allow anyone to see him except the family. I felt like saying, "Hey, I am his brother in the Lord," just to see his doctor's reaction. I went to see his mother and we started talking and I felt reinforced by her words. She said with a faith as solid as a rock, "He's in God's hands, I know he is." The smile on her face alone was encouraging enough. Then I knew that the Spirit of God was in her heart. I really can't put it down in words. All I can say is that I was uplifted. The joy that I saw in her was incredible. At any rate, he regained consciousness about two weeks after that and day by day there was improvement. He went through surgery and the doctors told his parents that their son might die, but he didn't. Praise God! The healing power of Jesus is now healing him and a miracle is taking place in my friend's life. I've only skimmed over what's happened in his life. This notebook that I'm writing in wouldn't be enough for me to fill in about the healing power of God.

The encouragement that I've gotten from his parents has made me look at my life and my attitude toward my mom's situation. I've been reinforced in my spirit, through praise and in faith in the true living God. It's going to be the same healing power that's working in mom's life. Just the fact that God is dealing with the situation is enough for me.

May 12, 1977
The swelling in my mom's leg is still there. We brought her back to the hospital because the pain in her leg was so bad. Now she's been getting headaches off and on. The pain she's having is almost unbearable. Sometimes it's hard to face the situation. She's crying a lot and is in so much pain. Sometimes I wish God would take her away to be with him instead of suffering like this. I can really relate to what heaven is like. No pain and suffering and total peace and tranquility. Praise God, I can hardly wait to live in heaven.

May 14, 1977
Last night was the worst night so far. Our neighbors invited us over for dinner and my dad had too many drinks. We came home around midnight and then my dad went to bed. My sister then started crying and crying. I knew then that the moment had come when my mom's illness had finally caught up with my sister. I really wanted to help her, but she just yelled at me and told me to move out. She sobbed and cried for about an hour and then finally went to bed.

May 16, 1977
Today Mom came back from hospital. She's still in pretty bad shape. Dad is trying to solve the situation humanly but he's finding out it doesn't work. You've got to put your trust in Jesus in getting any problems solved. The peace that he will give us will never leave. When I think it's the darkest hour, then I find out that he's been there all the time. A lot of times now I really get lonely. I call up friends of mine and they're all busy and doing something else. There's no one to talk to as a Christian. It's hard, really hard. This is when God comes clearly into view—when it's just God, me, and dealing with the world. I've tasted the world and I honestly want to tell anyone who doesn't know Jesus yet, that God is tops. He is supreme. The Living Bible, in Colossians 2:10, says, "He is the highest Ruler, with authority over every other power." God has so much more to offer than the world. I've tasted what God has to offer and I've tasted what the world has to offer. Believe me, what God has for us is far better. He's got power over cancer, tumors, crying, doubts, sickness, and even death. God is better than any drug, booze, and keggers. For those reading who don't know Jesus, the earthly desires that you've tied up, ask Jesus to come into your life. He'll throw away the things that you're messed up with. He'll make your life so meaningful and give you a purpose to live. He'll take away the sins that you had and give you the gift of eternal life. This doesn't mean just life after death, but life now, the very moment you accept him into your life.

I just praise God because he's never left me, especially now when I really need him. His peace never leaves. You must realize that I'm not some big spiritual person. For those of you who know me, you know that I'm rotten to the core without his grace. I just praise God for showing me the way through the world's darkness. He has given me his light to follow and to walk in.

May 21, 1977
We have hired a full-time nurse to be with mom for the next couple of weeks. This really takes the burden off us as far as always keeping an eye on her. She's still in a lot of pain and there's a lot of tears. Chemotherapy has started. Praise God that there's no more radiation from the cobalt treatments. She's been sleeping a lot which I guess is good and she's eating a little better.

May 22, 1977
Praise God that the swelling in mom's leg has gone down tremendously. She's in a lot better spirits today. Anyway, things are starting to perk up. Our pastor came over today which was good.

For the past two weeks we've had our dinner brought in to us from our neighbors. I can't get over how much people are helping us. The love of God has surrounded us. He showed me many things through our neighbors and our friends. I think of how much our neighbors care for us and they have shown their love to us. Then I look at God's love, and the power that his love has. I've been shown our neighbors' love, yet God's love is still so much greater than these people who are loving on us. You can sit and dwell on the love of God all day long and yet not capture it as a whole.

He cares for us beyond our understanding. We can just pick out parts of the love that he has for us and we think it's a lot. But really we've only seen a very small, tiny portion that he has for us. The only person who has ever seen God's love as a whole is Jesus who is in fact God himself. I want to rely on Jesus for everything. God has shown us the love that he has for us through Jesus. Jesus Christ is the bridge over that pit that all of us have fallen into. This is the barrier that separated us from God for so many years. But again, Christ is the bridge over the pit called sin. He has provided a way out, Praise the Lord!

May 23, 1977
Today, the place where I work (Safeway) went on strike. When I was down there picketing, I was thinking about the people inside the store working our jobs and taking our places. I thought "these dirty, dumb, stupid people; they're taking over our jobs, and making the money were supposed to be making." Then I thought, "Wait a minute. Don't hate them, love them, do unto others as you would have others would do unto you." The Lord kind of showed me the fear the customers had with crossed or picket lines, for people were always standing near or in front of the doors. The people inside working were kind of scared too. Maybe they even felt bad. They were forced into this as the picketers were forced into the strike. Personally, I think strikes are part of the devil's work. He's behind all bad things, any disagreements, and hard feelings. As I'm writing this, I am turning a 180-degree circle. I want the strike the end. What I'm saying is the Lord has changed my mind today. It's funny how we always think we are doing the right thing and that we've got it all together then God says, "Wait a minute here", then proceeds to show us his way, which is the only way! I'm glad he does this because it shows me how much God is to me.

May 31, 1977
Sometimes we get so caught up in a relationship with God that we actually miss the boat. At least, it has been this way for me. For the past couple weeks, I've been walking with the Lord, but also kind of ahead of him. Sometimes we do this and miss the meaning of having a relationship with God and what it means to commit our life to him. We tend to slip away from God because of our lack of faith and we want to run our lives instead of allowing him. Once

you realize what this has done to you, you make a beeline back to home, back to Jesus. I'm so thankful that the doors are wide open when we come back. Renewing your faith every once in a while is not a bad idea. I'm reading a book now called *Born Again* by Chuck Colson, who was a special adviser to President Nixon. I was uplifted to hear his testimony to the fact that now he is walking with Jesus. He writes about the struggles he had with Watergate and President Nixon. He tells about the joy and peace he found when he came before the Lord. I was really encouraged as he told about this time and then he went over the basic things of Christianity. Sometimes we forget when we first received Christ and how good it felt. I believe it's good to drink milk before going back to solid food.

June 9, 1977

Things are still good. Mom's back in the hospital. She went back in last night because she's not eating and if she does eat, it comes right back up. Would you believe that the once 150-pound Janet Riggs is now down to 108 pounds? Praise the Lord her spirits are still high. It's so great that our bodies can take so much beating, yet God is still there holding her soul high. I look back at Corrie Ten Boom and how she was so physically beaten and yet her spirit showed God's love in the Nazi prison camp. It was God in her, supporting her, and uplifting her. Praise God!

Have you ever had Satan just trying to stir up trouble inside with temptations and attempting to make things go wrong? It's been like this during this past week. Today, just to name a few problems, my car broke down and it's going to cost sixty dollars to fix it. A good friend is mad at me because of something I said. Another very good friend is moving to California and I won't see him until this fall. Some other friends are kind of slacking off from God and this really burns me up because it's right after graduation and now is one of the times they need God the most. My mom's back in the hospital, and I've got to pick one college to go to this fall and I don't have too much time left. Well, it sounds like a lot but I've lifted them all up to the Lord.

June 19, 1977

Mom's been back in the hospital for the past week or so and now she's back home. She was at chemotherapy every day in the hospital. She got a reaction and sores started to come out all over inside her mouth. All in all, she's feeling kind of bad. The thing I realized is that it's been four months since I started writing in this journal. It was kind of hairy the first couple months but you know, I've been praying for her healing. For us right now, each day means another day of life. The longer the time period of her living, the smaller the chances are of her leaving us to live with the Lord. Each day means taking another step closer to coming out of the woods with Jesus as our guide.

June 25, 1977

Things are looking good, Praise the Lord! Mom is in much better spirits now and has hardly any pain. The thing that has been sticking in my mind is the power of prayer. It comes down to the verse in Matthew 7:7 (NASB), "Ask and you shall receive." To ask in Jesus' name and it will be given to you. I have prayed in Jesus' name that God will heal my mother and now it seems to be an answered prayer. Let me rephrase this, all prayers are answered; it's just some of the answers that aren't seen or known to us. But have faith that the Lord is dealing with that prayer. He deals with every prayer that is made as an offering to him. This is a fact. Do you think he doesn't care for his children? We are the children of God and our name is in heaven. By praying, we communicate with God. We talk to him and he talks to us through his Spirit. Prayer is so simple, yet people make it so difficult. I believe God is dealing with my prayer. It's being answered. I can see with my eyes that it's being answered.

June 29, 1977

Yesterday morning, my mom went into a coma. My dad and my sister are really taking it hard. But you know, if mom dies, she'll be living with the King of kings, and the Lord of lords. She'll be face-to-face with the creator of the universe. I am really blessed when I think about this. Our pastor, Pastor Roe, has been really great to us. Today I went to the hospital to see her. Before I left I told her to take care of herself and that Jesus was with her. Right now, as I write, she is totally out of it and she can't talk. I've never even mentioned Jesus and my relationship with him to her before. I'm anxious to hear what she has to say when she can talk again. When people are in a coma, I've been told that they can hear everything. Praise the Lord!

July 1, 1977
Mom came out of the coma on June 30. Praise the Lord! She's still very weak. My dad and my sister are taking this very hard. My prayer is that they may have the peace that I have that God has given me. I've been told that people have wondered, including my dad, why I'm taking this so good. I feel free to talk about my mom's illness to anybody. I have given it up to the Lord. In return for this, his love, along with his joy and peace becomes even stronger in my spirit. I just praise God for giving me this. The King of kings and the Lord of lords gave it to me, and there is nobody and no situation that could take that away from me. My mother is God's possession just as I am. My mother is going to receive the gift of the eternal life just as I have. PTL!

Today my mom is in the hospital, I told my mom just before I left that Jesus was with her. She kind of shook her head and said, "Uh Huh." She probably was thinking, "Oh here we go again, my son the Christian." I thought to myself, well that's too bad. God's done so much for me and I wanted to share it with her one last time. She's got nothing to fear from death as close as it is to her. It's just Jesus on the other side.

9

O DEATH, WHERE IS YOUR STING?

"O death, where is your victory?
O death, where is your sting?"
(1 Corinthians 15:55 ESV)

"The LORD is my shepherd; I shall not want.
He makes me lie down in green pastures.
He leads me beside still waters.
He restores my soul.
He leads me in paths of
righteousness for his name's sake.
Even though I walk through the
valley of the shadow of death,
I will fear no evil, for you are with me;
your rod and your staff, they comfort me."
(Psalm 23:1-4 ESV)

The last entry from my journal:

July 3, 1977
Today will probably be the last time I'll be writing in this journal. Today my mom died at Allenmore Hospital at

4:30 p.m. There's not much I can say other than about a month ago I received this Word from the Lord:

> My child, you may not see me now and the healing work that you asked for. My will is that you wait for me, strive to do my will. From now until the dust settles remember that I am with you. After everything settles, you will be praising me in the works I have done.

I wasn't really sure that this was a word from God when I first received it. But now I know it's true. God has been glorified in my mother's death. My mom is now in the very best care that I can ever imagine, living with the Lord in heaven. God taught me so much in these past months that I can't write it all down. Our pastor, Pastor Roe, has been a tremendous help to me and my family. Our pastor showed me that Jesus has the victory over death and that we can believe in him. I simply praise God for being the God that he is and the love that he has shown me through my friends.

The day she died the timing couldn't have been better. Our pastor gave her communion, and I saw her right afterwards and stayed and talked to her for about two hours. I left about half past two in the afternoon. Praise be to God for the strength that I have now and for giving me life after death. Someday I'll stand in front of the Lord in heaven worshiping him and praising him with my mom right beside me. Thank you, Jesus. I cannot express my love for the friends that I have. They uplifted me when I was down and they were happy when I was happy. God told me to write this notebook, as it's my journal during this season. I believe this with all my heart. Thank you, God. My prayer is that you may receive the peace that only God can give. Thank you, Jesus, for giving us the victory that we have over death. Nothing in the world can separate us from the love of God.

Thanks for reading this. Amen.

My Lord and my Father, thank you for such a fantastic day!

> Those who know the Lord never cease giving thanks for all the wonderful things that he has given us. The new life in Christ cannot be put down in words. If we tried to write everything down on paper about the new life in Jesus Christ, all the books in the world wouldn't be enough.
> Todd Riggs, 10:13 p.m. July 10, 1977.

It was Sunday morning on July 3,1977. I headed off to church. After the service, my buddy Eric and I had plans to head to a lake near us for an afternoon of waterskiing and being on the water. Before I headed out to the water, I made the decision that I was going to go to Allenmore Hospital to see my mom. I pulled into the hospital parking lot, and as I was walking from the parking lot, I met our pastor who was just leaving the hospital. Pastor Roe looked at me and said, "I gave your mom communion and read her some scriptures. I think that she will be happy to see you."

I smiled and said, "Okay, thanks for coming in to see her today." I walked into the hospital that afternoon like I always did. I walked into her room as I had done many times before. I walked into the room, and I saw my mom. It looked like she was in a coma. Her eyes were open, and she was staring at the wall. I took hold of her hand and talked to her about my day. She never made eye contact with me. I remember looking at her body. At one time, she was a tall and beautiful, athletic woman. She had a contagious smile and laugh. Now, I was looking at a woman who was barely seventy pounds. Her body reminded me of someone in the Nazi death camps. She was wearing a scarf bandana. I realize that I had developed a tolerance of her looking this way. I told her that I loved her. I looked at her in the eyes, and said, "Jesus is with you mom. Right? Jesus is with you." I heard her mumble the words, "Uh huh." I responded, "I love you mom, I will see you tomorrow." I then walked out of her hospital room. Little did I know that this was the last time that I would see her.

That Sunday afternoon has played out in my head a million

times over the years. I have so many regrets and questions from that day. Why did I go skiing that afternoon? Why didn't I know that mom was so close to death that day? Why wasn't my dad there at the hospital that afternoon? Did we really know how close to death she was? Why didn't the hospital staff tell us to come and be with her while she passed? Why didn't I comfort my sister when I found her crying, standing alone in our driveway? Why was my dad drinking over at the neighbors that day? What will happen now?

After visiting my mother that afternoon, Eric and I headed out to a small lake near the area of Longbranch. It was a great afternoon of being on the water and skiing. By late afternoon, we brought the boat in and Eric brought me back to my home on Wollochet. I got out of his car at the end of our road at the antique store. With my slalom ski, gloves, and vest in hand, I walked down Picnic Point Drive, going toward the end of the dead-end street where our home was located. As I got closer to home, I noticed my sister was standing in the road. She was crying. It was though she was waiting for me. I walked up to her and asked, "What happened? What's wrong?"

She looked at me and continued crying and said, "Mom died. Where were you?" I turned around and continued walking up the road toward our house. I looked and saw the cars; dozens were in our driveway. I walked down our steps and walked into the house. The house was full of people.

My dad was in the living room and walked up to me and said, "Your mother died this afternoon." There was this pause between us.

I looked at him and said, "I'm okay. Are you okay?"

My mom's two best friends, Audrey Hemphill and Barb Rossi walked up to me and comforted me. Audrey hugged me and said through her tears, "Todd, I'm so sorry. Your mother was a great lady. She was my best friend." Barb was also crying and also gave me a big hug. She looked at me and said, "Your mother was a great lady. If you need anything, just come over. I'm so sorry." She then took my hand and walked me to our little kitchen and looked at me in the eyes and said, "I know that you are a young man of strong faith.

You will need to hold on to your faith tightly in the weeks ahead. You know Jack attends Mass every week. If you need to talk to him, just come over, okay?" Barb and her husband Jack lived three doors down from us. I remember being so heartbroken for Audrey and Barb. I knew that I went numb the moment that my sister told me the news out on the driveway.

What complicated things that afternoon was that no one knew what lake Eric and I were skiing on. When the word got out that my mom had passed, my dad didn't know where I was. So he asked several of our friends on the bay to drive around searching all over Wollochet and nearby Gig Harbor in an attempt to find me. When I finally had walked in the door that afternoon, there was a sigh of relief in the house that I had come home.

Our home was filled with people for the rest of the afternoon and into the evening. Our friends all around Wollochet Bay were with us well into the night.

I called my friend, Eric, my afternoon skiing buddy, and told him the news of my mother's passing. To this day, I still remember his comforting words, "Todd, I am so very sorry." I called our pastor, Pastor Roe, and told him that my mom had passed. He invited me to come over to his home. I left the gathering at our home and drove to his home next door to Peninsula Lutheran Church. His wife greeted me at the door, and we sat around their kitchen table and talked. I can still remember the look on their faces. In the midst of my numbness, they came alongside me and spoke words of comfort and healing. Even some brief smiles appeared as we spoke of the fond memories of my mother. Pastor Roe also comforted me by walking my dad and me through the funeral arrangements, and offering to be with us when we were meeting with Haven of Rest Funeral Home and Cemetery.

After everyone left later that night, my dad and sister went to bed. I remember hearing my sister crying herself to sleep. I can still recall the emptiness in our home; the grief was overwhelming. I also cried myself to sleep that night. When I got to sleep, I knew that my world was caving in, and I couldn't stop it. It was profoundly comforting to know that I had Jesus to hold on to. More importantly, he had a hold of me, and he wasn't about to let me go. My dad told me that my mother had written a letter to me several weeks before she passed. She also wrote a letter to my sister. He handed it to me. I remember reading the letter. I was numb. I didn't shed a tear. My emotions were stuffed deep down in my being. Through my mother's sickness and death, I had learned to turn off my emotions. It wasn't until my clinical training that I slowly began to give myself permission to share my emotions with others. My mom taught me many things. She taught me the importance of gratitude. Periodically, when we traveled across the Narrows Bridge into Tacoma, she would look out over the water and say, "Please, be thankful for living here. There are so many others who are less fortunate than we are."

The next day was the Fourth of July. It was a special day in the area, as many of the families that lived on the bay came together for the celebrations. In this particular year, we all met at the home of a family who lived directly across the bay from us. Their son was a friend of mine. One of the great things about hanging out with him was that he had a man cave in a separate cottage on the property. There were many times that my buddy Dave and I would spend the evening with him, playing pool and being introduced and listening to the music of the Allman Brothers. It was always a special time together. But, on this Fourth of July, the entire bay knew of my mother's passing. My dad, along with my sister and I, went to the gathering the day after my mom had passed. I knew that people knew what had happened. Everyone was heartbroken and silent. Standing outside, I saw my buddy Dave walk over to the party from his house down the block. He walked up to me, gave me a big hug, and said, "How are you doing? Are you okay?"

I looked at him and replied, "Yeah I'm okay, hanging in there."

I don't remember much else about that day other than a conversation that I had with my father on the beach. At one point in the afternoon, I looked down at the beach, and I saw my dad sitting around the fire. He was alone. I walked down to the fire and joined him. "How are you doing?" I asked.

He responded, "Todd, you need to know right now that you are the one who is holding this family together. I can't do it. I have lost your mother." I looked at him as he was speaking, and I noticed that there were tears rolling down his face. He was looking into the fire and said again, "Right now, you are the one who is holding this family together because I can't."

I don't remember anything else from that day. That night the three of us went back to our house. Once again, the house was quiet and our grief was overwhelming.

The next day, we started taking care of my mother's funeral arrangements. Pastor Roe came with us to Haven of Rest Funeral Home and he quietly sat with us through the funeral planning. I was so grateful for his willingness to be there with us. We had already called my mother's brother, Uncle Eric, and his wife, Auntie Dorie. It was reassuring that my mother's family from Minneapolis were coming out for the funeral. My dad asked me to call all of our friends that I thought should know and to let them know of my mother's passing. I knew that my father was not in the position emotionally to make the calls. I can still remember standing in my parents' bedroom calling to tell our friends from Alpental and Lakewood the news.

I had no thoughts of why I was the one calling our friends and family. It wasn't in my wheelhouse at the time to ask questions. I was on autopilot, and I had to push through it. My dad was incapacitated and my fourteen-year-old sister was in deep grief. There were several memories in my past I was very intentional about not visiting. When I allow myself to think about my sister's grief in the early years, I would always fall into a very dark place. It took me several years to not feel guilty for not being a better brother during this time of deep and significant loss. She had no coping skills, and to this day, I wish that I had in my being the awareness, the strength, and the tools to come alongside her.

> When a daughter loses a mother, the intervals between grief responses lengthen over time, but her longing never disappears. It always hovers at the edge of her awareness, prepared to surface at any time, in any place, in the least expected ways.[1]

As I look back, that week was so surreal. In the coming days, our family from Minneapolis came out and stayed with us. Our family had a private viewing at the Haven of Rest Chapel. My mother looked beautiful. Her funeral was held the next day at our church, Peninsula Lutheran, with six of our closest friends being her pallbearers. These men represented our friends from Wollochet and Gig Harbor, along with our friendships from Alpental and the mountain. We had a full house. I didn't cry at the service. I don't know why. I fought back the tears, but as I look back on that day I wanted to be strong for my family. We all proceeded to the cemetery for a small grave-side service where my mother was finally laid to rest. I watched one of the pallbearers, our dear family friend Brian from the mountain, carrying my mom's casket to her open grave, weeping uncontrollably as he walked. I felt so bad for him, as he also loved my mom. Then we gathered again at the house. I remember being aware that two of my mom's closest friends, Barb and Audrey, made the choice to not come to the funeral or the graveside gathering afterwards, because it was too painful for them.

Later, my dad asked me to walk outside, down our deck, and go into our basement to bring up more cases of beer for the gathering. As I was walking back up the stairs carrying two cases of beer, our pastor walked through the front door. He looked at me and paused, smiled, and said hello. I was embarrassed to have the cases of beer in my hands. Yet, I think he knew that I was ashamed that he saw me. He also knew that I was raised with a lot of alcohol in the home, and he knew of my sobriety.

Over the next couple of days, my dad informed me that we were heading north to Sekiu. He wanted to take my sister and I to his favorite fishing spot. It was a place that both my mom and dad, along with several couples from Wollochet, went to fish every summer. However, this time our trip there was to get away, clear our thoughts, and grieve. When he first asked me, I firmly said that I didn't want to go. I wanted to be with my friends who were part of my college Bible study. I said no several times to him. I found myself needing to get away from him. He was grieving, needy, and broken. His grief had sucked the life out of me. I said no. However, one of my dad's closest friends named Dale approached me privately and had asked to talk to me. He asked me, "Todd, your dad needs you. He needs his family to head up to Sekiu for some fishing and get away. Can you do this for him?" I told him that I would. But only for two or three days because I needed to be around my friends.

So, the next day we all headed to Sekiu to fish. Dale, his son Scott, my sister, my dad, and I spent two to three days on the northwest tip of Washington state and fished for salmon and halibut. When we came in and went to our rented cabins that night, I experienced a huge panic attack. I woke in my bed to find I had broken out in hives, and I couldn't sleep the entire night. I had internalized my grief, and it was starting to catch up to me. The next night after a full day of fishing, I again broke out in severe hives and with my heart pounding in my chest, I simply couldn't sleep. My mind raced all night long. On the third day, I drove home by myself in my Volkswagen Bug. When I got back to our home on Wollochet, I called my friends and they gathered around me that night and came to my side. It was a gathering that I will never forget. They all came alongside me and comforted me in my grief. Little did I know at the time, but they all spoke prophetic words into me. Later that night, we all drove up to Seattle and went to see Barry McGuire in concert. My dear friend Eric came with me and was looking after me. In fact, Eric watched my back for the next several months. The night of the concert was anointed, as Barry spoke into me through his stories and songs and his love of Jesus. He was promoting his new album *Have You Heard*. I was ambushed when he sang his song, "There Is a Peace":

> Oh, have you heard?
> There is a peace, The Prince of Peace,
> and He can ease your troubled minds.
> He came unashamed, to die for you and me,
> now we come to Him on bended knee.[2]

I will never forget that night in Seattle. God and I had connected. I was ministered to on such a deep level. I was with my friends, and a contemporary Christian music artist that held a special place in my heart. Most importantly, God's presence overshadowed me. I knew in my heart that things were going to be okay. Several years later, I was able to talk to Barry personally and thank him for that night. I remember him telling me, "Todd, it was all about Jesus that night. It had nothing to do with me." Shortly after that powerful evening, my family returned from Sekiu, and I made the decision to drive down to San Jose, California, to see my close friend Mike. I called him and asked if I could come and visit; he was thrilled and encouraged me to come. When I told my dad, he simply looked at me and said, "You're doing what? You're driving to San Jose? Okay, have fun."

I left the next day. I can't begin to tell you how therapeutic the drive was. I met people as I drove southbound down I-5. I slept in my car two nights. I arrived in San Jose, and Mike and his family received me with open arms. For three days, they wanted to hear my story. They wanted to hear about how my mom died. Mike had told me before that he loved my mom, and he knew that my mom loved him. Mike's family loved the Lord, and they poured both their love and his love into me. Mike took me away for a day, and we drove into Santa Cruz and walked the beach. Mike made a fire on the beach and we both barbecued steaks watching the sun set. Mike currently sings with the San Francisco opera, but back then he would sing just for my mom, especially when she was sick. He had a way to make her smile even when she was in so much pain. Mike had also applied to Peninsula College, and we were both thrilled that we were going to be roommates in the dorm. I drove home the next day, and there I made contact with my dear friend Bret, who also showered a lot of comfort and compassion over me. My friends kept me going.

The next week, I went back to work at Safeway. My coworkers were so kind to me. I worked about five more weeks at the grocery store before I reported to Peninsula College in Port Angeles. It was close to three hours north of where we lived and was located at the base of the Olympic mountain range on the Strait of Juan De Fuca. I had been accepted and was excited to leave for college in September. I gave my notice at work and began to prepare for college.

After the funeral, my dad threw himself into work. He was gone a lot. I don't remember where my sister was. What I do remember was the void that I felt after everyone left the house. My family from Minneapolis went back home, most of my friends stopped checking in on me, and our friends on Wollochet went back to their lives. Over the next two to three weeks, we were trying to get back to normal, whatever that was. Little did I know then, but I was really depressed. The grief really hadn't caught up to me, until now. One afternoon when no one was home, I walked into the kitchen and saw my mother's pill box on the shelf. All of her cancer and pain medications were still on the shelf in our kitchen. My dad had not gotten rid of them yet. I took the box and all the pill containers in my hand. Then, I put all the medications and spread them out on the kitchen counter. I dumped all the pain medications into my hand and looked at them. I was holding close to fifty or sixty pain pills. All I could think was that I didn't want to live the rest of my life without my mother. The other thought I had was that I didn't want to live my life with my dad. I wanted to die. With the pills in my hand, I stood in the kitchen by myself and thought, "You can do this. This is your out." After what seemed like an eternity, I dumped the pills back into their containers and walked out of the kitchen. I felt empowered. I could have taken all of my mom's pain killers that day, but I chose not to. On that warm summer day, I chose to live. Shortly after this experience, I heard a song by a young Christian songwriter by the name of Scott Wesley Brown. As I listened to the song's lyrics, I knew in my heart that this song spoke to what my heart was crying out for in declaration:

> You make me feel like I'm falling in love for the very first time in my life. You've given a spark, to this empty heart, you gave me a reason to live.
>
> I've been up and down, and all around, everywhere a man can go. I've been in and out, all about, looking for a love that I can know... Jesus.
>
> But you make me feel like I'm falling in love for the very first time in my life. You've given a spark, to this empty heart, you gave me a reason to live.
>
> I've been long and wide, and way up high, there was nothing I wouldn't do. I've been here and there, everywhere, and all the time looking for you... Jesus.
>
> You make me feel like I'm falling in love for the very first time in my life. You've given a spark, to this empty heart,
>
> you gave me a reason,
>
> you gave me a reason,
>
> you gave me a reason,
>
> you gave me a reason,
>
> you gave me a reason to live.[3]

One memory from that time was when I was cleaning the house

one afternoon. Everyone was gone and the house was empty. I told the Lord shortly after my mom died that I wasn't going to cry because I needed to be strong for my dad and my sister. I had asked the Lord to give me a prompting before I was going to have a good cry and let me break down by myself with him alone. When I was vacuuming the house, something deep in my heart began to rise up and started to flood my entire being. I dropped what I was doing in the house, grabbed my keys, and ran up the steps to my car in the driveway. By the time I got into my car, and started driving in reverse out of the driveway, the flood gates burst open. By the time I drove to the main road, I was sobbing uncontrollably. I remember thanking the Lord for honoring my prayer. I wanted to grieve in solitude and only be with him. He was the only one who was truly safe in my life. I have always known that he wept with me that day.

10

LEAVING HOME

"The LORD will fight for you,
and you have only to be silent."
(Exodus 14:14 ESV)

"When something bad happens,
you have three choices.
You can let it define you, let it destroy you, or let it let it
strengthen you."
– Unknown

"Behind every scar, there is an
untold story of overcoming."
– Unknown

I had about seven weeks between my mother's funeral and the day that I packed my car and headed to Port Angeles for college. I went to the airport and picked up my friend Mike, whom I had just spent a week with in San Jose. We packed up my Beetle and drove up to Port Angeles to started our first semester as full-time students. I was so grateful to have one of my best friends as my roommate. At the time, it broke my heart to leave home with my dad and sister in so much grief. Many nights I would walk around the campus alone praying and crying out to God for relief from the pain and grief. Too numerous to count were the nights that ended up with me walking alone out to the middle of the football field in the dark. There, I would lie on my back and look at the stars above me, and at the waters of the Strait of Juan De Fuca, and cry for hours. In the middle of my tears, the Lord and I would have conversations where he would speak tenderly to my heart, and he would comfort me. His presence was so strong and so healing to me. I had so many questions, and really no answers. He had promised me months before my mom passed away that as I trusted him, his name would be glorified through my mom's death. I had to weigh that out against the fact that I was angry, depressed, and wanted to fight the need of accepting of what had happened. The very fact that I was alone in my grief and not back home in my family's chaos was a double-edged sword.

During my mom's illness, my dad had pulled away even more than usual. He really didn't let people get close to him. It was one thing to party with people on the bay or at the mountain, but he kept his true self private. He had a lot of narcissistic traits. It wasn't until after I started my clinical training, that I had realized I was raised in home with a narcissistic parent. At times, my father was grandiose and was attracted to success. He loved people's admiration. He had a difficult time showing empathy. There were two sides to my father. There was the private side and then there was the public side. No one knew the secret side of my father. No one. I tried to check in with my father at least once a month by phone. Our phone calls always left me yearning for home, but I knew that things weren't good. I found out later that things were spinning out of control. My father was throwing himself into work and started to get out into the dating scene. What I didn't know was that he left my sister in the dust. I found out later that my father simply gave my fourteen-year-old sister his credit card and told her to live her life. At the time, I had no idea that my father had done this.

Back at school, I had thrown myself into classes. I remember that I purposely enrolled in a death and dying class, along with a writing class. I wanted to study death and dying, and I wanted to write about my life and my mother's death. That semester I did both. One evening, a friend who lived on the same floor of the dorm I lived in gave me a message stating that my dad had called and I was to call home. I called my dad back using the pay phone in the dorm. He informed me that one of my close friends named Jack had taken his own life. My dad briefly tried to console me on the phone, but when we hung up, I walked back to my room fighting back the tears. I closed the door, fell on my bed, and cried myself to sleep. I thought to myself, "Jack? Why? You took the out. How could you do this?"

I also remember making the decision to attend a church in town that was close to the college. I went to the Sunday morning service, and after the service, I remember shaking hands with the associate pastor and talking with him. While he was shaking my hand, I told him that I was a new college student in town and asked him if there were any opportunities to help with the youth program in his church. He smiled at me, and with a sense of relief he told me, "Why yes, we always need help." I told him that I was available to serve in any way. He told me when the youth group was meeting next week at the church, and he invited me to join him. So the next week, I attended the church's youth group for the first time. It was pretty mundane and sterile. The second week the associate pastor couldn't attend and asked me to lead the meeting. We met at someone's home. At first, there was an awkward silence, and the kids were restless and quiet. So I opened the meeting and began to tell my story of what the Lord had done in my life. I ended up giving my entire testimony that evening. I was surprised that when I spoke of my personal encounter with the Holy Spirit, they all started to look at each other with big grins on their faces. I was a little confused and knew that something was about to be disclosed. One of the kids, named Steve, told me that while they were on a church retreat they all had a very personal encounter with the Holy Spirit. He explained that they were praying and in worship, when the Holy Spirit had simply manifested himself to the group with a display of the different gifts of the Holy Spirit. Some had received a new fresh encounter with his presence, some a new prayer language, some healing, and some personal words of prophecy.

I sat there and listened to each of them tell their personal stories of their encounter with the Holy Spirit. I was amazed and blessed. I was grinning from ear to ear in my heart as I realized that God had visited this group of high school students on two to three different occasions around the area of the Olympic Mountain Range when they were together. I remember whispering to myself, "This is just like you, Lord. You responded to their hunger for you." That night they also told me that they had brought back their stories of their encounter back to their church. Their church told them that what they had experienced was all emotional hype, and they were encouraged to disregard their encounters. When they told me this, I have to admit, my spirit was grieved.

I remember that somewhere in my introduction to this small group of Port Angeles High School ragamuffins, I made a commitment to the Lord that I wanted to come alongside of them, mentor, and teach them about what they had experienced in the Olympic National Forest. Little did I know that for the next two years I was to pour my life into this group of kids. We spent our first year together going through a book on the gifts of the Holy Spirit. We also met on a regular basis in the church sanctuary where we simply waited on the Lord. We would usually meet at night, and the church's live-in caretaker would let us in. It's like he knew. He knew that we were wanting to meet, to press in, to wait, and to minister to the Lord. He never told us no. We would assemble in the church's sanctuary and pray and wait for him. During one of these times, we were lying on the floor next to the altar. I was prompted to ask one of the young men named Steve, who was one of the high school leaders of the youth group, if he would like to go to the piano and play. In the dark I heard him say to me, "Sure, the Holy Spirit just prompted me to go to the piano and play."

I told him, "Well, go for it." He walked up to the piano located next to the altar, sat down, and began to play. I had brought a tape recorder with me that night, and I pushed record as soon he started. Now, this fifteen-year-old kid had very few piano lessons and a beginner's musical ability to play the piano. The music he made that night contradicted his inexperience. As he started to play, I remember that the whole sanctuary was filled with the presence of the Lord. He was playing in the Spirit. The Spirit of the Lord danced on the piano keys that night. The sanctuary was filled with the Lord's celebration, with his joy, healing, love, and peace. Whatever darkness that was in our hearts when we arrived at the sanctuary that night was dispelled as heaven's music filled the room. He played nonstop for almost thirty minutes. This young man played as though he was an accomplished pianist. When he finished, several of us were overwhelmed with God's presence. Some of us laughed, some cried, some were speechless and in awe of what we just experienced. One ninth grader spoke up and said that he had been to the doctor that afternoon with severe pain in his arm. He said that the pain was gone now. Others reported, when we attempted to process the encounter afterward, that as the music played, headaches disappeared; sadness, anxiety, and depression had lifted. One of my favorite parts of the evening was when Steve finished, he turned around and looked at all of us and said, "Wow, that was really cool! How did I do that?" That night, all of us were led into an encounter that we would never forget. I had the whole event on tape.

> **Bible study without
> Bible experience is pointless.**
> – Bill Johnson[1]

One weekend shortly afterwards, I visited my friend Eric at the college he attended. I gave the tape to Eric and asked him to have his teachers listen to the tape. The music department at the college listened to the tape and came to the conclusion that the person who had played the piece was an accomplished pianist. They were surprised to hear that the young man who played the piano on the tape had only a little over a year of piano lessons.

When it came to school, my first semester at Peninsula College living in the dorm was a great experience. My close friend from high school, Mike, was my roommate, and we had a wonderful semester living in the dorm. I made a lot of great friends during my two years living in Port Angeles.

Some of my favorite Peninsula College memories include the art of rock touching. In this exercise, usually done at night, a handful of us would go down to the harbor spit, a man-made landform. The Coast Guard station was at the very end of it. The waters of the Strait of Juan De Fuca were on one side of the spit and the harbor was on the other side, where the waters were calm like glass. Sometimes the waves were between three and five feet high, and would break up on the rocks of the shore. On the open-water side of the spit, we would stand on the shore and dare each other to run out into the water, touch the farthest rock away from shore, and run back to shore before the next wave would come in and crash onto the rocks. It wasn't really that dangerous, but most of us usually got fairly wet. Depending on the tides, sometimes we would have to run out thirty or forty feet to the farthest rock, and then run as fast as we could back to the beach before the waves came crashing in. There was always a lot of laughter and fun. The person touching the rock farthest away won and always got their hot chocolate paid for by the rest of the gang while we warmed up at a local restaurant and, of course, dried out. Our conversations on those evenings were always precious because we talked about our lives and where we had come from.

Another thing all of my friends and I would do was to climb into our cars and drive up to Hurricane Ridge at night. Port Angeles boasted the fact that anyone living in the city could go from seawater to snow in less than thirty minutes. Hurricane Ridge was the top of the mountain that overlooked the city. The daytime views of the

Olympic Mountain Range, including Mount Olympus, from the top of Hurricane Ridge were breathtaking. At night, my friends and I would head up to the top of the ridge and chase deer that were feeding at night. I still remember being at the top of the ridge on a clear night with only the moon shining down on us. Even at night the view was breathtaking. Attempting to touch the herds of deer on top of the ridge made it even more fun.

In my social group of friends, there was a tremendous amount of vulnerability, acceptance, and care for one another. It was a healing balm in my heart regarding the grief that was still in my heart.

I was extremely grateful that the handful of Christians in our dorm made the decision to meet for Bible study on a regular basis early in the morning before classes. That small group of close friends became my main spiritual support. I continue to be friends with some of them even to this day. It was through that group that I met the youth pastor at the Assemblies of God church in town. His name was Craig and he was taking classes at the college when we met. I was so intrigued by the fire in his soul and his love for the Lord. Over the course of the fall, he and I became friends. I was already attending a church in town and helping out in their youth group, yet I was hungry for more of the Holy Spirit, so I started to attend his church on Sunday nights.

I liked Craig, and he began to mentor and disciple me on a weekly basis. We started to meet at his home on a weekly basis shortly after I began to attend his church. I learned a great deal during my time with him. He was very familiar with YWAM. He talked openly about reading the Word of God on a daily basis, along with being open to miracles, signs and wonders, and encounters with the Holy Spirit. One night when we were meeting at his home, Craig was teaching on the topic of faith and our need to step out of our comfort zones. As he was teaching, he put his very young toddler up on the mantle above his fireplace. As he was teaching about faith and comfort zones, he proceeded to step away from the fireplace and got on his knees about five feet away from the fireplace. Craig looked at his daughter and clapped his hands and said, "Sarah, jump!" I will never forget his daughter's face. With the look of reckless abandonment, Sarah proceeded to jump off the mantle and into Craig's arms. My initial reaction was that of absolute astonishment. I was stunned.

I was thankful that Craig immediately consoled all of us in his living room by telling us that he had been working on this exercise with his daughter for the last several months. He proceeded to teach us a very simple principle of walking in faith. He told us that in the very beginning he would do this exercise daily with his daughter. He would put Sarah up on the mantle and simply hold her close to his face. He would slowly, inch by inch, move his face away from his daughter until she felt comfortable. Eventually, Craig would put Sarah up on the mantle and he would no longer hold her, but simply speak to her. When she became comfortable with that posture, he began to step away from the mantle, inch by inch, and slowly lower himself onto the ground. Over the course of weeks, he would kneel on his living room floor and ask Sarah to jump off the mantle. As he taught us, he commented that every time he asked Sarah to jump, Craig would always catch her. Being caught by her father was all she ever knew. She trusted him. Her trust grew with every encounter she had with her father regarding the mantle.

I sat there in his living room and listened. For the first time I realized something. Often the Holy Spirit will take our heart to places where our mind will never be able to understand.

Shortly after that evening, I was driving down from the college into town. Driving down the road, I caught the view of Port Angeles Harbor with all the boats tied up to the docks or the buoys out in the middle of the harbor. Some of these were large, gorgeous schooners and other wooden vessels. My spirit knew that these majestic ships were not meant to be buoyed, but to sail the open seas. The Holy Spirit started to minister to my heart as he showed me a valuable lesson: we were never meant to be buoyed up in a calm harbor either. When we surrender our lives to Jesus Christ, we become a new creation. As the Apostle Paul wrote, "Therefore, if anyone is in

Christ, he is a new creation. The old has passed away; behold, the new has come" (2 Corinthians 5:17 ESV).

Becoming a new creation means becoming a prototype—a one of a kind. We have been created to be his workmanship, and we become part of God's family. We all serve at the pleasure of our King. Prototype. Did you hear that word? We are all one of a kind. When we accepted Jesus Christ into our hearts as our Lord and Savior, God put his spiritual DNA into our spirits. From that point on we became part of his family; we became his royal nobility. Just like what I saw in the harbor that day, we are all expensive schooners, which have been created by the God himself. We were never meant to live in the harbor, but to live out on the open seas. We were created to have our masts filled with the winds of the Spirit and to ride the swells and the big waves. It's part of our DNA. Each schooner is meant for the high winds and the open waves. As I realized my value, I made a commitment to God. I told him that during my lifetime I never want to spend a lot of time in the harbor. That I was open for him to take me out into the open seas where ever he wished. I was his, and he was mine.

Occasionally on the weekends, I would drive home from college. It was so different. During the fall of my first year of college, my dad and I were close. As the weeks went on, he became more and more distant. He began dating women only several months after burying my mom. Each time I came home, more and more I felt like I was infringing on his environment, even though I think he dreaded being alone. So, during the first year after my mom died, things were becoming more chaotic at home, less engaging, and more distant. My sister, who was in high school, and I were becoming a burden to him. I look back and can now say that my sister was the biggest victim in this. I had the luxury of grieving on my own while I was in my first year in college. I didn't have to deal with the chaos of home. I found out later that my dad and my sister had a huge falling out. I was told that she was acting out her grief of losing her mother. I was grateful that I had the solace of friends in college, along with my harbor friends to fall back on. I continued to throw myself into college life and the church high school youth group in Port Angeles.

During December of 1977, my dad made the decision that we were not going to have Christmas at our house on Wollochet or in Lakewood with our extended family. On this particular Christmas after my mother's passing in July, the Riggs' party barge had come to a dead stop and the music had died. My father, my sister, and I felt like orphans. It was clear that my father wanted to leave the familiar. He chose, for the three of us, to head to the mountain for Christmas. Alpental had always been a place of retreat for all of us and a place of extraordinary memories of playing and resting. Now, we would also remember a wonderful lady. However, my father was engulfed in pain from the grief of losing his wife and our mother. I was not allowed to ask questions. For those couple of days, we stayed with our friends, the Nelson family. They lived on the summit as well, and their family took us in. They didn't ask any questions. They made us laugh. They knew that my dad, my sister, and I were in a cloud of grief. Their family encircled us and loved us in the silence. They embraced us. Wayne and Carolyn Nelson and their children made us part of their family that Christmas.

Back then, I had my old Volkswagen Beetle with its Porsche engine in the back end. On Christmas Eve, I took the Nelson kids and my sister Kris inner tubing behind my Beetle around the area parking lots. That night was filled with laughter – laughter for all of us. That evening, we forgot about our loss. We chose to forget our past hurts and pain, and we also chose to not allow our fears of the future to engulf us. I never got a chance to thank the Nelson family for taking us in that Christmas. Wayne and Carolyn later moved to Fairbanks, Alaska. A couple of years later, they lost a son who was in serving the military. Wayne went on to become mayor of Fairbanks, and has since passed on. That year at Christmas, the light that had been in my life was nearly snuffed out, but I look back and remember that God's flame faintly flickered in the darkness. Abba's hope that he had instilled in me had never left.

After Christmas, I went back to college and started my second semester. My good friend Mike had made the decision to not to return to college and headed back to San Jose to live with his parents, so I had my dorm room to myself. I was continuing to serve as a volunteer in the youth group. I was encouraged by the dorm Bible study and the fellowship of my Christian friends who lived in the dorm. I was also introduced to Victor, an interesting man who helped teach a political science course that I had enrolled in. He was passionate about politics and was involved in the Kennedy administration. According to him, his position was rated with a GS grade which was one number below the President's cabinet. He attempted to get out of politics as a Washington insider, but he ended up having a nervous breakdown when his superiors in Washington, DC, told him that he had to stay. When I took the class, I befriended him and quickly found out that he was also a Christian. My friendship with Victor became close, and I also met his wife Sharon. They invited me over to their home outside of Port Angeles.

Both Victor and his wife Sharon taught me many things. The most important thing they passed on to me was the value and truth of the scriptures. Politics and world events should always be viewed through the lenses of scriptures and Jesus' mission. Victor also spoke of having a discernment and balance between the role of the Holy Spirit and politics. He was also the first of many intellectuals that would eventually cross my path and didn't scare me. He was a brilliant man who also had an incredible sense of humor. If it weren't for him, I know that I wouldn't have passed my political science class. Victor and Sharon also became aware that I had lost my mother and that my home on Wollochet was imploding. They listened and prayed with me, and we studied the Bible together on a weekly basis. Most notably, they loved me unconditionally.

That spring I applied to be a resident assistant in the dorms and was offered the job. The Lord opened up this door as I was running out of money for school and being a resident assistant meant that my room and board were paid for. God was providing for me to continue with school.

I continued to pour my energy into mentoring the kids from church on a weekly basis. God always met us in powerful ways whenever we came together. On one occasion, two of the young men from the group and I drove up to the top of Hurricane Ridge on a crystal clear, moonlit evening when we could see the Olympic Mountain Range off in the distance. That night we prayed together and went before the Lord as we gazed out over the mountains. We asked the Holy Spirit to come and to visit us with his presence. As we were praying, the inside of my little Volkswagen Beetle filled with the fullness of heaven. We became aware that he was bringing us into his sanctuary. We were listening to the Archers, a Christian music group, on my music system in the car. They were singing these words:

> I will praise Him, praise Him.
> The warmth of His Love abides in me.
> I will praise Him, praise Him.
> Sweet Communion we share, He'll set us free.
> And I will praise Him, praise Him.
> The warmth of His Love abides in me.
> Praise Him, Oh Praise Him.[2]

As the Holy Spirit filled my car, heaven's hope, strength, reinforcement, grace, forgiveness, and his peace filled my inner being. The two young men who were with me were filled with his Spirit once again and began to speak in other languages. It was a precious time that I will never forget. I was reliving my encounter with the Holy Spirit out on the dock in Rosedale. Everything in my racing mind came to a full stop that night. I realized then that one encounter with the One has more healing and impact than years in a therapist's office. His Anointing has the power to do that. Love always wins.

That spring, as the Father's grace continued to fill the youth group, the opposition from the church to shut it down became more apparent. The person who was in the cross fire was the youth pastor at the church. He had invited me to come and serve as a volunteer. I don't think that he really knew what hit him. He was not prepared for the visitation that occurred in his youth group. All I know was that I was committed to see those kids grow and embrace what they had received. During this season, God was everywhere. There was growing opposition with what was happening in the youth group. In religious circles, people often can say mean things and their words can be cloaked as their convictions, when in reality they are simply afraid of the spiritual unknown.

> "When greatness is inside of you,
> it has to be drawn out.
> Sometimes, it's the attack that draws the greatness out."
> – T. D. Jakes[3]

I went home that summer and lived with my close friend Eric. We rented a duplex in Gig Harbor for the summer. I worked for a construction company and poured concrete for residential homes on the peninsula. I hated it. It was hard work for a day's wages. I was miserable. My dad was gone for most of the time as he was busy dating. For a second time, I took some of the kids from the Port Angeles youth group to the Christian rock festival in Oregon called Jesus Northwest. On the way home from the festival, my car's oil light went on and the rest is history. We almost made it back to Port Angeles before the car's engine froze up. After the festival, I no longer had a car. I was stranded.

That fall of 1978 I headed back to Port Angeles. Again, I was a resident assistant and I was privileged to work on the weekends at Hurricane Ridge over the winter as a lift operator for some extra money. I was already receiving my mother's social security death benefit of approximately $120 a month. One night, I received a phone call from my dad saying that my uncle Eric from Minneapolis had passed away. He asked me to join him that weekend to fly to Minneapolis and attend the funeral. I hung up the phone in the hallway of the dorm and wept as I walked to my room. I cried to the Lord, "No, Lord. No. Not him, not my uncle. Not him too." Shortly after, I got on a plane with my father and flew to the Twin Cities. On the plane ride my father and I sat together and about halfway through the flight, he leaned over to me and asked me, "Can I talk to you? I've been seeing this woman and we have been spending a lot of time together. I would like to marry her."

A long pause ensued. All I thought was, "We are flying out to the Twin Cities to bury my mother's brother. Why are you asking me this?" I looked at him and I decided to take the high road, "Wow, Dad, that's great. I'm happy for you." Nothing more was said. We got off the plane and cared for my grieving family in the Twin Cities, and buried my uncle Eric. Watching my cousins in their intense grief, triggered my grief all over again. It was a tough couple of days. My dad and I got on a plane and returned to Seattle. As we got off the plane, my dad was very angry. He stormed off the plane in the airport at Sea-Tac and marched down to the baggage claim. He wouldn't talk to me. To this day, sixteen years after his death, he never told me why he was so mad that day. My imagination tells me that he told our Minneapolis family in their time of grief that he was happily intending to marry a woman. His announcement to them was most likely met with rebuff. My father never knew how to give out empathy well because it was never offered to him.

At the end of the first semester I made the decision to resign from my role of resident assistant at the college. An incident happened in the dorm during the fall of that year that really terrified me. One weekend, when both the resident managers and the other resident assistants were gone off campus, several students decided to have a dorm party. As the party started, I went into the dorm area and reminded everyone that they had to keep things under control and take the alcohol off campus. They ignored my multiple requests to take their party off campus. I sat in my room and listened to the commotion. As the night went on, two entire floors of one wing broke out in chaos. People were severely intoxicated and began to destroy the dormitory. They broke lights and ransacked the rooms. I remained in my room absolutely terrified with the door locked. I didn't know what to do. I was in shock and was paralyzed. I finally fell asleep and woke up the next morning. An eerie silence filled the dorms the next morning. I opened up my door and walked down the stairs to the hallway of the rooms that were decimated. All the lights were busted out. Markings painted the hallways. Glass was everywhere, yet no one was seen. I was in shock. Several days later, those who were responsible for the destruction of the dorm were expelled from the college. I was relieved, but several weeks later I resigned from my resident assistant position. I wanted to devote my remaining months in Port Angeles to mentoring the kids at the church. The opposition was growing within the church to put the fire out that was happening in the hearts of the youth. One weekend, when I was having lunch in the college cafeteria, I looked up and saw my friend Eric walk past the window. Wondering what he was doing here, I left the table and greeted Eric at the front doors. "What are you doing here?" I asked.

"Yeah, I hitchhiked up from PLU," he replied. Eric had caught a ride from Tacoma to Port Angeles to spend the weekend with me, and I was thrilled. He came up to see me that weekend because I had told him of the church's opposition to the Holy Spirit's impartation in the youth. That night, we were not prepared for the encounter that we had with the presence of Jesus. After we both had fallen asleep in my dorm room, Eric woke up in the middle of the night because, according to him, I was restless and snoring. He just couldn't get back to sleep. He begged, "Lord, can you please make Todd roll over? Please make him stop snoring."

Then after a long pause, I immediately sat up in my bed, and I started speaking in another language in my sleep. According to Eric, I cried out in a booming voice, "Oh boy, here it comes!" At that point in my dark dorm room, Eric saw a swirling wind that filled the room.

He began to rebuke the encounter, and immediately his spirit was quickened. He was told to stop because he was witnessing the Holy Spirit. Eric experienced a rushing wind blowing through the room. The room began to swirl with a blue light. The room was 'charged'. He looked toward the door of the room and witnessed two beings in the Spirit, who walked through the door and stood on each side of the doorway, as guards of my room. It reminded him of when the secret service agents guard the President. Eric watched, as the presence of the Holy Spirit came through the door and filled the room. At this point, the Spirit of God spoke to Eric to get up, leave the bedroom, bring a tablet and a pen, and walk down the hall to the bathroom. As soon as Eric walked into the bathroom, he hit the floor and was on his knees. For the next hour or so, the Holy Spirit spoke over him a prophetic word that he was to give to me. When it was all over, Eric came back to bed. The next morning, Eric sat me down and told me what had happened. When he told about the blue swirling light that he saw, I was reminded of what I saw as a little boy when the large piece of blue and white cloth passed over me while I was in bed. Eric then handed me the prophetic word that he heard the Father speak to him. Eric spoke the Father's words over me, and I received encouragement from heaven. There was a passage from the scriptures, found in Jeremiah that was part of the message. Once again, I felt and received his love over me. I heard him speak, "Well done, Todd." That morning, both Eric and I were overwhelmed by the grace of our Heavenly Father. I was reminded that he loved me, and that his favor had grown in me.

I knew that eventually I had to say goodbye to this handful of anointed and highly-favored group of high school kids who had experienced an incredible encounter with Abba. I wanted to make sure that I was part of Abba's 'sealing the deal' by spending a lot of time with them before I left and went back home to Wollochet Bay.

11

THE SUMMER AT ALPENTAL

"The LORD is near to the brokenhearted
and saves the crushed in spirit."
(Psalm 34:18 ESV)

"The world breaks everyone, and afterwards,
some are strong at the broken places."
— Ernest Hemingway[1]

In the spring of 1978, I left Port Angeles and returned home to Wollochet. I had applied and been accepted at a Bible school known as the Lutheran Bible Institute (LBI) located in Issaquah. They had a four-year youth ministry program that I was interested in. My dad had remarried, so as soon as I returned home from college I began looking for work. But first, my father decided to fly me out to Reno with both him and his new wife for a sort of coming-of-age twenty-first birthday gift. We flew out to Reno for the weekend and my dad made it clear that the weekend was all about my twenty-first birthday. In Reno, I was greeted at the gate by a chauffeur who escorted us to the waiting white limousine. The driver handed me a glass of champagne as I got into the back of the car. Looking at my dad, I saw him smiling.

The limousine drove us to the hotel where I got out of the car. I turned to my dad and said, "Dad, people are staring at us."

He responded smiling and suggesting, "Well, I know that Cher is in town. Maybe they think that you are her new boyfriend." I was embarrassed, and I looked to the ground as I walked into the hotel. When we got to my room, my dad handed me seventy-five dollars for gambling money and said, "I want to teach you how to work the slots and how to play Blackjack." I was already feeling uncomfortable, but for the rest of the afternoon and evening I was his student. He made sure that he taught me the art of staying in and walking away. We did the same thing the next day.

That night, my dad had purchased tickets to Reno's biggest show known as *Hello Hollywood!* I had no idea what I was getting in to. In the opening act, the front end of a 747 came out on stage. Then the dancing started and over a hundred topless dancers and performers came out on stage. I was in my seat, and I desperately wanted to go back to my room.

"Why did he buy tickets to this show?", I thought. "He knows that I'm heading to Bible College in two months." I sat in my seat and got through the show. Afterwards, I remained quiet as we walked back to our rooms. I had not wanted to disrespect my dad by walking out of the show, but when I arrived back in my room that night, I sat down on the bed and told God that I was sorry. I asked for his forgiveness for not walking out of the show. The next morning we flew back home. There weren't a lot of words spoken.

It became clear in the first couple of days after I arrived back home that I was an intruder. My father had made the decision to demolish and level our old home and rebuild a new home on the property. Meanwhile, both he and his new wife were living in her home in Federal Way. He eventually told me that I was not welcome to live in the home on Wollochet.

However, I had heard through the grapevine that our close family friend, Brian, who was living up on the summit on the mountain, was willing to hire me for the summer to work on a construction crew building homes in the Alpental Valley. My dad conceded to allow me to live in our family condominium in the valley while I worked for Brian during the summer. I called Brian and he offered me the job as a laborer.

The next critical issue was the question of transportation. I didn't have a vehicle anymore, and I had no way to get up to the summit. My dad refused to allow me to use any of the vehicles that he had. I recall several times when he went into rages making it clear that I couldn't live with him or use his vehicles. He made it clear that I was responsible for my own transportation to get to the mountain. I walked next door to our close family friend named Jack, and told him about the situation. I was on the verge of tears and extremely upset with my dad. Jack was very close to my dad, and tried to help me by telling my father that he had a Ford Pinto that was not being used and that he was willing to allow me to use the vehicle for the summer. My father became very angry at Jack and shouted at him, "Absolutely not!"

Jack snapped back and told him, "Dave, the car will simply stay in our driveway if Todd doesn't use it!"

My dad, getting more and more angry, responded back to Jack, "Stay out of this!" My dad turned around and walked back into his yard. Jack simply shook his head at me. I was stunned, but I was also relieved. For once, someone else was on my side when it came to my dad's rages, selfishness, and lack of empathy. The next day, my new stepsister offered to take me to the Tacoma bus station, and with my bags packed, I took the Greyhound bus to the summit. I got off the bus and walked into the valley to our family condominium at Alpental. As I was walking on the long road it started to rain. Everything I had got wet. Hatred toward my father filled my heart. How could he do this to me? I felt rejected, alone, and empty on the inside. The family that I knew was no more. My mom was dead. The man that I knew as my father was no longer the man that I knew and loved. I had growing contempt toward him, and for the moment, God was hiding from me.

Monday morning came and I started to work on the construction sites in the valley at Alpental. It was hard work. By the end of the day, I would come back to my condo and be exhausted. I had to walk everywhere, so I spent a lot of time in the condo reading scripture and spending time in prayer during the evenings. On the weekends, I would hike all around Denny Mountain. I was by myself a great deal of the time. On one occasion, I was at a job site by myself picking up lumber and the tools. I was praying and crying out to God. I now know that I was in a deep depression. I was crying uncontrollably and sitting down on the newly-poured concrete foundation telling the Lord, "It's just you and me, Lord. I can't do this anymore. I'm done. If this is the way my life is going to be, then I'm out. Take me out. I want to go home and be with you." I stared at the mountains that surrounded me, which I was so familiar with, and took a deep breath. His peace surrounded me. It was the same peace that I had felt after I fell off the cliff as a boy. It was the same peace that I felt in my heart when I had surrendered my heart to Jesus. After a couple of hours, I got back up and went back to my condominium. I was exhausted. When I allow myself to think upon those memories from that summer, I am reminded of Psalm 139 and the song written by Shane & Shane called "Far Too Wonderful":

> You wrote the story of my life
> You go before you fall behind, yeah
> Before a breath beyond my death you are with me all the way to everlasting
> Oh I can't run, I can't hide
> Even darkness is a light
> From the lowest place to the highest praise You are worthy
> Amazing love how can it be
> Far too wonderful for me
> There's only one thing left to say You are worthy, oh
> Search me God and know my heart
> Try me, know my anxious thoughts, yeah
> Find the weakness in me and lead me in the way Everlasting

> Oh I can't run, I can't hide
> Even darkness is a light
> From the lowest place to the highest praise You are worthy
> Amazing love how can it be
> Far too wonderful for me
> There's only one thing left to say You are worthy, oh
> You formed me in my mother's womb
> You know my frame, my flesh, and bone
> Oh, how wonderfully made
> Oh I can't describe it's way too hard
> You see me through and through and call me loved
> What a wonderful grace, oh
> Oh I can't run, I can't hide
> Even darkness is a light
> From the lowest place to the highest praise You are worthy
> Amazing love how can it be
> Far too wonderful for me
> There's only one thing left to say You are worthy.[2]

The good news of that summer was that I worked with a great crew. Brian knew that I was in a dark place and he looked after me. Earlier in this writing, I spoke about how my dad took Brian under his wing when he was around seventeen years old, when my dad was the general manager at Alpental. I think that Brian was returning the favor to me, and I was grateful that he made sure that I was okay. I also worked with a young man named Jeff. He was an interesting guy with long hair and a big beard. He weighed no more than 130 pounds, and he could play a fierce harmonica. Working together, we talked about everything as we dug ditches, poured concrete foundations, and picked up excess wood and debris from the job sites. I ended up telling him about my faith and relationship in Jesus Christ throughout the course of the summer, as he led most of our conversations about Christianity. He had so many questions, so I responded the best way I could by simply telling him my story of encounters with this man named Jesus. I simply told him, when he asked, of what God had done for me and how he had changed my life. I enjoyed our casual conversations while we worked. I think he did too. I found out a couple of years later that he had surrendered his life to Jesus as well. I learned that Jeff had spoken at a church where my friends were in the pews. Jeff told his testimony that night and spoke of our summer together mentioning my name and sharing our conversations that created a hunger in him to seek out Jesus. I'm thankful that he found what I had found. He found Jesus, and like Jesus, we need to live and walk with an awareness that the Father's blessing is upon us.

After several weeks of working that summer, Brian came to the house where I was working and sat down next to me. "Todd, your dad called me this morning. Your grandmother passed away yesterday. I'm sorry."

I just stared at him. "Wow," I replied.

I left the summit the next day and headed back to Wollochet. My grandmother had been battling cancer for a while, cared for by my cousins Nicole and Leslie who were staying with her. Her memorial was beautiful and was held at the cemetery chapel with my entire family there. She was buried in a cemetery in Tacoma where the rest of the Cornell family were buried. Afterward, we went over to her home in Lakewood for a family gathering. Lots of laughter burst out that afternoon, so I don't remember the grief but the celebration of her life as a Cornell. Her father was Daniel Cornell. He was a Tacoma pioneer who had built several of the early buildings there. He also built Paradise Lodge on Mount Rainier. Daniel's father, my great-great-grandfather Ezra Cornell, built Cornell University.

That afternoon after the funeral, the grandchildren, including myself, were allowed to take anything in her home as a keepsake of our grandmother. I thought about her car. I walked over to my aunt Patti and asked the question, "What will happen to her car?"

Patti looked at my dad and told him, "David, Todd needs a car. Let him have the Buick." Dad agreed. I was relieved as I had a car again. I think I whispered a silent prayer of thanks to my grandmother. I drove back to the bay that afternoon with a grateful heart. The next day I drove back up to Alpental at the summit on Snoqualmie Pass. I worked the rest of the summer at the summit, and then I came back to Wollochet. In August, I was ready for my next adventure as I began a new school at LBI where I had enrolled in the youth ministries four-year program. My heart was set to be a youth pastor. I was ready to move on with my life.

12

A NEW BEGINNING

"Behold, I am doing a new thing;
now it springs forth, do you not perceive it?
I will make a way in the wilderness and
rivers in the desert."
(Isaiah 43:19 ESV)

"I lift up my eyes to the hills.
From where does my help come?
My help comes from the Lord,
who made heaven and earth.
He will not let your foot be moved;
he who keeps you will not slumber.
Behold, he who keeps Israel will neither slumber nor sleep.
The Lord is your keeper;
the Lord is your shade on your right hand.
The sun shall not strike you by day, nor the moon by night.
The Lord will keep you from all evil;
he will keep your life.
The Lord will keep your going out and your coming in
from this time forth and forevermore."
(Psalm 121:1-8 ESV)

As the first day of school approached, I drove to Issaquah and up the hill to Providence Point where the school was located. Its original campus was in Greenwood, a suburb of North Seattle; this new campus was purchased from The Sisters of Providence. As I turned into the entrance, I gazed upon the new campus, which included the chapel, classrooms, and dorms. "Wow, this place is sweet!" was my initial response as I parked my full car in the front parking lot of the campus. What struck me was its serenity. The Father's peace was on the property. I could feel it, and my spirit was drawn to it. The chapel stood majestically in the background, behind the classrooms. I parked my car, walked up the sidewalk and through the entrance, and stood at the front desk. A couple of students greeted me and I replied, "Hi, I'm Todd Riggs."

One of the students looked up and said, "Hi Todd, welcome to LBI. Here is your welcome packet and your dorm room number."

I grabbed the packet of information and went out to my car, drove around to the back of the campus, and unloaded my car. I knew in my heart that my new adventure had begun. The days that followed were days of orientation and over the next few weeks, I made new friends in the dorms. All of the students participated in a lot of activities together.

The highlights of my three years at LBI could never be contained in a book. It was the best three years of my twenty-one years of life. I was coming out of such brokenness and anger toward my father and continuing to grieve the loss of my mother. LBI was a place of healing for me. The Bible college's primary focus was 'Jesus Only', teaching the Word of God and letting the Word speak for itself to its students. The focus was also on having a personal relationship with Christ through his Word and sacraments. The college emphasized learning to listen to the Holy Spirit as the student read the Word of God thus providing a personal encounter with God through his Word. At LBI, I had the privilege of learning how to read the scriptures through the 'inductive method' of Bible study. Inductive Bible study consists of three component parts, which frequently overlap in practice. These three parts are observation, interpretation, and application.

The teachers who taught at the Bible college included Pastors Rismiller, Schweiss, Lunder, Hedman, Bloomquist, Dr. Knute Lee, Pickering, Stime, Pat Lelvis, and Josee Jordan. The pastors will forever be remembered by the students. They each taught their classes with such simplicity and clarity, yet each of their classes left a profound impact on the students. They taught with great authority and anointing. It was hard to miss. Then there was my favorite teacher, who quickly became my mentor. His name was Don Fladland, who was the department chair of the Youth Ministries Program and Director of Ministries at LBI. In his own right, he was one of a kind. People either loved him or despised him. He had an evangelist's and a pastor's heart. He took me under his wing shortly after we met, and I had the opportunity to listen to him talk about youth ministry. I loved to just soak it in. His enthusiasm was highly contagious and his laughter could be heard from one end of the hallway to the other. When he looked at me, I think he knew my heart was broken. I appreciated the fact that he always made me laugh and that he never condemned or looked down on me. Not once did he call me out, but he always called me up. He called me up to what God was calling me to. With tears, I can say that I loved him, and it was an honor to call this man my friend.

The community at LBI, which included both the faculty and students, gave me a lot of special things. They gave me love, respect, a great deal of encouragement, and a tremendous amount of laughter. The student body and staff offered me worth, value, love, acceptance, a sense of feeling capable, and the gift of community. It was exactly what I needed at that time in my journey.

At times, there was a lot of laughter on the campus. I was introduced to many great friends, and many of them I have stayed in contact with. I had the opportunity to host 'Insanity Night' during my first year. It was an evening filled with craziness and laughter. I looked quite dapper wearing my boxers and briefs together with a dress shirt, tie, and dress coat. It was a great evening of community.

All students and faculty met for chapel every morning during the week. During my second year, I was asked to lead the charismatic prayer group that met in the chapel every Monday night. Several times we had encounters with the Holy Spirit. On one Monday night, the son of one of the administrators came into the chapel. He had a cast on his leg and was using crutches to help himself walk. He asked for prayer from the group. After we prayed for him, he ran out of the chapel shouting that he was healed, leaving his crutches at the altar. I watched him as he ran out and I noticed that his face was radiant with the Glory of God. I will never forget it.

On another night, after an anointed prayer time, all of us were at the altar. At least seventy-five people were lying on the marble altar praying that night. When we were finished praying, two older women who had recently come back from the mission field walked up to me in the dark. The red Eternal Light candle was the only light in the chapel other than the moonlight that beamed through the stained-glass windows. They walked up to me and said they wanted to talk to me. "While we were all praying, we both looked over to you and parts of your face and your feet were glowing. We both looked at each other and asked, "Do you see Todd right now?" We both confirmed what we saw and made the decision to talk to you about what the Lord told us to tell you." I just looked at them in wonderment. They looked at me and said, "The Lord told us that you have been given the gifts of the prophetic and pastoral office. We are to confirm this within you." I just stared at them. In my heart and spirit, a series of doors flung open as they spoke to me. Something was activated in me, and I was overwhelmed by the presence of God. As Paul confirms, "And he gave the apostles, the prophets, the evangelists, the shepherds, and teachers" (Ephesians 4:11 ESV).

Learning to read the scriptures from the inductive method of Bible study was a new doorway for me into reading the word of God. It provided a way to make scripture reading relevant and personal, and often set me up for encounters with God and confirmed the Word itself, "For the word of God is living and active, sharper than any two-edged sword, piercing to the division of soul and of spirit, of joints and of marrow, and discerning the thoughts and intentions of the heart" (Hebrews 4:12 (ESV).

Even so, a lot of my Bible classes were not easy. Many classes were incredibly challenging to me because it required focus and my full attention on my homework and memorization.

The LBI campus was all self-contained as the classrooms, dormitories, chapel and offices were all interconnected from inside. We were able to get up out of our beds and go right to class and never go outside. What a luxury. I also gained new friends and threw myself into all the social activities on campus. For my first year at this Bible college, I owe a deep amount of gratitude to the second-year students who provided a rich deep community of acceptance and love. Outside of my college fellowship in Gig Harbor, this was also a community where I felt safe.

In the classroom, I was exposed to different Christian writers. Authors by the name of Andrew Murray, Watchman Née, A.W. Tozer, and others became mentors who were often discussed in my learning. I was enthusiastic to see that my book library was beginning to build.

In the Christian music scene, many contemporary Christian music artists had a great deal of influence on me. Keith Green was one whose music had a tremendous spiritual impact on me. His music was a loud voice in my life. So loud that I wanted to find out who was mentoring Keith. I contacted his mentor, Leonard Ravenhill, and we wrote letters back and forth. Leonard, who was in his eighties, was an established revivalist, author, and a sought-out speaker. He was also deeply committed to the prophetic ministry. He personally knew A.W. Tozer, Samuel Chadwick, and Smith Wigglesworth. His last handwritten letter to me is hanging on the wall in my home to this day.

As mentioned earlier, the music and teaching ministry of Tony Salerno and the ministry of the Agape Force along with the Bible teachers known as Winkie Pratney, Joy Dawson, Loren Cunningham, and others from YWAM continued to speak into my life. The ministry of the Agape Force had set up a base in Gig Harbor and YWAM had a Discipleship Training School (DTS) on Tanglewood Island, off Fox Island, right across from Wollochet Bay.

The early years at LBI could best be described as a season of growth for me. I had a great deal of zeal, but very little wisdom. I had a great deal of experience with the Lord. I was exposed to several powerful encounters and experiences with Jesus, but I lacked many things including a working knowledge of the scriptural foundation to enhance what I encountered with God. My three years at the LBI gave me the foundation that I needed.

Several members of the faculty and even some students saw me as a loose cannon who had a hard time submitting to authority. Other faculty members were able to see past the zeal and lack of wisdom into my pain. They were able to validate and accept me. They saw my heart and never judged me. I will be forever grateful for Don Fladland, Eldon Pickering, Dr. Don Douglas, and Arlie Rue, who were able to see past my insecurities and pain, and who embraced me.

Once, I was walking past the acting dean's office when I heard him ask, "Todd, can you come in here?"

"Sure, what's up?" I replied.

He leaned back in his chair and stared at me. "I can't believe you've gotten this far. What do you think you are doing here? You've conned your way through your time here and you know what? I know who you are. You're going to be just like my brother. He ended up spending his whole life on a barstool."

I simply just stared at him in disbelief. "Really? You really think that about me?"

I got out of my chair in his office and walked out. I shared the confrontation with several of my faculty advisors, and I knew from the looks on their faces that they were extremely irritated by what was spoken over me that afternoon. One of my advisers told me that he would take care of it and that he would talk to the acting dean.

Even though I was experiencing deeper acceptance from my peers and most of the faculty, I was still struggling with bouts of depression and deep episodes of social anxiety. I continued to have symptoms related to Post-Traumatic Stress Disorder (PTSD). I often covered it up with grandiosity, confidence, and humor. Little did I know that the Lord was starting to break down the walls that I had built around me to cover the pain.

One morning I was late to class and rushed out from my room in the dorm. As I was walking toward the chapel, a beautiful second-year student walked right past me. When she walked by me, the Holy Spirit whispered to my heart, "You're going to marry that woman." I turned around and watched her walk away. "What? Really? What? What just happened?" I whispered to myself.

Shortly after that brief experience, this young lady was on my radar. I loved her smile. I loved her outgoing personality. She was one of the resident assistants for the women's dorm. I often saw Jesus in her face, especially when she smiled. I was in love. She kept her distance from me over the next few months, but I found out later that she was watching me. Over the next several months we became friends.

At the same time, my contact with my father was on a limited basis. I was on my own. He was busy in his new marriage, and I felt that he had no time for me. We only made contact with each other when I reached out to him. He was traveling a lot with his wife and was attempting to build a new life for himself. My father never came to my college graduation, my graduation from graduate school, or my ordination later. At LBI, I was already very disappointed in him. My disappointment grew deeper in the years ahead.

The summer came, and I worked on campus. Several working students and I painted the interior of the campus which, needed a facelift of colors. I wasn't welcome to come back to Wollochet that summer, and I was glad that I had a free place to live and work to help pay for the next year's tuition. The young lady, Cheryl, whom I had my sights on, was working at Glacier National Park for the summer. She came back to Washington to work at LBI in September. On the first day she came back, I met her in her office and asked her to come with me to Redmond to pick up more paint. On the drive back, we were talking, and I told her that I was thinking about dating. She asked the question, "Who do you want to date?" I responded, "You." This, my friends, is when the romance started.

I started an incredible second year that fall. By then my girlfriend, Cheryl, was working for Don Fladland who was the department chair for the youth ministries, campus ministries, and alumni departments. Two high-school graduates from the Port Angeles group were now attending LBI as well. The fellowship within the campus student body was so powerful and intoxicating. We had chapel every day along with classes and student activities. I was asked to be the student leader of the youth ministries volunteers that ministered off campus on a weekly basis. I also served as the leader of the weekly Monday night charismatic prayer group.

One day, an older Lutheran pastor, who was also a student by the name of Bob Johnson, came up to me in the hallway after class. He asked, "Todd, can I talk to you?"

I said, "Sure. What's up?"

He looked at me and said, "I need you to meet a man who is my pastor. His name is Bob Whipple. He and his wife Helen live in Stanwood, but I really think that you need to meet them."

I looked at him and was aware of his intensity, so I replied, "Okay, that sounds good."

He replied, "He will help you grow in your spiritual giftings. I think that you two will get along great."

That week, I called Bob Whipple and arranged a meeting with both him and his wife. I drove up to Stanwood from the campus in Issaquah. Our first meeting will remain in my memory forever. Bob and Helen were both in their sixties. We met for around three hours and he spoke of his relationship with the Lord. He spoke of the encounters he had throughout his life. He spoke with authority and with a sense of deep intimacy with the Father. He told me about the group that he shepherded known as The Lord's Company. From that day on our hearts were knit together. I grew to love Bob as a spiritual father and shared honestly with him about my relationship with my own father. Bob had a unique way of validating my father wound, but also had the ability to offer a perspective on how my father saw the world and saw me. He affirmed me on a deep level, yet he didn't talk down my dad. He simply offered a perspective. I was able to receive it. Little did I know that God was beginning to heal my father wound.

During that time in the summer, I lived on campus. Besides working for the school as a painter, I also was a lifeguard for the Seattle Sonics basketball camp that was held on campus during the summer. I worked for Lenny Wilkins, the coach of the team at the time, and he paid me cash. A big perk was being able to meet the different team members. Most notable was Jack Sikma. The two of us roasted hotdogs in an outdoor fire pit reserved for those who attended the basketball camp. It was great money at the time and I still have fond memories of that summer at LBI.

All the while, I did not know that my dad was tearing down our old cottage home on the bay, which was in deep need of repair. He was newly married, and he and his wife had made the decision to tear down the old structure and rebuild their home. They left the bedroom wing intact. While they leveled the cottage on the bay, my father made the decision to have a garage sale and sell everything in the old house. They made the point to not tell my sister and I about the garage sale. So, one weekend they sold all of the furniture from our childhood home, including all of the belongings of my sister and I, my mother's antiques, along with her Tole paintings, and other art that she had made. All of our childhood things that were in the attic were given away or sold without our knowledge. I found out later that several of my mother's friends on the bay came to the garage sale and purchased several of my mom's art pieces so that they could be saved for my sister and me. I have been told that from that point on, there were awkward tensions between our friends on Wollochet and my dad. My dad had crossed a line. When I heard about the garage sale and the secrecy, I went numb, and then I imploded. Everything in the former cottage home was gone. All of my childhood items that were in the small attic were gone. I was grateful that my friends and the families that I grew up with from the bay came, and either claimed or purchased items of importance for my sister and me, and then later handed them off to each of us. I realized that I no longer knew my father. The man that I knew had disappeared into a new marriage, a new life, and left his son and daughter behind. When I heard what had happened, I came down to Wollochet on the weekends. I was told that my mother's hope chest and other items were packed away under the detached garage. I asked my father for permission to get some things that were packed away. After giving me permission and telling me where the key was, I managed to get as much stuff as possible packed into my car and drive back to college, where I stored the items with my girlfriend Cheryl. I was conflicted as I wanted to be happy for my father and his new life, but was resentful in the way he went about it.

In the winter of 1981, I was interning at Glendale Lutheran Church as a youth ministries intern under the supervision of an amazing youth pastor. I was living with families in the youth ministry. I was honored to be at this church which was, at the time, the largest Lutheran church in the Pacific Northwest and embraced the Lutheran Charismatic Renewal. I served under leadership who embraced the things of the Spirit and taught openly the importance of having a personal relationship with the third person of the Trinity, known as the Holy Spirit. Sitting under the youth director was an anointed time for me. His passion and enthusiasm for kids to know Jesus was contagious. After my internship was completed, I came back to the college.

During that summer, Cheryl and I were continuing to get to know each other. Our relationship was moving forward. I knew that

I loved this woman, and I made the decision to ask her to marry me. That summer, we drove down to Pike Lake, near the LBI campus. We walked around the park and sat down on the beach.

"Do you want to marry me?" I asked.

She looked at me and replied, "I think that's a great idea!"

"Then let's go look for a ring this weekend." We kissed and hugged and walked to the car. We had no money. The one thing we did have was our love and God's smile. It was the best decision that I have ever made outside of following Jesus. Thirty-five years ago, I watched my bride walk down the aisle as we were married in the LBI chapel in March of 1982. It was a glorious day. All of our friends from LBI were there. Several of Cheryl's family and friends from Minneapolis were in the wedding. Most of my friends from Wollochet Bay were there.

Following the wedding, my dad threw an after-the-wedding bash at his home on Wollochet. I was later told that it was quite the party. Several years later, I was talking to my aunt Dorie who had flown in from Minneapolis for the wedding. She told me that there was some tension at the party because several of our friends wanted to talk about the memories of my mother from the earlier years. With my dad's remarriage, he was uncomfortable talking about them. So in the middle of his party, celebrating my and Cheryl's new marriage, he made a bold statement to everyone who was there. He declared, "From this day on, Janet's name will never be mentioned in this house again."

I wasn't there, but was told that an awkward silence followed. The families who lived on the bay were quiet, yet the party went on. I am grateful that I was not told. When my aunt told me this over two decades later, when we visited her in Starbuck, Minnesota, I was stunned, angry, and resentful. My father's declaration was hidden from me. My friends from Wollochet knew how hurtful it was. After the wedding, my dad would only talk about my mom when we were alone and only when I talked about her. I had no idea that he had said this after our wedding.

Fortunately, I had the Word to guide and direct me, "Strive for peace with everyone, and for the holiness without which no one will see the Lord. See to it that no one fails to obtain the grace of God; that no 'root of bitterness' springs up and causes trouble, and by it many become defiled" (Hebrews 12:14-15 ESV).

And even a warning, "For if you forgive others their trespasses, your heavenly Father will also forgive you, but if you do not forgive others their trespasses, neither will your Father forgive your trespasses" (Matthew 6:14-15 ESV).

When I returned to the campus, Cheryl and I started a house church that met each week. The group consisted of LBI college kids, who were hungry for more of the things of the Spirit. We had different teachers from LBI come, teach, and lead our group in prayer and ministry. It was a tight knit group, and we all learned a great deal during our time together. Our ministry time had an atmosphere anointed with the Lord's presence. The Lord was eager to show us who he was. When my wife Cheryl was working in Glacier National Park during the past summer, she became close friends with a young woman named Mary Hooley. Mary came back to the Seattle area and joined us in our house church; she was a new Christian. She would come over to our house, and we would sit for hours while she asked us questions about her faith and God, whom she was so hungry for. She was so filled with wonder and optimism. Her walk with Jesus was contagious. Her questions about the person of Jesus were naive and yet deep. Two years later while we were in Missouri attending seminary, Cheryl received a letter from Mary's parents. In their letter, we were told that Mary was abducted from her home and murdered in California. The authorities had found her body on the beach several days later. After reading this, Cheryl and I wept and prayed for the rest of the afternoon. Even today this tragedy continues to remain a deep wound in our hearts, but our hope remains steadfast as we know that we will see Mary again. That night, after we read the letter from Mary's parents, we went out to dinner with the seminary's academic dean, who was also a good friend of mine. He prayed for us, but we knew that we would carry this grief the rest of our lives. At this point, I began to understand the fierceness of the shepherd's heart. I was aware that I had a shepherd's heart for those who the Lord had put under my care. I knew that I would protect them to the point of death whether it was my family, my friends on Wollochet, the youth in Port Angeles, our friends at LBI, or our house church members in Bellevue. My love and loyalty toward those who the Lord had put under our care was intense and fierce. With this revelation, I began to see the fierceness of the Father's love for us. This intense, fierce loyalty to the Lord's flock is in the heart of every Ephesians 4:11 pastor. Mary and Cheryl had spent their summer hiking together around Glacier National Park. A couple of years ago, my wife and I were in Yellowstone National Park on vacation and staying in a hotel just outside the park in Garner, Montana. One morning, I went out to the edge of the property and got on the swing with my morning coffee and had some quiet time with the Lord. As I was swinging and pondering the view of the mountain range that stood before me, I became acutely aware that I was not alone. "Lord, is that you?" I asked.

"Yes," he said, "and Mary is with me."

I began to cry. Cheryl walked up to the swing, and we began to swing together. Cheryl asked, "What's wrong?"

I responded by telling her what I had experienced. I said to her, "Jesus and Mary are watching us, and they are both with us right now, smiling at us."

Cheryl replied, "Mary loved the mountains." We held each other and wept for quite a while on the swing, as we watched the sun rise on the mountain range before us in Yellowstone National Park. It was a glorious day. A deep healing had occurred for both of us.

While we were ministering in our house church in Bellevue, a young man from Beltrami, Minnesota, joined us. He was fresh off the farm, full of himself, and into fast cars and the ladies. He came to one of our gatherings and was ambushed by the Spirit of God. He kept coming back for more. Our whole house group was hungry and wanted more of God, but this young man had a spiritual thirst that was deep. After several weeks, Tim came to our house gathering and announced that he had made the decision to leave the Bible college. He had been offered a job in Colorado, and he told me that he wanted to find a girl and marry her. He was leaving in the next couple of weeks. I told him that this was a crazy idea. I told him that I really wanted him to stay at LBI and with our house church, but he was adamant in going. Tim left LBI and drove to Colorado shortly after our conversation. Cheryl and I were heartbroken.

A couple of weeks later, I had heard the devastating news from Colorado that Tim had been involved in a motorcycle accident on Easter morning of April 1982. He had a broken back and other severe injuries which paralyzed him, so he could no longer walk. Our group started to pray for him. Shortly after Tim's accident, I had several recurring dreams at night that lasted almost a week. I dreamed that I walked into Tim's hospital room, and I heard a voice saying, "I do not possess silver and gold, but what I do have I give to you: In the name of Jesus Christ the Nazarene—walk!" I was prompted by the Holy Spirit to go to Colorado and pray for Tim. I had one problem; I had no money. So, I confided in my faculty advisor and friend, Pastor Eldon Pickering. I told him the story and my dreams. He just looked at me and smiled. "Todd, if you are to fly to Craig Rehabilitation Center in Colorado, then God must supply your needs."

I responded, "Yes, I agree!" I walked out of his office and simply surrendered this whole thing to the Lord. Several days later, I received a check in the mail from Tim's parents. I opened up the letter, and there was a check. I called the airlines that same day, and they told me that the cost of a same-day round-trip ticket to Denver would be a certain amount. The check in my hands was the same amount of the plane ticket. I was flying to Denver!

I could write another book about what happened that day. I flew into Denver. I requested that my friend, Pastor Bob Johnson would join me in my prayer time with Tim. Pastor Bob was living in Denver, and a pastor of a church in the area. Bob was a former student and also a former board member of LBI. As I have mentioned earlier, Bob was instrumental in introducing me to his pastor, Bob Whipple. What happened that day, will stay with me the rest of my life. When we arrived at the rehabilitation center, we met Tim in his room. I walked in, and it was the same identical room that I saw earlier in my dreams.

We walked into the hospital room together thinking that we were going to pray for this young man for total healing. We came before the Lord and began to pray. After a few moments, my older pastor friend looked up at me. I also looked up at him. What we didn't know until we saw each other, that the Lord had spoken a prophetic word to both of us at the same time.

"Did you hear that?" he asked.

"Yes, I did." I replied. We then spoke the word out loud to each other at the same time. The young man that we were praying for, looked up at us with a big question mark on his face. I then said to Pastor Bob, "It would seem that you and I are to anoint this young man right now into the office of Apostle. That is what I heard."

Looking at me, he replied "Yes, that is what I heard as well." We brought Tim up in his bed. Pastor Bob was standing at the bottom of the bed, and I stood on the side of the bed, and we began to pray. As we began to pray and anoint my young friend with his back broken, the presence of Jesus filled the room. At one point during the prayer time, the Lord spoke prophetically into my young friend Tim. After we anointed him with oil, and prayed for healing, we both laid our hands on him and watched the Lord set him apart for the Apostolic office and ministry. I looked up, and all I could see was light, a light so bright that the only way I can describe it is that it was like 747 landing lights, two inches from my eyeballs. I looked around the room in the brilliant light trying to see where Bob was. I couldn't see him anymore as the light filled the room as Jesus was speaking his words over this young man. All I heard were his words, "Praise you, Holy Spirit. Praise you, Holy Spirit," over and over. Pastor Bob was face down on the floor in worship. Tim was sobbing in his bed. Jesus was physically in the room with us that day. His presence, glory, beauty, holiness, anointing, and joy were all there. It maybe lasted no more than ten minutes. Jesus spoke over my friend in the hospital that day in 1982, telling him that he was commissioning him to start new works around the world. Today our good friends, Tim and Dena Stromstad, have started orphanages in Haiti, Guatemala, and Costa Rica. I am thankful that the Lord is true to his Word.

I flew home that night, back to my dorm in Bible school. I tried to talk about what happened in Colorado, but I couldn't speak about it without weeping. My mentor and pastor, Bob Whipple, gave some good advice on that day. He said, "Todd, you've been in his Glory. No one will be able to understand you and really know what happened. You will need to wait until he gives you permission to speak."

As I allow myself to reflect on that powerful encounter during our time when we were in the light of heaven, when Jesus was in the room at Craig Rehabilitation Hospital, all of my earthly fears vanished. While I was in the light, all doubt disappeared. I knew in my whole entire being that I was in the presence of his all-consuming-furious-Agape-love. I knew that I was loved, all of me, and all hints of self-hatred disappeared. It was a foretaste of heaven, and I look forward to going back into that place of resurrection power and glory and not leaving it for the rest of eternity.

In the following spring, my wife Cheryl was laid off from her administrative assistant position at LBI. I graduated that spring with a BS degree in Youth Ministries. One afternoon during the week of graduation, one of the school's faculty members, Pastor Don Baron, president of the Lutheran Bible Institute in Hawaii, approached me in the hallway. He looked at me and said, "Todd, please, please don't ever leave the Lutheran church, as we need more obedient rebels like you."

I remember looking at him and saying, "Thanks Pastor Don, I won't." After graduation, I left my position as a youth director at a church in Bellevue and went to work at a rehabilitation facility in the same town, which is a suburb of Seattle. While working there, I had become friends with a man who became one of my closest friends and confidants. His name was Don. Our close friendship lasted over two and a half decades. We worked almost every day together serving children who had special needs. I could write a whole chapter about Don and our friendship together that spanned over the years. I learned more about the ministry of signs and wonders, miracles, and deliverance from him than anyone else. He went to be with the Lord a couple of years ago, and his passing has left a hole in my heart that has yet to be filled.

During those months, Cheryl and I made the decision to go to a small seminary south of St. Louis, located in Hillsboro, Missouri. This seminary appealed to me because the entire faculty were former Lutheran Charismatic Renewal pastors who had left the denomination to be part of this unique ministry training school. The school's vision was to train men and women who were called to the five-fold ministries of Ephesians 4:11. As I was going through the application process of this seminary and graduate school, I realized that I was not coming back to the Pacific Northwest for a long time. I quit my job at the rehabilitation center, and I worked at my childhood home at Alpental Ski Resort as a chair lift operator during the late fall and winter where I skied for free. We continued to have our house church in our home. I was tutored in New Testament Greek for half of the year to help prepare for seminary. When the resort closed for the season in the spring of 1983, I resumed my work at the rehabilitation center through the summer, but we also applied at a Lutheran retreat center known as Holden Village in the heart of the north Cascade Mountains. We were accepted to serve on their volunteer staff for the month of June. We were thrilled.

We left our home in Bellevue and served on staff at this unique village. To get to the village required a boat ride and then a bus ride up into the mountains into the self-contained village. We both were required to work four hours a day, five days a week. I served in the grounds and landscaping crew while my wife Cheryl served in the children's day care. It was a wonderful time as Cheryl and I were getting settled in our marriage. We went on hikes together every day. The foods that we ate were organic. We both lost weight during that time, yet we ate very well. We were outdoors for most of the day when we were there. It was a time of rest as we both were preparing to head to St. Louis for seminary. It was what we needed. After our four-week stay at Holden Village, we drove home and began to pack for our new adventure to move to the Midwest.

In July, we packed all our belongings in a U-Haul truck, and with our car in tow, we headed for Minneapolis. We stayed there for about thirty or forty-five days and then moved to St. Louis in time for me to begin seminary in September. Little did Cheryl and I know that this was the starting point for our new grand adventure together.

In 1985, almost two years later and several weeks before graduating from seminary and being ordained as a pastor, I had an extremely powerful encounter with the Lord. A young prophetic teacher came into the school and was prompted by the Lord to lay hands on all the graduating students. For two hours, this young man prayed and laid his hands on all of us who were graduating from the seminary, one by one. When he came to me, I remember that I simply shut my eyes in prayer. As I felt his hand on the top of my head, I immediately felt a fire all over my body. I started to sweat as he began to prophesy over me. He then stopped speaking and said, "My goodness, you are hot!" I responded and said quietly to him, "I'm really warm right now." We were standing in front of the church, in front of the congregation which included the other students and faculty members. The man took his hand away from my head, and said, "This has only happened once before to me. The last time this happened, there were blisters on my fingertips after praying for someone in the prophetic. It's happened again tonight. This man is a prophet!" My eyes were closed again, and I was still feeling an intense heat around my body. He then continued and spoke the following words over me:

You are like the prophet Micaiah to this generation. You will become familiar with rejection, and you will be familiar with pain and suffering. Your life and ministry will be characterized by these words, but know this, the Lord will reward you by knowing him in his inner chamber, in the inner chamber of the Lord.

When we were done, I opened my eyes and turned around. I remember that all I could see was light. I was once again in the light of his presence, just like I was in Colorado. I spoke out to Cheryl who was sitting in a pew not far from the altar and said, "I can't see you Cheryl, where are you? All I see is light." I heard many people in the pews quietly laugh. I remember hearing several people worshipping the Lord.

That night was a powerful night for me. Once again, something was activated in me. Everything that the young man said to me in his prophetic word has come to pass. Currently, in my counseling practice, I talk to people every day who are filled with despair and who are emotionally broken, or who are suffering and in pain. I have learned that the inner chamber of the Lord is a wonderful and holy place. The man that prayed for me that night went on to serve as a campus leader and a well-known prophetic teacher for the school known as Christ for the Nations, which is located in Texas.

After graduating from seminary with a Master's of Divinity, I was involved with a church-planting project in Iowa. After two years in church planting, we moved to the Twin Cities where I was offered a clinical position in a mental health hospital.

I can honestly tell you that sometimes I feel I have lived an entire lifetime in so many ways those many years ago. I know that I'm not the same person I was when I was raised on the waters of Puget Sound, yet I am incredibly grateful to both of my parents for raising my sister and I on Wollochet Bay. It's been forty-eight years since I slipped off that ten-story cliff as a boy. I still have periodic sleep terrors and symptoms related to Post-Traumatic Stress Disorder (PTSD) from the fall, being run over by a truck, and the motor cycle accident that left me physically scarred. I am so thankful that I can walk and run, even though the doctors told me that I would not be able to walk long distances because of my leg injuries I sustained when the truck rolled over me. I am grateful to Jesus for healing me of my second- and third-degree burn scars on my legs from the motor cycle exhaust pipe that burned into my leg. Today, I have no scars.

I have wrestled with periods of both depression and social anxiety all my life. The Lord has healed me from the scars of my sexual trauma, which has helped me come alongside other men and women who have had similar histories. Some of the tests that I've taken over the years suggest that I might have a splash of a high-functioning form of autism, formerly known as Asperger's Syndrome. We left the parish ministry in the late 1980s so that I could pursue a career in mental health. After working for almost four years in an inpatient hospital setting, I became a Licensed Independent Clinical Social Worker. I now have a thriving private practice in the Twin Cities. I remember when a teacher in YWAM told me once that our walk with the Lord is similar to what God did with Moses. First, God got Moses out of Egypt, then God got Egypt out of Moses, and then God sent Moses back into Egypt as a free man, with a song of deliverance on his lips to set God's people free. This is exactly what God has done for me. He actually does the same thing for all of us. In the area of our hurt and pain, we can learn to reign. When God gets a hold of pain, he takes what was meant for evil and destruction, and transforms and heals it for his glory. Everything Jesus touches, he liberates. My mother's cancer and death were the seeds that God used to plant me in the field of mental health. Today, I find myself the most comfortable when I am with people who struggle with mental health issues. Those who are emotionally broken and hurting are my people. It's where I belong. These folks are now my congregation.

13

ANOTHER VISIT FROM AN OLD ADVERSARY

"He made the storm be still,
and the waves of the sea were hushed."
(Psalm 107:29 ESV)

"The LORD your God is in your midst,
a mighty one who will save;
he will rejoice over you with gladness;
he will quiet you by his love;
he will exult over you with loud singing."
(Zephaniah 3:17 ESV)

In the fall of 1999, I was home alone one evening when the phone rang. It was my father on the other line. I picked up the phone and said, "Hey, Dad. How are you doing?"

"Hi Todd. I'm great! How are you doing? I'm calling to let you know that today was my final day working. I am officially retired! I wanted to call you and tell you."

I replied, "Wow, dad, that's great! Congratulations! I'm so happy for you. You deserve this day. You finally made it!" After a long silence on the other end of the phone, I asked, "Dad? What's up?"

Then I heard his words, "I'm sorry how I treated you as a boy. There were times when I didn't treat you very well. I'm sorry."

I listened to his words. I thought to myself, "Something is wrong. Why is he saying this to me?" But I responded, "Dad, it's all good. I forgave you a long time ago."

He then shot back, "Todd, you had an extraordinary childhood. You experienced things that most people don't experience in their entire life."

I responded back, "Yes, Dad, we had an extraordinary childhood. We did! I wouldn't trade any of it for the world." We talked for about fifteen more minutes. I then hung up the phone. In the silence, I remember looking at my parents' skating pictures that hung on our basement wall. I was numb and in tears. I had waited all my life for an apology from my father and he had just offered it to me. I walked up stairs and told my wife Cheryl what had just happened. Deep within me, something was activated in my spirit. There were no words to what the Lord did in my heart after I hung up the phone, but I now know that I had the permission from the Lord to share my story.

It was early March of that next year, almost five months since I had heard from my father. The phone rang, and then I heard my wife's voice from upstairs, "Todd, it's your dad."

I went upstairs and took the phone. "Hi Dad. It's good to hear your voice. Thanks for calling me. So how are you doing?"

"Hey, Todd. How are you?" he responded. I heard his voice. It was different.

"I have something to talk to you about." Then there was a long pause. I waited in the awkward moment. He continued by saying, "I saw my doctor this week. He told me that I have cancer in my pancreas. It's stage four."

"What?" I said back to him.

He responded, "We are going to fight this thing. We will take every measure necessary to beat this thing. We are going to fight it."

"I can't believe this," I again responded.

His voice over the phone replied, "I will keep you posted Todd."

I said, "Okay! If you need anything, Dad, just call me. Do you want me to come home? I will if you want me to."

He replied, "No, not now. We have a lot to do."

"Okay," I replied. "I love you dad." I hung up the phone, and I was in shock.

I whispered, "Okay cancer! You foul disease! Listen to me! You are not going to take my dad. You took my mom, and you are not going to take my dad as well!"

During the next several days, I retreated into my own private world. My old adversary known by the word cancer had raised up his ugly head again, so I buried myself in my work attempting to turn off my feelings. I attempted to be the adult. I attempted to turn off the worry. I lost my internal war. I was a wreck.

In April of 2000 I came home from work, and my wife met me at the door and told me that my dad had passed away. I just looked at her with a blank stare. We hugged for a long time. She looked at me and said, "You are going to be okay, but we have to figure out how to tell Josh and Alyssa that their grandpa Dave is gone." I immediately thought about our two children. They loved their grandpa Dave.

I sat the four of us down in our living room. "I have to tell you some extremely bad news," I said to them. The three of them just stared at me. I looked at them and said, "Grandpa Dave has died." After I said the words, I started to weep uncontrollably.

My wife Cheryl grabbed my hand and whispered, "There it is, let it out Todd." My daughter saw me and began to weep as well. She had never seen her father cry before. My son, with tears in his eyes, simply stared out the window in our living room. My wife was stoic and kept herself together. I was immediately brought back to the memories of my sister, crying while she waited for me to come home that afternoon from waterskiing to tell me that our mother had died. Watching my children respond to grief will be something that I will never forget. I just wanted it to all go away. Grief and loss was a part of my adolescence, and now my children were touching grief for the very first time. It was unbearable to watch.

That evening I booked the tickets to fly out to Seattle to be with my family and my father's wife. I went to her home in Federal Way. Graciously, she had requested that my dad's body be held at the funeral home until I had the chance to say good bye. I drove to the funeral home alone and walked into the building. On the way from the airport to the funeral home I was intentional in listening to soaking music. I remember listening to the song by Jaci Velasquez called, "I Will Rest in You". I let the song's chorus speak into my soul while I drove to the funeral home:

> Take me back to You
> The place that I once knew
> As a little child, constantly the eyes of God watched over me
> Oh I want to be
> In the place that I once knew
> As a little child, fall into the bed of faith prepared for me
> I will rest in You
> I will rest in You
> I will rest in You
> Tell me I'm a fool
> Tell me that You love me for the fool I am
> And comfort me, like only You can
> And tell me there's a place
> Where I can feel Your breath like sweet caresses on my face again.[1]

In the surreal atmosphere, I walked alone into the prepared room where my dad's body was located. I walked into the room and saw my dad on a bed with a blanket that came up to his neck. I walked up to him and simply looked into his face. He looked so tired. I put my hand on the blanket that covered his chest, and kept my hand there for several moments. I then whispered, "Lord, what do you want me to do?"

The Lord spoke to my heart, and he gently whispered to me, "You are to anoint him for burial."

"All right, I will do that." I then took out my small flask of anointing oil, and anointed my father with the sign of the cross. I also anointed his eyes and his ears as well. I again asked the Lord, "Now what do you want me to do?"

He gently whispered again to my heart, "You are to speak over his body the Blessing of Aaron, the priestly blessing."

"All right", I responded. I then spoke the following words from Numbers 6:24-26 (NASB) over my dad's body:

> "'The LORD bless you, and keep you;
> The LORD make His face shine on you, and be gracious to you;
> The LORD lift up His countenance on you, and give you peace.'
>
> I pray this in the name of the Father, and the Son, and the Holy Spirit."

I looked into his face one last time and said, "I love you, Dad." The Lord spoke to my heart again and said, "Todd, your father has spent a lifetime looking for the Father's blessing. He traveled the world seeking a father's love and had never found it. He never found what he was looking for until now. It was only in death and through his son's words that he could find it. He didn't have to earn it, but you offered it freely to him today. It is done."

I walked out of the room in the funeral home, got in my car, and drove to Anthony's Seafood Restaurant where my close friend Don Pursel and I met for dinner. That night, as I reviewed that day with him and we talked about my new awareness of now being an orphan of sorts, Don turned to me and stuck out his pinky finger toward me. He told me to stick out my pinky finger toward his. He then looked at me in the eye, his pinky finger grabbing mine and said, "I pinky swear that we are brothers for life." I looked at him and thanked him. We then enjoyed the rest of our seafood meal at one of the finest restaurants in Seattle. I drove back later that night to Burien, where I was staying with my cousin, and I threw up my meal. It was quite a day.

When I flew home, I was ready to get back to the familiar and my family. Little did I know that three weeks later, my wife's father was going to die with complications of bone cancer. Bob was a good man. He had a hard life. He was an 'Archer Bunker' type of guy who was rough on the outside, but had a soft side that rarely came out. He surrendered his life to Jesus shortly before he passed. It was an incredible thing to watch the softening of his heart to God as he approached death.

As I look back over the decades of my life, I am acutely aware of the grief and loss that have been my constant companions. They have shaped me into the man that I am today. I am reminded of an old song by Barry McGuire. The lyrics are from the poem written by Robert Browning Hamilton:

> I walked a mile with Pleasure;
> she chatted all the way;
> But left me none the wiser
> for all she had to say.
> I walked a mile with Sorrow;
> and ne'er a word said she;
> But oh! The things I learned from her,
> When Sorrow walked with me.[2]

My father and I had the chance to reconcile in the months prior to his death. I had come to the conclusion years ago that my dad would never be able to give to me what I needed emotionally. The tides turned when I accepted that he was not able to give me emotional validation when it was never given to him. He grew up without a father, as he lost his father as a young child. His wound grew in him, where he searched for love, acceptance, and validation in other things that the world had to offer. My father wound began to heal when I realized that he could never give to me what was never given to him. The way he showed his love for me was through provision. He provided for me and he offered me a childhood that he referred to as 'extraordinary'.

Every time I make shrimp cocktails, the same thing happens. My wife and I drift off into my memories of my father. When I was in college, and then later in Bible school, every time I came home to visit my dad, he always served me shrimp cocktails as I walked through the door into our home on Wollochet. It was his way of saying to me, "I miss you; you're important to me. And I'm glad you're here." On one occasion, when I flew in from St. Louis while I was attending seminary, I was in Seattle for a brief visit. I took the ferry across from Seattle to Bremerton. When I arrived in Bremerton, I walked to my dad's car and in the backseat on a silver platter was an extremely large shrimp cocktail waiting for me.

I've learned a great deal in my life's journey. I have just scratched the surface of my lifelong learning curve.

> Everybody fails, errs, and makes mistakes. We have all heard the saying, "To err is human, to forgive, divine." Alexander Pope wrote that over 250 years ago. And he was only paraphrasing an ancient saying that was common during the time of the Romans. Recently I came across something called "Rules for Being Human." I believe this accurately describes the state of many of us:
> Rule #1: You will learn lessons.
> Rule #2: There are no mistakes—only lessons.
> Rule #3: A lesson is repeated until it is learned.
> Rule #4: If you don't learn the easy lessons, they get harder.
> Rule #5: You'll know you've learned a lesson when your actions change.[3]

Throughout my career as a pastoral clinical social worker, I have shared a parable known as 'The Wall' in my counseling sessions with clients. All of us get wounded in life. We are wounded and hurt by relationships and events that have entered our lives. Some of us, including myself, sought bricks every time we were wounded. We use the bricks that we gather to build large walls around us. For each wound that occurs in our lives, another brick is added to the wall. By the time we realize what has happened, we have built a wall around us so high that we can't get out, and also people can't get in to help us. The only way the wall can come down is to ask for help. With God's help, and those he sends our way, brick by brick, our wall will come down. Then, God sends us out to help others with their walls, and help them take their bricks down.

Next, I would like to share with you a conversation that I had with the matriarch of my paternal family. Over a year ago, I flew out to the Pacific Northwest to interview my aunt Patti for more information about our family history that was needed for this writing. I captured my interview with her in the following chapter.

A Boy From Wollochet

My dad, skating and performing a hand stand on the ice.

My dad, skating and performing a cantilever.

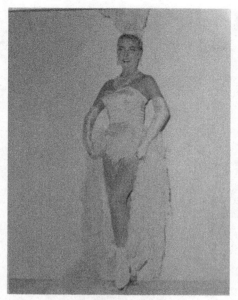

My mom in her figure skater's costume.

A family picture taken while Dad was general manager of the Alpental Ski Resort – 1969.

My dad with his plane – during his skating years.

My dad with his Mercedes – during his skating years.

On Wollochet Bay – I am driving the Connelly ski boat.

My Dad and I.

My grandmother Florence Cornell – French Riviera – late 1950s.

My sister and I – Christmas in Sun Valley, Idaho – 1970.

My parents – Christmas in Sun Valley, Idaho – 1970.

My mom and I having a moment on the beach – 1963.

My Dad's Sister – Aunt Patti.

On Crystal Mountain as a boy.

Preparing for a ski race as a boy at Crystal Mountain.

Looking at the Olympic Mountain Range from the top of Hurricane Ridge.

On the top of Denny Mountain in Alpental Valley above the cliff that I fell off.

14

THE TALES OF GENERATIONS GONE BY

In the summer of 2015, I had the privilege of visiting the Pacific Northwest to do some research for this writing. Our matriarch, my father's older sister Patti, is almost 90, and for an hour I heard about the stories that will be passed down through the next generations in our family. It was an honor and a privilege to listen to Aunt Patti and her husband, Uncle Don, tell the old stories over the course of that summer afternoon in Olympia. Don and Patti have five children who are my beloved cousins: Janne, Nicole, Leslie, Daniel, and Deirdre. Patti began by telling her early memories of her childhood. Florence Cornell was my grandmother. Grandmother was an extraordinary lady. She was one of two daughters of my great-grandfather Daniel Cornell. Daniel was one of two sons of my great-great-grandfather Ezra Cornell. Ezra Cornell founded Cornell University.

> The founding of Cornell University brought together all of the themes that were important in Ezra Cornell's life: his deep and abiding concern for education, his interest in agriculture, his philanthropic impulse, and his political sense. The opportunities also were there. In 1862 the Morrill Land Grant Act had been passed, appropriating public lands to aid state agricultural and mechanical colleges. By 1864,

Cornell's family, his personal philanthropies, and the Public Library required only a small part of his considerable fortune. He had been elected to the New York State Senate, where he made the acquaintance of Andrew Dickson White of Syracuse. Through discussions with White, the idea of a university grew in Cornell's mind. When the Legislature met in 1865, White introduced a bill in the Senate "to establish the Cornell University and to appropriate to it the income of the sale of public lands granted to this State." After much political maneuvering, the bill was passed in the Assembly on April 21, in the Senate on April 22, and was signed by Governor Reuben E. Fenton on April 27. The first meeting of the Board of Trustees was held on April 28. Cornell endowed the university through an outright gift of $500,000, to which would be added the sum realized by Cornell's purchase of the Morrill land scrip from the state.

Ezra Cornell was closely involved in all aspects of the new university. He superintended construction and purchased equipment, books, and collections. On October 7, 1868, Inauguration Day, 412 students, the largest entering class admitted to any American college up to that time, came to Ithaca. Cornell gave a brief address, concluding with the University's newly adopted motto: "Finally, I trust we have laid the foundation of a University—an institution where any person can find instruction in any study.[1]

As my aunt Patti reminisced that day, she spoke of her grandfather Daniel as a very nice man. They originally moved to the Pacific Northwest from back east in Ohio. Both Daniel and his brother Ernest moved to San Francisco where they went by train. They got off the train in Portland, where in her words, "It was so crowded", and they then made the decision that they didn't want to live there. The two of them went by horseback up to Tacoma. That is where they ended up and started their own company and began to build homes. Daniel Cornell ended up living in a home on the north end of Tacoma.

> Ernest C. and Daniel Cornell, natives of Ohio, moved to Tacoma in the late 1880s. The brothers started working in the contracting business immediately, and for a while partnered together. By the late 1920s they helped create the firm of Albertson, Cornell Brothers & Walsh, a large business which constructed roads, erected power stations and a large part of Fort Lewis during World War I. The firm's average payroll included between 400 and 600 men, although to build Fort Lewis the firm employed more than 10,000 men. Daniel Cornell later became vice president of the Washington Paving Company. Both the brothers were active in community affairs, particularly with fraternal orders, and were members of the Masons, Knights Templar, Scottish Rite, Elks, and the Union Club.[2]

According to my aunt Patti, they always had lovely Thanksgivings and Easters. In my interview with her she said:

> My grandmother's name was Sarah, and she was a grand lady. Sarah was the first woman in Tacoma to buy her own car, which was a Model A. Sarah had two daughters, Florence and Hazel. My mother, Florence Cornell, was an aristocrat. She was an extraordinary woman who experienced the deaths of two husbands, and had the agility, perseverance, and where-with-all to raise three children in an era when this was unheard of. My father's name was Norman Riggs. He was raised in Portland and owned a Frigidaire dealership and moved to Tacoma when he lost his business. He became a draftsman and during the depression there were no jobs. He became very sick and died from high blood pressure when your father, my brother, was five years old and I was ten years old.

My aunt Patti continued reminiscing and told me that my grandmother Florence survived breast cancer in a time when women were cut open brutally in surgery. She was a woman who spent a lot of time on Mount Rainier, watching her father build Paradise Lodge. She also witnessed her father build most of the early buildings such as the Tacoma train depot and the first Episcopalian and Presbyterian churches in town. As a young woman, my grandmother lived in Ketchikan, Alaska for a short time when my great-grandfather was asked to build a fort in the town in the early days. As a young boy, I can remember that my grandmother always smiled, and always wore dresses or skirts when she was working in her rose garden. She was a proper lady. She never spoke evil of anyone. Our family's memories of Thanksgiving will always remain infamous. Grandmother always hosted Thanksgiving in her home in Lakewood. She also always hosted Easter by having our entire family over to her home, where there was an Easter egg hunt in her backyard rose garden. On Easter, she always bought presents for us. These were the best of times, growing up during the holidays with my extended family in the Pacific Northwest. I was always put into training weeks before the holidays to remember on which side of the plate the salad dish was placed and to also remember which fork to use for the salad. At Thanksgiving, there were always seven grandchildren in her home in Lakewood. It was an extremely humorous fiasco for the grandchildren in our attempts to have proper manners around her. She raised three wonderful children, who were our parents, aunts, and uncles. In her later years she was able to travel Europe and spent a lot of time there. Her fortune with the Cornell trust fund was lost due to poor money management from her financial advisor.

My grandmother had a son from her first marriage who was twelve years older than my dad. My grandmother, as a babysitting and parenting tactic, would drop my dad off at the Lakewood Ice Arena. This was where he learned to skate. With the lack of a father figure in his life, my dad was able to have relationships with the coaches and skating teachers at the arena. At an early age, my father became a talented and gifted ice skater. Sonja Henie found him at the Lakewood Ice Arena when he was part of a comedy team with his friend Larry Ham. In high school, my grandmother pulled my dad out of high school because of the way the math teacher was treating my father. They moved to Sun Valley, Idaho, as did Larry, and they finished high school and continued with their ice skating comedy routine under the supervision and watchful eye of Sonja Henie. After their high school graduation, they joined the ice show. After my dad left, my grandmother owned a toy store. As I grew up watching my dad, I was aware of the father wound in him. He never talked about it.

My dad had a half brother. His name was Bill Donnelly. When my grandmother's first husband passed away from the flu during World War I, Bill went to live with my grandmother's father, Daniel Cornell. My uncle Bill was then sent to the University of Washington. My dad, aunt Patti and uncle Bill enjoyed their family beach place on Vashon Island.

I have never talked about my uncle Bill a lot. Simply because of the man he was. Growing up, my memories of him consist of both he and my aunt Susan flying out to Tacoma from Washington, DC, and visiting us about every five or six years. They would stay with my grandmother. My dad often told stories of his older half brother. They were all true. Bill was an interesting man. He joined the marine corps at an early age. He served in World War II. My dad told me that he was one of the first marines to reach Pearl Harbor after the Japanese bombing. Uncle Bill never spoke any words of what he witnessed that day he arrived at Pearl Harbor. He later went on to also fight in the Battle of Iwo Jima. After the war, he went on to receive his law degree. He initially was going to join the Schnel Law Practice in Tacoma, but soon found himself bored with the thought of spending all day drawing up wills. Shortly after that, Bill was recruited and hired on by the first director of the FBI, J. Edgar Hoover. He spent his entire career in the FBI, living in Washington, DC, after he married my aunt Susan. Susan worked for the Canadian Embassy. They never had any children. Growing up, I was told that my uncle was in charge of all communist affairs in the United States with his work in the FBI. My memories of my uncle were that of seeing him on my grandmother's backyard patio during one of their visits, in warm clothing and always wearing his dark sunglasses. He was a quiet man. As a boy, I wanted to ask him questions like, "So, who really killed Kennedy?" or "What's it like working for the FBI?" I would try and get the nerve to ask him, and my dad would always give me the glare. That meant, "Don't you dare ask him anything stupid." I always caved to my dad's glare. My dad told me once that during the Bay of Pigs crisis, my aunt and uncle had their car packed with their belongings, along with food, and a bottle of whiskey just in case they had to leave Washington, DC, on a moment's notice.

There were a lot of fascinating things about my uncle Bill. First, he was my dad's older half brother. Second, he was a veteran and saw things in Pearl Harbor after the bombing that he would never speak of. Third, he served his country in the FBI, and fought the war on communism in the United States for over twenty-five years. To a young boy, he was the figure that represented the cloak and dagger. It was like we had a spy in our family and my uncle was one of the good guys.

When he retired, my aunt and uncle bought a waterfront home in Rosedale, minutes from Gig Harbor. My dad once told me that one of my uncle's friends from Washington, DC, also retired shortly after he did and bought a waterfront home a couple doors down from my uncle. I was also told that Bill and his friend would often sit out on their decks sipping cocktails after dinner. His friend was a former *Air Force One* pilot. He flew *Air Force One* home to Washington, DC, with Kennedy's body on board, back from Dallas on that horrible day in November, 1963. My dad often said, "Oh, to be a little mouse under the deck and be able to listen to their stories..." These stories were never heard or retold. For me, this is one of the reasons why I stop, pause, and reflect on those who served and died so that we could live in freedom. At his death, my uncle requested that there would be no memorial or funeral. He was buried in Arlington National Cemetery with full military honors. He was a private man who requested a private death, but lived life large. He is one of my heroes. Lastly, another thing about my uncle Bill was that I was able to buy his Tiderunner boat after he died. Over the years, several of my friends have asked me, "So why don't you get rid of your old ski boat and buy a new Malibu boat?" My response to those who have asked that question has simply been, "Not on your life, this is my uncle Bill's boat. It's a keeper."

I asked my aunt Patti during our time together if she had any favorite recollections of her and my father when they were kids. She responded by sharing more of her memories of the beach house on Vashon Island:

> My younger brother David, your father, was a live wire. He went out and got a paper route when he was around four years old. Guess who had to go out with him and roll up the papers? I had to pull his wagon with all of his stuff in it. I had to go collect with him because he was not good at collecting money from people. We were very close, and I looked after him.

My mother's name was Janet. She was born in 1937 and raised in south Minneapolis in a middle-class home. She graduated from Roosevelt High School and then joined *Holiday on Ice* and met my father while on tour. My parents fell in love, and got married while they were on tour. I was born in the summer of 1958. My parents made the decision that my mother would quit the show and take care of me, and my dad continued to skate to provide for us. My mom went to work for a radio station known as KJR in Tacoma and I was placed in day care with a woman who our family called 'Momma Bev'. We continued to live in the Lakewood area of Tacoma and moved to a small home on Leona Lane when I was around four years old.

I never knew either of my grandfathers. My mom's father, Evert Williams, died several months after I was born. My mom's mother, Ida Williams, died shortly before I was born. They raised their family in Minneapolis. Grandfather Evert was born in May, 1900 in Sweden and as a young man immigrated to Minneapolis. He was a street car conductor in south Minneapolis. Evert's parents, Villiam and Anna Prest, stayed in Sweden. As the story goes, Villiam's last name changed when he beat up a priest in Sweden as a young man. My maternal grandmother, Ida Christina Eklund, was born in June, 1906 in Stanchfield, Minnesota. She and I share the same birthday. I have been told many times by my cousins that my grandpa Evert would stop at the bar from time to time on Lake Street in Minneapolis while he was working and have a 'bump'. He then would finish his bus route. I smile every time that I hear the story, as it was his routine.

My mother had an older brother named Eric. He owned a cement and concrete business in the Twin Cities. They had three children who are my beloved cousins: Jamie, Bart, and Preston (Pepper). Since I had no relationship with my grandfathers, both of these men have held an enormous sense of fascination and awe for me.

In the following chapters, I want to share with you some of the things that I have learned over the course of my life. First, I want to write about two topics that have been strong pillars in my spiritual journey. One is learning to step out of our comfort zones. The second pillar is encountering the powerful and awesome love of the Father. I have had the pleasure of talking with people all over the world about these two subjects. The first, I had to learn to step out and take risks, the second, I had to learn to receive. They both brought me into deep encounters with the Lord. You are about to read portions from my sermon notes. As you read the next two chapters, you will sense the flow starting with the goal, then the problem, and then the solution.

15

COMFORT ZONES

"Life begins at the end of your comfort zone."
— Neale Donald Walsch[1]
"To get something you've never had you have to do something you've never done."
— Unknown

As I look back over my life, I've come to a sobering reminder that God always wants me to come out of my comfort zones. Growth is always outside of comfort. As I have finished telling my story, I would like you to pause and then take a deep breath. As I begin to talk about this topic regarding comfort zones, I would ask that you would open up your heart to the Lord Jesus, so he can speak to you concerning his desire for you to step into the things of God in a new fresh way. I've learned a lot over my life about how to step out of what is familiar and to walk into a deeper trust walk with Jesus. As Jesus' followers have learned to follow him over the years, I realize that he is calling, and even wooing, each one to follow him more deeply. He is calling each of us out of the areas of life that are complacent and at ease, and leading us to his holy place.

To do that, we need to understand the Father's heart and his purpose in our lives as he wants to fashion us into his image. We need to believe what he is doing before we see it happen. This believing has the power to transform us from a natural people into a supernatural people. In my story, I've already shared about Pastor Craig asking his daughter Sarah to jump into his arms off the fireplace mantle. Thus, the kingdom of God is opposite of what we would consider in the natural. For example, all of us are bombarded with society telling us that we need to have more and more money; therefore, we need to save. Yet, in God's kingdom to have more, we need to give more away. When we take care of the things of the kingdom, the kingdom will take care of us. Matthew 6:33 (ESV) confirms this, "But seek first the kingdom of God and his righteousness, and all these things will be added to you." If we want a manifestation of God's kingdom in our lives, we must believe it before we see it. We need to learn to see with the eye of faith and not the natural. We need to learn to walk in the simple truth that he will not quit me, but that he has already equipped me in Christ.

Some of us are living like a person who is spending all their time trying to get into an overstuffed recliner when we are unaware that we have already been sitting in the recliner all along. You see, God put us in his recliner chair when we called out to him and when we became part of his family.

What I've learned over the course my life is that God wants to convince us that we are powerful in him. I think sometimes we look too much at ourselves and not enough on Jesus.

What I'm talking about here is to have the ability to walk in this world with a consciousness of God's way and power. We need to get it into our hearts, and then walk in it.

We will be out of our comfort zones. So, I want to stir us up in the area of learning how to step out of our comfort zones. In the Old Testament, several examples of men and women show us how to step out of what they knew to be familiar and to step into the things of God. When I think of individuals like Noah, Abraham, Caleb, Joshua, and Elijah, I see these men as listening to the voice of God and moving out of their comforts to follow him.

Looking at Hebrews 11, otherwise known as the faith chapter, one sees numerous accounts of normal men and women who moved outside of their comfort zones and accomplished great things for God. Also, when we follow God out of our comfort zones, we give God freedom and permission to move on our behalf. Then, the Lord steps in and puts to death something in us so that more of his life can be manifested in us.

Let's take a look at a lesson from America's history. In 1519, Captain Cortes landed in Veracruz to begin his great conquest. Upon arriving on the shore, he gave the order to his men to burn the ships. Retreat is easy when options are available. We all hang onto possible exit strategies and exit doors. These are our safety nets just in case something really bad happens. But being more honest with ourselves, we would say, "This is where I am at just in case I get really, really scared."

In 1996, I was at the Billy Graham Crusade in Minneapolis when the Holy Spirit began to speak to my heart by asking me the question, "Are you willing to give your life away to me?" I thought to myself, "Lord, you know the answer to that." He again asked me the same question two more times. Little did I know that he was starting to prepare me for a new chapter of ministry that would include short-term missions. Two months later, I was in Estonia, Russia, and Finland serving in the shadow of three spiritual giants. My mentor, Don Fladland, asked me to join two of the pastors, including Don Richman, the director and founder of East European Missions Network. Two months later after returning from a trip, I was in the rural countryside of Atenas, Costa Rica. I had the privilege of serving under the missionaries with Children of Promise. Soon after this prophetic encounter, I was asked to come alongside a group of young men and mentor them. We are still meeting on a regular basis. These men are known as the Minneapolis Band of Brothers. I have found in my journey that whenever we put ourselves in a position before the Lord to learn obedience, he will take us out of our spiritual comforts and into a deeper life with him. Author and motivational speaker Jack Canfield says it this way, "Everything we want is on the other side of fear."[2]

I have found that the Lord takes great pleasure in us when we step out of what we know to be secure and normal Christianity, into a life of radical obedience to him. What we consider as being fanatical for Jesus, God sees as normal Christianity. Can we pray for God's deliverance from comfortable, normal Christianity? Nothing is normal about Christianity. When Christianity is boring, something is very wrong.

Jesus invites us to have encounters with him. Having one encounter with Jesus Christ can take the place of five years in a therapist chair. One of the primary ways I know to set us up with encounters with God is by reading his Word daily.

The scriptures tell us, "The name of the LORD is a strong tower; the righteous man runs into it and is safe" (Proverbs 18:10. ESV).

I want to be in a place of absolute dependence on Jesus, to lift my heart to him and to declare that he is my hope, my security, my defense, my life, my past, present, and my future.

If you would like more Bible references to how God dealt with man's comfort zones, check out the three Hebrew captives in Daniel 3:16. You could read the story of David where he danced before the Lord in a loin cloth in worship in 2 Samuel 6. It's incredible to read that David danced before the Lord and was lost in worship. I don't think he cared who saw him. The prophet Hosea was told by the Lord to marry a prostitute as a symbol of the Lord's faithfulness to the nation of Israel.

Also, the New Testament speaks of many other people who stepped out of their comfort zones. Here are some more awesome testimonies related to Jesus' ministry:

> The Centurion. Matthew 8:5-10
> The sick woman. Mark 5:24-34
> The sinful woman. Luke 7:36-50
> The 10 lepers. Luke 17:11-19

Even the disciple Peter was called out of the boat in Matthew 14:22-33. In order for Peter to step out of the boat, he needed three things: faith, assurance, and obedience. What I find fascinating in the story is that Jesus provided an opportunity for all three things to happen. What I've learned over the years is that when God is going to lead us down a path requiring faith, he will provide the means to make it happen. The Lord Jesus himself was called out of his comfort zone by his heavenly Father:

> "Have this mind among yourselves, which is yours in Christ Jesus, who, though he was in the form of God, did not count equality with God a thing to be grasped, but emptied himself, by taking the form of a servant, being born in the likeness of men. And being found in human form, he humbled himself by becoming obedient to the point of death, even death on a cross. Therefore God has highly exalted him and bestowed on him the name that is above every name, so that at the name of Jesus every knee should bow, in heaven and on earth and under the earth, and every tongue confess that Jesus Christ is Lord, to the glory of God the Father" (Philippians 2:5-11 ESV).

"There is safety in complacency, but God is calling us out of our comfort zone into a life of complete surrender to the cross. To live dangerously is not to live recklessly but righteously. It is because of God's radical grace for us that we can risk living a life of radical obedience for him."[3]

One of my life lessons has been simply that God is ready to assume full responsibility for a life that is totally yielded to him. God never leads us into, but out of, our comfort zone and ease. God is waiting for us to step out into a walk of dependence on him. He wants so very much for opportunities to reveal himself to all of us through his Word. I believe that all Christians need to step out of the familiar, which allows him to reveal his character. He wants opportunities to show himself. He wants to build faith in all who seek him. The prophet Amos tells us, "Woe to those who are at ease in Zion" (Amos 6:1 ESV).

This is a prayer for all of us: "Lord, take us deeper into your heart, no matter what, no matter the cost, even if I'm the only one standing, I'm willing to stand alone."

Can we agree with the apostle Paul when he wrote, "that I may know him and the power of his resurrection, and may share his sufferings, becoming like him in his death" (Philippians 3:10 ESV).

Our Father God is always saying to us, "Come. I've got so much to show you."

When God says come, he is always drawing us out and is asking us to join him into embracing things that are better for us than what was before.

"And he brought us out from there, that he might bring us in and give us the land that he swore to give to our fathers" (Deuteronomy 6:23 ESV).

Listen to the apostle Peter when he wrote these words, "But you are a chosen race, a royal priesthood, a holy nation, a people for his own possession, that you may proclaim the excellencies of him who called you out of darkness into his marvelous light. Once you were not a people, but now you are God's people; once you had not received mercy, but now you have received mercy" (1 Peter 2:9-10 ESV).

Listen to the "Comes" of scripture.

Come into a place of safety.
"Then the Lord said to Noah, 'Go into the ark, you and all your household, for I have seen that you are righteous before me in this generation.'" (Genesis 7:1 ESV).

Come into good fellowship.
"The Lord has promised good concerning Israel" (Numbers 10:29 NASB).

Come for personal cleansing.
"Come now, and let us reason together, says the LORD: though your sins are like scarlet, they shall be as white as snow; though they are red like crimson, they will be like wool" (Isaiah 1:18 NASB).

Come for a satisfying portion.
"Come, everyone who thirsts, come to the waters; and he who has no money, come, buy and eat! Come, buy wine and milk without money and without price" (Isaiah 55:1 ESV).

Come for rest of soul.
"Come to me, all who labor and are heavy laden, and I will give you rest" (Matthew 11:28 ESV).

Come at the King's urgent invitation.
"Again he sent other servants, saying, 'Tell those who are invited, "See, I have prepared my dinner, my oxen and my fat calves have been slaughtered, and everything is ready. Come to the wedding feast"'" (Matthew 22:4 ESV).

Come to the Gospel feast.
"But he said to him, 'A man once gave a great banquet and invited many. And at the time for the banquet he sent his servant to say to those who had been invited, "Come, for everything is now ready"'" (Luke 14:16-17 ESV).

Come at the threefold call.
"The Spirit and the Bride say, "Come." And let the one who hears say, "Come." And let the one who is thirsty come; let the one who desires take the water of life without price" (Revelation 22:17 ESV).

I have learned along life's journey that obedience to the Lord always requires me to step out of my own comforts and out of the natural into the supernatural realm of his kingdom. But the problem is simply that this doesn't come. And usually it's because of my own fears and pride. Not only do many followers of Jesus live in their spiritual comfort zone, but so do many churches. So, how do we move past all of this? The first thing we need to understand is how we let our fears become roadblocks to receiving.

Many of us fear emotions.
"But the fruit of the Spirit is love, joy, peace, patience, kindness, goodness, faithfulness, gentleness, self-control; against such things there is no law" (Galatians 5:22-23 ESV).

Many of us fear that we will be deceived.
"Or which one of you, if his son asks him for bread, will give him a stone?" (Matthew 7:9 ESV).

Many of us have a fear of phenomena and manipulation.
"Now the Lord is the Spirit, and where the Spirit of the Lord is, there is freedom" 2 Corinthians 3:17 ESV).
"and you will know the truth, and the truth will set you free" (John 8:32 ESV).

"The Spirit of the Lord God is upon me, because the LORD has anointed me to bring good news to the poor; he has sent me to bind up the brokenhearted, to proclaim liberty to the captives, and the opening of the prison to those who are bound" (Isaiah 61:1 ESV).

Many of us fear getting hurt by others.
Many of us have fears that have been caused by wrong theology.
Many of us fear rejection.

Winkie Pratney, a Bible teacher with YWAM, said once that fear comes from one of four things:

1. When we put our confidence in ourselves.
2. When we put our confidence in someone else.

3. When we put our confidence in a circumstance.
4. When we put our confidence in the devil.[4]

Other reasons to remain in comfort zones are:

- Anxiety
- Complacency—when everything is going too smooth
- Feelings of inadequacy
- Potential financial instability
- Lack of spiritual vision
- Lack of faith
- Pride

Pride is the biggest hindrance in developing intimate relationships, spiritual or otherwise. Pride must be surrendered and that includes the pride of being too comfortable to join in whatever God is doing at the time. There is also the pride of our mind. "And my speech and my message were not in plausible words of wisdom, but in demonstration of the Spirit and of power, so that your faith might not rest in the wisdom of men but in the power of God" (1 Corinthians 2:4-5 ESV).

There is also the pride of analyzing everything, with the intent of staying in control of our relationship with God. Our pride can go as far as trying to set our own terms with God.

So when should we expect to be drawn out of our comfort zone?

- When other people are talking about change.
- When everything is okay around us.
- When we are in need.
- When we are open to what God is doing.
- When a teachable heart is present.
- When the river of our soul is dry.
- When we are not being challenged spiritually.

Early on, in my walk with Jesus, I had to deal with my false assumptions about how God worked in my life. I had learned that I had at least four misbeliefs in my Christian faith:

1. Whatever God was doing, I had to understand it, or it is not from him.
2. The Holy Spirit will never do anything against my will.
3. If it is truly God, I will not be afraid.
4. God is tidy and is always proper.

If we press into his presence, we can learn to lay these false assumptions on the altar, using the Word of God as the blueprint and then ask the Holy Spirit to call us out of our spiritual comfort zones. We want to allow him to bring us into a deeper walk of obedience to him. How do we learn to walk out this life of radical obedience to our Father God? How then do we step out of our complacency and into a life of complete surrender to the cross?

First, receive and step out in faith.
"Now it is evident that no one is justified before God by the law, for 'The righteous shall live by faith'" (Galatians 3:11 ESV).

Second, learn to take risks.
"And without faith it is impossible to please him, for whoever would draw near to God must believe that he exists and that he rewards those who seek him" (Hebrews 11:6 ESV).

Third, be persistent.
"And Elijah said to Elisha, 'Please stay here, for the LORD has sent me as far as Bethel.' But Elisha said, 'As the LORD lives, and as you yourself live, I will not leave you.' So they went down to Bethel" (2 Kings 2:2 ESV).

"So he departed from there and found Elisha the son of Shaphat, who was plowing with twelve yoke of oxen in front of him, and he was with the twelfth. Elijah passed by him and cast his cloak upon him. And he left the oxen and ran after Elijah and said, 'Let me kiss my father and my mother, and then I will follow you.' And he said to him, 'Go back again, for what have I done to you?' And he returned from following him and took the yoke of oxen and sacrificed them and boiled their flesh with the yokes of the oxen and gave it to the people, and they ate. Then he arose and went after Elijah and assisted him" (1 Kings 19:19-21 ESV).

Fourth, come to him as a child.
"At that time the disciples came to Jesus, saying, 'Who is the greatest in the kingdom of heaven?' And calling to him a child, he put him in the midst of them and said, 'Truly, I say to you, unless you turn and become like children, you will never enter the kingdom of heaven'" (Matthew 18:1-3 ESV).

Fifth, press in and take what God offers.

Sixth, learn to soak in the Spirit.
"And no one puts new wine into old wineskins. If he does, the new wine will burst the skins and it will be spilled, and the skins will be destroyed. But new wine must be put into fresh wineskins" (Luke 5:37-38 ESV).

Seventh, trust God with yourself. Then GO for the Kingdom!
Stay hungry for more of God, count the cost, and pay the price. Step out into his strength. Ask God for direction, then run with him!

I learned as a boy that Jesus died to have a love affair with me. I learned that the highest place in the heavens is on my knees, at his feet!

Here is a challenge—ask God for opportunities to follow him out of your comfort zone every day this coming week:

When you step out...
- You will be surprised.
- God will meet your need specifically where you are at.
- You will move out from faith into experience.
- God will reveal his character.
- You will develop a deeper attitude of gratitude.
- You will welcome doors to open in the future because you will have had firsthand knowledge that God always keeps his written and spoken Word.

16
THE ROYAL LAW OF LOVE

"God is moving us from a people who are only interested
in a visitation,
to a people who are hungry for a habitation."
– Leif Hetland[1]

The Father's love saved my life. I struggled as a young boy with self-hatred from my childhood sexual trauma. I was raised in an extraverted family where my introversion wasn't validated or nurtured. I hated myself because I wasn't living a life worthy enough to have been spared from death from my cliff accident. Someone else perished, and I had lived. I struggled continuously to make my life count.

During my mother's illness, my ability to trust joy was diminished despite the great deal of joy in my early years growing up. When my mother's diagnosis hit our family, I began to fear joy, even the Lord's joy. In Tim Sledge's groundbreaking work in his book *Making Peace with Your Past: Help for Adult Children of Dysfunctional Families*, he writes:

The Process of Shame's Work

1. Shame comes from growing up in a dysfunctional family.
2. The shame develops into a shame-based identity.
3. The shame-based identity begins to have a drastic impact on thoughts and actions.
4. Some behavior creates its own shame.
5. One learns to deny the presence of shame in life, using various tools of denial.[2]

As I slowly healed in the early years, I learned to trust the Father's joy in my life. In fact, he began to teach me that the joy of the Lord was my strength (Nehemiah 8:10 ESV). I also began to learn how my family fostered the fear of joy. The irony was that none of us knew that this was happening at the time. These are some of the traits in families that fear joy:

1. They are unpredictable.
2. They are not sure that the future will come to pass.
3. They do a lot of waiting.
4. They may produce people who think both well and poorly of themselves.
5. They may foster a desire to prove self-worth through achievements.
6. They encourage wearing masks.
7. They may not esteem heroes.
8. They live on the emotions of one or more focal family members.[3]

I had to claim the joy of the Lord as a major battleground in my life. I had to go after it and seek it with all my heart. I have always found it in his presence. "You will make known to me the path of life; In Your presence is fullness of joy; In Your right hand there are pleasures forever" (Psalm 16:11 NASB).

I began to learn to move beyond the fear of joy by addressing these three issues learned from Tim Sledge's book:

1. I had to ask myself the following the question, "On whom am I depending?"
2. I had to learn to clean out the closets of my past.
3. I had to learn to live in the here and now.[4]

After my mother's diagnosis when I was in the ninth grade, I lost part of my youth. I learned to become a caretaker. I learned that children who have come out of trauma put on armor. They become bulletproof. I learned that to survive, I had to turn off my emotions. I learned to survive in a difficult family situation due to the alcoholism and cancer.

In order to heal, I had to address my past. I had to learn to allow the Lord to speak into the areas of my life where there was loss. I had to be intentional in remembering the positive memories of my past. And lastly, I had to develop a childlike faith.

As a boy, I hated myself because of my bald spots on my head, my teeth, and my speech problems. In my adolescence, I drank alcohol to cover up my feelings of inadequacies and my feelings of shame and worthlessness because of the traumas. Deep down, I felt that I was unworthy of love. Then Jesus opened the door of my heart, and I let him come in. He showed me what love is. Jesus has taught me that love is the currency of heaven. His love for me has transformed me.

> "If you really fulfill the royal law according to the Scripture, 'You shall love your neighbor as yourself,' you are doing well" (James 2:8 ESV).

Learning to love ourselves and loving others has a ring of nobility connected to it. It is both a royal and a legal mandate from God the Father.

"For God so loved the world, that he gave his only Son, that whoever believes in him should not perish but have eternal life" (John 3:16 ESV).

God himself modeled this action when He sent Jesus to come and live among us.

There was a man named John who followed Jesus during his earthly ministry. John was one of Jesus' disciples and a man who knew Jesus intimately. He was there when Jesus performed some of the biggest miracles. John saw things that I could only long for. John was known as the 'Beloved'. Many believe that John was Jesus' best friend. Of all the things that John could write about and use specific words to describe Jesus, he chose one word, love.

"Beloved, let us love one another, for love is from God, and whoever loves has been born of God and knows God. Anyone who does not love does not know God, because God is love" (1 John 4:7-8 ESV).

John uses the word "love" more than twenty-five times in the fourth chapter of 1 John.

The Apostle Paul wrote to the believers in Corinth, "Be watchful, stand firm in the faith, act like men, be strong. Let all that you do be done in love" (1 Corinthians 16:13-14 ESV).

Paul wrote again in the letter to the Galatians, "For the whole law is fulfilled in one word: 'You shall love your neighbor as yourself.'" (Galatians 5:14 ESV).

Paul told Timothy, "The aim of our charge is love that issues from a pure heart and a good conscience and a sincere faith" (1 Timothy 1:5 ESV).

The apostle Peter wrote, "Above all, keep loving one another earnestly, since love covers a multitude of sins" (1 Peter 4:8 ESV).

Jesus himself said, "And because lawlessness will be increased, the love of many will grow cold" (Matthew 24:12 ESV) (referring to the end times).

Do you love your enemies? As I ask this question, I am reminding you and me that love is a command. In the books of the New Testament, love is always the theme!

Love is the mark of the Christian. It's not about crosses around our necks, or bumper stickers on our vehicles. It's not whether or not we are in a particular Bible study, or youth group, or attend a specific church. It's never been about charismatic phenomena, speaking in tongues, prophecy, or whatever. "A new commandment I give to you, that you love one another: just as I have loved you, you also are to love one another. By this all people will know that you are my disciples, if you have love for one another" (John 13:34-35 ESV).

> "As the Father has loved me, so have I loved you. Abide in my love. If you keep my commandments, you will abide in my love, just as I have kept my Father's commandments and abide in his love. These things I have spoken to you, that my joy may be in you, and that your joy may be full.
>
> This is my commandment, that you love one another as I have loved you. Greater love has no one than this, that someone lay down his life for his friends. You are my friends if you do what I command you. No longer do I call you servants, for the servant does not know what his master is doing; but I have called you friends, for all that I have heard from my Father I have made known to you. You did not choose me, but I chose you and appointed you that you should go and bear fruit and that your fruit should abide, so that whatever you ask the Father in my name, he may give it to you. These things I command you, so that you will love one another" (John 15:9-17 ESV).

So how much should we love others? The answer is simple, just how God loves us! The answer is really that simple.

Did you know that Jesus gives the world the right to judge our love? In America, sixty years ago, non-believers had a higher moral standard than the church has today. Think about it!

There are several types of love in the Greek language used in the first century.

> **Philia:** a "friendship" or a "social" type of love. It represents tender affection. Phileo is never used in a command to men to love God; it is, however, used as a warning in 1 Corinthians 16:22. It is an unselfish love, ready to serve. It is the word of genuine affection—heart love. It is seen in the name, Philadelphia (brotherly love). Jesus had this kind of love for his closest disciple, John (John 20:2) and for Lazarus (John 11:3).

> **Eros:** generally having to do with sexual love. From this term derives the English word "erotic." This word, however, is never found in the New Testament.

> **Storge:** a "maternal" type of love. This term was primarily employed of family affection.

> **Agape:** Love of a willing choice. A spirit that sees the other person as good no matter what they have done.

The word Agape is used in the New Testament to describe the attitude of God toward his Son. This word is used to convey his will to his children concerning their attitude toward one another and toward all men. It's also used to express the essential nature of God.

Love can be known only from the action that it prompts. It was an exercise of divine will in deliberate choice. Love had its perfect expression among men in the Lord Jesus Christ.

> "For the love of Christ controls us, because we have concluded this: that one has died for all, therefore all have died" (2 Corinthians 5:14 ESV).

> "But God, being rich in mercy, because of the great love with which he loved us, even when we were dead in our trespasses,

made us alive together with Christ—by grace you have been saved—" (Ephesians 2:4–5 ESV).

In respect of the word agapeo as used of God, it expresses the deep and constant love and interests of a perfect being towards entirely unworthy objects, producing and fostering a reverential love in them toward the giver and a practical love towards those who are partakers of the same, and a desire to help others to seek the giver.

The source of this quote has been disputed over the years, but it's message is timeless and potent. "Go out and preach the Gospel, and if you must, use words."[5]

But it's hard to love others who get under our skin!

"Love does not die easily. It is a living thing. It thrives in the face of all life's hazards, save one – neglect."[6]

The Church has had a difficult time over the centuries with the Biblical truth of sacrificial love. It goes against our nature. Our old self shows his ugly face from time to time and we find ourselves making inner vows that we will not love our enemies.

The very Spirit of Christ that dwells within us then begins to weep because within his character, at the inner core of his heart, radiates unconditional, selfless, sacrificial love. Because of a lack of love in the way of interactions with each other, denominations have been formed. Until we begin to see that love covers a multitude of sins, that to "love one another" is at the very core of the Christian life, there will be no unity in church of Jesus Christ.

There are many reasons why we choose to not love others. The first and foremost reason is that we all get in the way of what God wants to do. I'm talking about the rooms that we have in our own hearts where we don't allow the Lord to look at and to deal with. Remember what's in the middle of sin? It's the big "I."

Another reason why we choose not to love others is because of our own fear. Anxiety is also rooted in fear. If we step out of our comfort zone, many of us have a belief that we're going to get hurt or even punished for doing so. Fear keeps us from moving in the life of God and has a tendency to stop us dead in our tracks and makes us look into ourselves. When we end up doing that, we make the choice to not step into the path that has been made by God. The misbelief that rattles around within our thinking is this: "I'm going to screw up; I'm going to fail." Some of us come from families where we were never given permission to fail. Some of us have come out of abusive homes in past relationships where we have learned to fear as a way to survive. The apostle John wrote these words, "There is no fear in love, but perfect love casts out fear. For fear has to do with punishment, and whoever fears has not been perfected in love" (1 John 4:18 ESV).

Another reason why we choose not to love others or ourselves is because of pride and jealousy. Some of us say words like, "I just can't, and I won't love that person because I'm better than that. I will not go down that low. I can't love those who have hurt me. I'm not going to do this, and I'm not going to let my hurt go. I am going to hang onto my pride, it has gotten me this far. I can't love those who are less fortunate than me. It's too awkward, and I just don't have it in me."

I am indebted to a handful of friends who chose to come alongside me and show love to me when I was so lost and afraid in the days of my youth. So many people went the extra mile for me and loved on me when I didn't deserve it. They chose not to turn their back, but intentionally entered my world. They all knew that I was a mess, but they offered kind words, encouraging support, and their smiles and laughter. They saved my life.

To honestly look at the royal law of love and Jesus' command to love others, we need to start with the fact that we do not have the capability or the capacity to love by ourselves. But I know someone who can show us the way. For those of us who have surrendered our lives to Jesus, we know that he lives in the center of our being. He is known as Messiah, the carpenter from Nazareth, whose name is Jesus. He has given us the power to love those who have hurt us and even anoints us to love the unloving. Through the Spirit of the living God, he can teach us how to love the unloving, even the perpetrators in our lives, and all those who have brought harm to us through their acts of betrayals. If we allow him, God the Father can, and will, even enable us to Agape others, to love others. In my own journey, I have learned that he delights to come into our broken relationships to become the bridge, when we make the choice to love others with his love. His unconditional love that has been poured out upon us through Jesus Christ is the greatest force in the universe. God's unconditional love can take a heart of stone and make it flesh. His unconditional love has the ability to take something that was meant for evil and make it a blessing. His love can bring something that was dead and bring it back to life. It can heal anything that has been destroyed. God's unconditional love brings hope to the hopeless, and life to the lifeless. It happened to me, it could happen to you. To love others in this way, is a command in scripture.

> "And this commandment we have from him: whoever loves God must also love his brother" (1 John 4:21 ESV).

In all of the books in the New Testament, love is always the theme. This love is not necessarily seen by the crosses Christians wear around their necks, the bumper stickers posted on the back of their cars, or the magnets on their refrigerators. Nothing is more powerful in heaven's arsenal than the unconditional love of God the Father. Love is the currency of heaven. God is love, and love always draws in the lost. God's unconditional love will be the greatest single tool that will bring a town to Christ, thus fulfilling the great commission.

In order for that to happen, we need to heal. Believers need to heal. Some have made decisions to not love certain people for whatever reasons and have many justifications for that decision. But the truth is that a mighty outpouring of God's love will change both believers and nonbelievers. In truth, to love one another is a challenge. Only by seeing God's people obeying his commandments to love one another in the manner described in the royal law, written in the book of James, will other people see Jesus. A Christian is the only person who could love the person he doesn't like. What if the following statement is really true?

> Take the person you love the least, and that's the maximum love you have for Jesus Christ.

> "A new commandment I give to you, that you love one another: just as I have loved you, you also are to love one another. By this all people will know that you are my disciples, if you have love for one another" (John 13:34-35 ESV).

The question that is before all of us is this: how much should I love? The answer is simple, as much as God loves me. Am I willing to be God's pipeline of his unconditional Agape to those around me? Walking with Jesus means that we understand that we were created to be a living example of what happens when the love of God transforms a human being—totally embraced in the reality of being wrapped up in, motivated by, and empowered by the love of God the Father. In essence, we are kingdom dispensers in this world. The Father's love is sacrificial, unconditional, giving, and selfless. The apostle Paul writes in 1 Corinthians 13 that love is to be our aim. Paul also wrote to the church in Rome the following words, "but God shows his love for us in that while we were still sinners, Christ died for us" (Romans 5:8 ESV).

New Christians may find it difficult to accept the fact that God loves them just as they are because much of the world operates by conditional love, which offers approval and acceptance on the basis of performance. So, in coming to Christ, there is often a natural tendency to assume the necessity to strive to deserve our blessings, such as monetary wealth, loving families, and solid careers. Divine love, however, can never be earned by human effort. Absolutely nothing can be done to make God love more or less (see Romans 5:8, and 1 John 4:8). The problem is that many of us understand this intellectually, but have trouble believing it deep down in our hearts.

I talk about the love of God everywhere I go around the world. The people who know me well know that I can't stop talking about God's unconditional love for us. No matter what has occurred in the past or what is happening right now, our Abba's love has been freely given. God pours his love upon us without exception—no ifs, ands, or buts about this issue. He did not begin to love you at the moment you invited him into your life. Nor did he begin to love you when you first started to go to church or when you rose from the baptismal waters. In truth, God never started to love you. He simply always has. From the creation of the world, God knew you and loved you. In return, Abba tells us to do the same:

"We love because he first loved us" (1 John 4:19 ESV).

Also, consider what King David wrote in the Psalms:

"Where shall I go from your Spirit?
Or where shall I flee from your presence?
If I ascend to heaven, you are there!
If I make my bed in Sheol, you are there!
If I take the wings of the morning
and dwell in the uttermost parts of the sea,
even there your hand shall lead me,
and your right hand shall hold me.
If I say, 'Surely the darkness shall cover me,
and the light about me be night,'
even the darkness is not dark to you;
the night is bright as the day,
for darkness is as light with you.
For you formed my inward parts;
you knitted me together in my mother's womb.
I praise you, for I am fearfully and wonderfully made.
Wonderful are your works;
my soul knows it very well" (Psalm 139:7-14 ESV).

Are you rejoicing in the father's love, or are you withdrawn and depressed? Do you exude peace, or do others see you as anxious? Is your life characterized by power and purpose, or by fear? Recognizing the amazing truth of God's unconditional love is life-changing. Prayerfully open your arms to his powerful love today.

17

THE THINGS THAT I'VE LEARNED

When I left the congregational ministry in 1987, the Lord led me into the field of mental health. I worked for over four years in an in-patient hospital working with children and adolescents who were struggling with multiple diagnostic issues, and with adults who struggled with sexual addiction. In 1990, after four years, I became a Licensed Independent Clinical Social Worker, and started my private practice. During the time when I worked in hospitals, I had the privilege of being supervised and trained by some of the most gifted clinicians in the Twin Cities. Because of the training involved for licensure, I had the opportunity to work through my issues with people that I trusted. To be licensed in the state of Minnesota, I had to participate in four thousand hours of supervision and training. That is almost two solid years of therapy, training, and supervision. I am constantly learning and growing in my field. First and foremost, I had to address my deep-seated pain and character flaws as someone who grew up in an alcoholic family. Slowly, the Lord began to show me what I had learned in my family, where alcohol was the drug of choice. My healing started when I embraced my identity in who I was in Christ. I let go of the past, and who I was in the past, a person who was filled with a world of hurt. I realized that my attempts at cleaning up the old me was like giving a corpse plastic surgery (see Galatians 2:17-21). The old me was crucified with Christ. He didn't just die for me, he died as me. I learned to ignore my old nature. I learned that the struggle with the old me was over and that I no longer had to fight something that was dead. I knew that any future work of inner transformation was going to come from a renewed mindset. In her groundbreaking work, Dr. Janet G. Woititz identifies thirteen traits of adult children of alcoholics. The Lord was relentless in his dealings with me in the given areas listed below:

1. We become approval seekers and lose our identity in the process.
2. We are frightened by angry people and any personal criticism.
3. We either become alcoholics, marry them, or both, or find another compulsive habit such as being a workaholic to fulfill our sick abandonment needs.
4. We live life from the viewpoint of victims, and we are attracted by that weakness in our love and friendship relationships.
5. We have an overdeveloped sense of responsibility, and it is easier for us to be concerned with others rather than ourselves; this enables us not to look too closely at our own faults, etc.
6. We get guilt feelings when we stand up for ourselves instead of giving in to others.
7. We become addicted to excitement.
8. We confuse love and pity and believe we love people when we actually pity or rescue them.
9. We have stuffed our feelings from our traumatic childhoods and lost the ability to feel or express our feelings because it hurts so much (denial).
10. We judge ourselves harshly and have a very low sense of self-esteem.

11. We are dependent personalities who are terrified of abandonment and will do anything to hold on to a relationship in order not to experience painful abandonment feelings, which we received from living with sick people who were never there emotionally for us.
12. Alcoholism is a family disease; and we become para-alcoholics and took on the characteristics of that disease even though we did not pick up the drink.
13. Para-alcoholics are reactors rather than actors.[1]

I learned early on when I first met Jesus, that the mind is the battleground. Thoughts are the battle bullets. The Apostle Paul wrote that a good thought life is the believer's first step to the pursuit of holiness. He said in Romans 12:1-2 (ESV), "I appeal to you therefore, brothers, by the mercies of God, to present your bodies as a living sacrifice, holy and acceptable to God, which is your spiritual worship. Do not be conformed to this world, but be transformed by the renewal of your mind, that by testing you may discern what is the will of God, what is good and acceptable and perfect."

If thinking is negative in the beginning, chances are that behavior will reflect that negativity in the finish. With the Lord's help, followers need to control their own thought life or thoughts will be the controllers. Thoughts of today are previews of coming attractions tomorrow, every thought must be taken captive to the obedience of Christ (2 Corinthians 10:4-5 ESV).

Please consider a few suggestions on how to control thoughts:[2]

> **Pray.** The first step is to pray, asking God to help us control our thinking (Philippians 4:6-8 ESV).
>
> **Meditate on the Word of God.** Our minds are like recording tapes. We have recorded a bad past and bad thoughts. Think good thoughts (Philippians 4:8 ESV).

Memorize scripture. King David wrote, "I have stored up your word in my heart, that I might not sin against you" (Psalm 119:11 ESV).

Know God. Our lives should be centered in discovering God. Make a commitment to get to know his character and his nature.

Keep a record of past encounters. The Bible is a full record of the faithfulness of God. God has not changed. Trace the encounters of God's faithfulness in your own life. Discover the face of Christ in all your ups and downs. Keep a personal notebook. Remember what God has done.

Become accountable. Jesus never sent a disciple on a mission alone. We need one another.

Sing aloud to God. Under the oppression of adversity Martin Luther said, "Let's sing a Psalm and startle the devil." When we worship, we learn to practice the beholding-becoming principle (2 Corinthians 3:18 ESV). When we worship, we learn to behold the King of Ages. We become what we behold. God inhabits the praises of his people (Psalm 22:3 ESV).

Practice what you know. "Do not merely listen to the word, and so deceive yourselves. Do what it says" (James 1:22 New International Version). Practice what you know. Gain control of your thoughts, and your life will take shape.

As we grow in our faith and in emotional wellness, we need to be aware of the roadblocks to our growth. Here are five that I teach my patients in my clinical practice.

1. Busyness
2. Resistance
3. False Assumptions

4. Distractions
5. Fear[3]

These five roadblocks will always keep us from moving into the next breakthrough. I'd like to propose that what we need to do, is to learn to move in the opposite spirit and emotion when these roadblocks come up. So, instead of busyness, we ask the Lord to move us into his rest. Instead of resistance, we yield to his hand, instead of living a life of false assumptions, we embrace the truth of his Word in the scriptures. Instead of distractions, we focus on the one thing, and that's him. Instead of fear, we embrace his love for us. It will always be easier to take care of other people than to take care of ourselves. As I tell my patients when we talk about learning about self-care, an empty cup can't fill an empty cup. God is more concerned with the condition of our hearts, than he is our behavior because he knows that once he has our hearts, eventually everything else will follow.

I learned early on in my spiritual journey with Jesus that prayer, worship, and reading scripture are the most effective ways that I deal with my periodic anxiety and ongoing sensory issues. There is also a powerful principle known as the 'Beholding/Becoming' principle. It's a very simple truth. We become what we behold. Whatever we choose to look upon will eventually have an impact on us. When I am in a place of anxiety, depression, or sensory overload, I choose to look to Jesus. Over the years, and through my training, I have learned a great deal about the topic of self-soothing skills. These skills have helped me in my own struggle with anxiety and periodic revisits of PTSD. I have found that there are two things that can lower the stress hormone known as cortisol in my body during these times. The first one is diaphragmatic breathing. This is done by contracting the diaphragm, a muscle located between the thoracic cavity and abdominal cavity. When breathing is done this way, air enters the lungs and the belly expands. Our cortisol level decreases when we learn to breath this way. Every time we breath in, we activate the sympathetic nervous system in our body which is responsible for our fight, flight, or freeze responses. Every time we exhale, we activate the parasympathetic nervous system, which is responsible for our need to 'rest and digest.' The second tool that has helped me are self-soothing exercises. When we use our five senses to relax, our body will respond accordingly, and our cortisol levels will decrease as well. I teach my clients to make five separate lists, one for each of our five senses of sight, hearing, taste, touch, and smell. I teach them to try to label at least three things on each list that works for them to help them to relax. When they become stressed, they have the list to fall back on.

In my clinical practice, I teach my patients different principles surrounding the topics of mindfulness. Mindfulness is a state of active, open attention on the present. When you're mindful, you observe your thoughts and feelings from a distance, without judging them good or bad. Instead of letting your life pass you by, mindfulness means living in the moment and awakening to experience.

Here are some words that are connected to mindfulness:

1. Non-judging
2. Patience
3. Beginner's Mind
4. Trust
5. Non-striving
6. Acceptance
7. Letting Go
8. Gratitude[4]

In order for me to heal and to come to terms with my past, I had to understand one thing taught by Dr. Henry Cloud, "We change our behavior when the pain of staying the same becomes greater than the pain of changing."[5] I needed to learn to take responsibility for my choices and behavior. I also had to look deep into my own motivation and learn to overcome the secondary gains. In other words, to identify the issues that kept me stuck, I had to look at the reasons why I was stuck. I had learned in my training that all behavior has a social purpose. I eventually had to make a commitment to follow through with things and have a willingness to take risks. Lastly, I needed to stop 'flying by the seat of my pants' and, with the help of the Holy Spirit, I had to define and visualize my goals for the future.

In their book *The Freedom from Depression Workbook*, Les Carter, PhD and Frank Minirth, MD share twelve points in helping people walk out of depression. Their points are listed below:

1. Be aware of the indicators that tell you that changes are needed.
2. Know that anger can be uncovered and choices can be made regarding its purpose.
3. Become committed to healthy boundaries and assertions.
4. Believe in yourself. Know your worth and value as a person.
5. Refuse to be a perpetual victim of past or present abuse.
6. Allow time for natural grief to run its course.
7. Know that the best way to be in control is to resist the craving to be in control.
8. Make allowances for painful truths.
9. Understand how your personality can predispose you to depressive feelings.
10. Be open minded as you consider the medical aspects of depression.
11. Reveal your struggles with thoughts of death. Allow others to know you thoroughly.
12. Be committed to positive attitudes that can bring balance to your emotions.[6]

I teach in therapy that anger turned inward often converts into depression. Our anger is always connected to unmet expectations.

Our anger is also fueled by feelings of rejection and invalidation. With that said, most important is that we need to know that our anger points us to our vulnerabilities and our feeling unprotected. I had to learn skills to help me when I was feeling vulnerable and when I needed to feel secure. Once I learned that my anger was not a bad thing, but that it is actually a God-given tool, I was able to use my anger as a tool and not a weapon. From early on, I had learned to implode when I felt anger. My father's rage had taught me to keep as many of my emotions inside as I could. Before my mother was diagnosed with cancer when I was fourteen years old, my anger was not an issue for me. When the diagnosis came, the family shifted. It's hard to explain, other than whatever emotions that we all had, all went below the surface. The unspoken rule was, "Let's not talk about what's right in front of us; yes, we all saw it, but we are not to speak about the cancer and our fears about losing our wife and our mother." Instead, there were rules that were set in place. Two of them, I remember well.

1. The good times will be enshrined, and the bad times will be forgotten.
2. If someone says, "There's a problem here", that person then becomes the problem.

For many years, I blamed my father for creating these sets of expectations in our family. Later in life, I realized that this was simply not the case. My mother was trying not to die. My father wanted to play, party, and make great memories just in case his wife should die. It was madness. In the midst of the chaos, I met Jesus. He began to speak truth to me, as he led me into his Word. Whatever small amount of trust I had in my family had shifted, and I slowly started to trust Jesus. It's been over forty years since I welcomed Jesus into my heart. He has never lied to me. He has always spoken his truth to me. He has never been mad at me or disappointed in me. There have been hundreds of times when he has brought me into encounters with him, where he has asked me to lay down my hurt, my grief, and my pain before him. When I have surrendered, he has always met me and has healed my heart, piece by piece.

Several years ago, when my aunt Dorie passed away, I made the decision to meet with a grief therapist and process her death. I was having several grief responses that were resurfacing in my life. I've never done grief very well. I made the decision to tell the therapist the cliff notes of my story. We met three or four times. I remember on one occasion, in one of our sessions, I was sitting on the sofa in his office. He was sitting on the floor, leaning up against the overstuffed chair sipping on his coffee. I don't remember what part of my story that I was telling, but I watched him put down his coffee and stare at me. He started to weep. I asked him, "What's wrong, why are you crying? You're not the one who is supposed to cry." He responded, "Your story is very, very sad. I am surprised that when you were a boy, there wasn't a homicide or even a suicide in your family." His response startled me. It was at that point I realized that in order to survive, I had turned off my emotions many years ago. I was simply telling him my story like I was telling someone the news. At that moment, in his office, I was determined to turn them back on again, no matter if I became a fool in the process.

There was one stone that the Lord wanted to take down off my wall. But I was resistant and it took a long time for my heart to begin to be open for his healing in this one area. I needed to forgive my father. My father's narcissistic injury occurred when he was a small boy, when he lost his father. I don't think that he ever fully recovered. The Lord began to speak into me a simple question, "How could your father ever give you what you needed, when he never received what he needed from his father?" Once I understood that, the healing came. Shortly after that revelation, I made the decision to forgive my dad. He had given me an extraordinary childhood. He gave me so many physical things. His gifts to me were his love language to me. I didn't see it until I was an older man. What I needed from him were his words. Later in life, he would always sign his birthday cards with, "I'm proud of you!" Because of my lack of forgiveness toward him, they were like an eyedropper of water dripping on a dried sponge. The Lord started to work on my heart. He started to show me that I needed to forgive my father, and he showed me some steps to follow. I am again grateful to Les Carter, PhD and Frank Minirth, MD for their material on the topic of forgiveness:

> I had to recognize wrong deeds to be wrong deeds.
> I had to recognize that my anger was not only normal, but necessary.
> I had to realize how ongoing bitterness was going to ultimately hurt me.
> I had to learn from my problems by establishing better boundaries in my life.
> I learned to refuse to be in an inferior position in my relationships and resist the desire to be superior.
> I learned to avoid the futility of judgments, letting God be the ultimate judge.
> I allowed myself permission to grieve.
> I learned the importance of confronting the injuring party if it was appropriate.
> I learned to find emotional freedom as I let go of the illusion of control.
> I made the decision to choose forgiveness because it is part of my life's mission.
> I had to come to terms with others' wrong deeds by recognizing my own need for forgiveness.
> And lastly, I made the choice to become a source of encouragement to other hurting people.[7]

Walking out these simple truths helped me to be set free. The late author H. Jackson Brown, Jr. described it well when he wrote,

> Twenty years from now you will be more disappointed by the things that you didn't do than by the ones you did do. So

throw off the bowlines. Sail away from the safe harbor. Catch the trade winds in your sails. Explore. Dream. Discover.[8]

I will end my writing here but before I do, let me leave you with some closing thoughts. The one main constant in my life has been Jesus. He has been my constant companion even through the darkest and happiest of times. I am so incredibly grateful that he saved me from myself and for what is to come. If you don't know him and want to, simply ask him to come into your life. Admit that you have sinned against him and turn to him. Then, believe in your heart that he can save you. Confess with your lips that you have surrendered your life to him. You have to tell someone. You can't do this journey by yourself. Talk to him through prayer. It's called conversation. Tell him everything that is on your heart. Lastly, get into a Bible study or a Bible fellowship that is committed to studying the Bible. Trust me on this, he is the Author and the Finisher of your faith. He will see you through to the end, and then he will be there at the finish line and you will see his smile.

EPILOGUE

As we come full circle, I want to bring you back to the point in time when my father called me and asked for my forgiveness and told me that I had lived an extraordinary childhood. I am grateful for my parents. As I reflect on bringing my writing to a close, I am thankful for my parents, as they taught me how to live life to its fullest. I love my family, and I hold no ill feelings toward them. I have no regrets. I have learned that when I surrendered my life to Jesus as a teenager, I had already experienced his encounters. Having encounters with my Abba has been an ongoing source of encouragement and strength in my life. He has spoken to me through his scriptures time and time again. I have been grateful throughout my life that he has pursued me. Even when I was in a place of doubt and fear, he has been relentless in showing me his kindness and faithfulness.

Recently in a therapy session, I mentioned that Jesus is less concerned about our sin and shortcomings than we are. Now that is grace. Over the last forty-two years of walking with Jesus, I have never met anyone who has been more kind, gracious, and loving toward me. I have gotten to know him through many experiences. Each encounter that I've had with God because of his Son Jesus and through his Holy Spirit, has changed me and brought me to a place of wanting more. His encounters with me, through his Word, have contained the seeds to change and set me free. I have learned so many things in my walk with Jesus, so let me leave you with one more word of encouragement. Be brave with your life. You won't regret it.

One summer afternoon, while I was writing this book, I met with my cousins who live in the Twin Cities to talk about what they wanted me to write about regarding our family's history of alcoholism. We spent the afternoon looking at pictures and telling stories of our parents and grandparents. We talked about our individual pain from living with an alcoholic parent. I asked them if there was anything that they wanted me to say in this writing. They responded with this statement: "Please tell the readers, especially the young readers, the three C's: We didn't cause it, we can't control it, and we can't cure it."

I am a boy from Wollochet Bay, and this has been my story, and it continues...

NOTES

Introduction

Chapter 1   The Early Years
1. Wikipedia contributors, "J. P. Patches," *Wikipedia, The Free Encyclopedia*, Wikimedia Foundation, Inc., modified December 7. 2016, accessed January 18, 2017, <en.wikipedia.org/wiki/J._P._Patches>.

"J.P. Patches (full name: Julius Pierpont Patches) was a clown portrayed by Seattle entertainer Chris Wedes (April 3, 1928 – July 22, 2012). The J.P. Patches Show was one of the longer-running locally produced children's television programs in the United States, having appeared on Seattle TV station KIRO channel 7 from 1958 to 1981. The show was live, unrehearsed improv with rarely more than two live actors on screen (Wedes and Bob Newman) but with frequent contributions from the sound effects man and off-camera crew.

J.P. Patches hosted his show twice a day every weekday for 13 years (plus Saturdays), then for the next 8 years did the morning show only, and finally for the last 2 years appeared on Saturday mornings only—for a total of over 10,000 hours of on-air time. The show premiered on April 5, 1958, as the second program ever broadcast by KIRO-TV, the first being a telecast of the explosion of Ripple

Rock in Seymour Narrows, British Columbia, Canada. The show was immensely popular in the Puget Sound area and southwestern British Columbia, with children as well as their parents, who enjoyed J.P.'s frequent use of double entendre and sly subversiveness. Two generations of viewers grew up as "Patches Pals", sharing the joyful zany antics of J.P. with their kids. At the peak of its run, the Emmy-winning program had a viewership of over 100,000 in its local markets."

2. Franklin Silverman, "Stuttering and Other Fluency Disorders," in *Stuttering and Other Fluency Disorders Third Edition* (Long Grove, IL: Waveland Press, 2004).

3. Greg Lange, "Earthquake rattles Western Washington on April 29, 1965.", *www.historylink.org*, posted March 2, 2000, modified May 5 2011, www.historylink.org/File/1986.

Chapter 2   Alpental

Chapter 3   My Introduction to Wollochet Bay
1. Josh McDowell and Bob Hostetler, *Josh McDowell's Handbook on Counseling Youth* (Dallas, TX: Word Publishing, 1996), p. 466.

Chapter 4   Peninsula High School
1. Brené Brown, *The Gifts of Imperfection* (Center City, MN: Hazelden Books, 2010), p. 26.

2. Tim Sledge, *Making Peace with Your Past: Help for Adult Children of Dysfunctional Families* (Nashville, TN: LifeWay Press, 1992), p .49.

3. Kristine Buffington, Carly B. Dierkhising, and Shawn C. Marsh, "Ten Things Every Juvenile Court Judge Should Know About Trauma and Delinquency," in *National Council of Juvenile*

and Family Court Judges (Reno, NV: National Council of Juvenile and Family Court Judges, 2010), www.ncjfcj.org/sites/default/files/trauma%20bulletin_1.pdf.

4. Jeff VanVonderen, "Breaking the Silence" (seminar presentation, 1990).

5. Charles Dickens, "Book the First: Recalled to Life" in *The Tale of Two Cities*, 1859, Unabridged, (Mineola, NY: Dover Publications, 1999), p. 1.

6. *The White Rabbit,* www.thewhiterabbit.net, 2017.

7. Erwin Raphael McManus, *The Artisan Soul: Crafting Your Life into a Work of Art* (New York, NY: HarperCollins, February 25, 2014), Kindle edition, pp. 3-4.

8. Erwin Raphael McManus, *The Artisan Soul: Crafting Your Life into a Work of Art* (New York, NY: HarperCollins, February 25, 2014), Kindle edition, p. 7.

Chapter 5   Early Memories Living on the Bay
1. "The Ship" and "World War II", *ussmissouri.org*, accessed January 2017, https://ussmissouri.org/learn-the-history/the-ship, and https://ussmissouri.org/learn-the-history/world-war-ii-1.

Born in the midst of World War II, the shipyard workers at Brooklyn's New York Navy Yard constructed the battleship in time for her launch on January 29, 1944 and commissioning as the USS *Missouri* on June 11, 1944 with Capt. William M. Callaghan in command.

The USS *Missouri* was the third U.S. Navy ship to be named after the Show Me state and the fourth American warship* to bear the name - there was a Confederate *Missouri* that was captured by Union forces during the Civil War but never commissioned as a United States Ship (USS).

*In the merchant fleet there were other ships named *Missouri*.

On September 2, 1945, in Tokyo Bay aboard the USS *Missouri*, representatives of the Allied and Axis powers met in solemn ceremony to "conclude an agreement by which peace can be restored". Following General Douglas MacArthur's introductory speech, representatives of the Empire of Japan were directed to step forward and sign the two copies of the Instrument of Surrender. General MacArthur then signed on behalf of all the Allied powers followed by representatives of Allied nations in attendance. General MacArthur concluded the ceremony by saying: "Let us pray that peace be now restored to the world, and that God will preserve it always. These proceeding are closed!" With those words, World War II was over.

2. Used by permission of Sea of Glass Music ©2015, from the 1976 album *Glow in The Dark* by Chuck Girard. (1976 Good News Records, 8319 Lankershim Blvd., North Hollywood, CA. 91605. Published by Dunamis Music/ASCAP).

3. Wikipedia contributors, "The Red Balloon," *Wikipedia, The Free Encyclopedia*, Wikimedia Foundation, Inc., modified November 20, 2016, <en.wikipedia.org/wiki/The Red Balloon>.

4. Neil Anderson, "232 Your New Skipper," in *Freedom in Christ Ministries*, accessed Jan. 2017, www.ficm.org.uk/node/446.

Chapter 6   Camp Hahobas
1. Leif Hetland, *Healing the Orphan Spirit Revised Edition*. Sonship Series Book 1. (Peachtree City, GA: Leif Hetland, September 19, 2013), Kindle edition, p. 16.

Chapter 7 The Storm Clouds Gather

1. Bill Johnson, *When Heaven Invades Earth* (Shippensburg, PA: Destiny Image Publishers, 2003), Kindle edition, p. 1.

2. Graham Cooke, *Hiddenness & Manifestation* (Kent, England: Sovereign World, 2003), p.12.

Chapter 8 My Journal

Chapter 9 O Death, Where Is Your Sting?

1. Hope Edelman, *Motherless Daughters: The Legacy of Loss, 20th Anniversary Edition* (Boston, MA: Da Capo Lifelong Books, 2014), Kindle edition, locations 922-923.

2. Barry McGuire, "There Is a Peace", title song from the album, *Have You Heard?* (Sparrow Records, 1977).

3. Scott Wesley Brown, "You Make Me Feel," Published by Songward Music. Used by Permission of Scott Wesley Brown/ Songward Publishing.

Chapter 10 Leaving Home

1. Bill Johnson, *Experience the Impossible: Simple Ways to Unleash Heaven's Power on Earth* (Grand Rapids, MI: Baker Publishing Group, 2014), Kindle edition, p. 73.

2. The Archers, "Praise Him," from the album, *Things We Deeply Feel*, written by Billy Masters, Don Aldridge, (Waco, Texas: Light Records, a division of Lexicon Music, 1975).

3. T. D. Jakes, Twitter post, March 1, 2016, 9:00 p.m., https://twitter.com/bishopjakes/status/704894237213597697.

Chapter 11   The Summer at Alpental
1. Ernest Hemingway, *A Farewell to Arms* (1929), quote source: http://www.quotationspage.com/quote/34122.html.

2. Shane & Shane, "Psalm 139 (Far too Wonderful)" from the album *Psalms II* (Label: WellHouse Records. All rights reserved, © The Worship Initiative, 2015).

Chapter 12   A New Beginning

Chapter 13   Another Visit from an Old Adversary
1. Jaci Velasquez, "I Will Rest in You," songwriters Brent Thomas Bourgeois and Michelle L. Tumes, (published by Lyrics © Warner/Chappell Music, Inc., Universal Music Publishing, 1999), http://www.metrolyrics.com/i-will-rest-in-you-lyrics-jaci-velasquez.html.

2. Barry McGuire, "I Walked a Mile," from the album *To the Bride* (song written by Barry Mann, chorus taken from poem by Robert Browning Hamilton 1975), http://lyrics.wikia.com/wiki/Barry_McGuire:Walked_A_Mile.

3. John Maxwell, *Leadership Promises for Every Day: A Daily Devotional* (published by Countryman, a division of Thomas Nelson © 2003, p. 269, from the book *If Life is a Game, These are the Rules* written by Cherie Carter-Scott, Broadway Books, a division of Bantam Doubleday Dell Publishing Group © 1998).

Chapter 14   The Tales of Generations Gone By
1. "The Cornell University – Ezra Cornell: A Nineteenth-Century Life", *Cornell University Library Rare and Manuscript Collections*, modified June 5, 1996, rmc.library.cornell.edu/Ezra-exhibit/EC-life/EC-life-11.html.

2. "North Slope Walking Tour", *Historic Tacoma*, www.historic-tacoma.com/wp-content/uploads/2016/08/north_slope_walking_tour.pdf.

Chapter 15 Comfort Zones

1. Neale Donald Walsch, *Habitsforwellbeing.com*, accessed January 2017, http://www.habitsforwellbeing.com/20-quotes-to-inspire-personal-growth.

2. Jack Canfield, Goodreads Inc., accessed 2017, http://www.goodreads.com/quotes/495741-everything-you-want-is-on-the-other-side-of-fear.

3. Steve Camp, "Living Dangerously in the Hands of God," from the album *Justice* (Chatsworth, CA: The Sparrow Corporation, copyright 1988).

4. Winkie Pratney (lecture notes, YWAM DTS class, Tacoma, WA, 1980).

Chapter 16 The Royal Law of Love

1. Leif Hetland, *Healing the Orphan Spirit Revised Edition*. Sonship Series Book 1. (Peachtree City, GA: Leif Hetland, September 19, 2013), Kindle edition, p. 53.

2. Tim Sledge, *Making Peace with Your Past: Help for Adult Children of Dysfunctional Families* (Nashville, TN: LifeWay Press, 1992), p .58.

3. Tim Sledge, *Making Peace with Your Past: Help for Adult Children of Dysfunctional Families* (Nashville, TN: LifeWay Press, 1992), p .67.

4. Tim Sledge, *Making Peace with Your Past: Help for Adult Children of Dysfunctional Families* (Nashville, TN: LifeWay Press, 1992), p .81.

5. This quote has been widely used, but its origin is unknown.

6. James D Bryden, "James D. Bryden Quotes," *Quotes.net* (STANDS4 LLC, 2017), accessed January 22, 2017, <http://www.quotes.net/authors/James+D.+Bryden>.

Chapter 17   The Things That I've Learned
1. Janet G Woititz, *Adult Children of Alcoholics* (Pompano Beach, FL: Health Communications, 1983), p.4.

2. E. Langston Haygood, "It's All in Your Mind: Steps to Controlling Your Thought Life", *Campus Christian's Ministry*, posted May 6, 2014, accessed February, 2017), http://www.campuschristians.info/reading-library/its-all-in-your-mind.

3. Marc Lesser, *Less: Accomplishing More by Doing Less* (Novato, CA: New World Library, 2009).

4. Jon Kabat-Zinn, *Mindfulness Attitudes*, © 2017, accessed January, 2017, www.mindfulnessattitudes.com.

5. Henry Cloud and John Townsend, *Boundaries with Kids: When to Say YES, When to Say NO to Help Your Children Gain Control of Their Lives* (Grand Rapids, MI: Zondervan, 1998), p. 72.

6. Les Carter, PhD and Frank Minirth, MD, *The Freedom from Depression Workbook* (Nashville, TN: Thomas Nelson, 1995), p. xiii.

7. Les Carter, PhD and Frank Minirth, MD, *The Choosing to Forgive Workbook* (Nashville, TN: Thomas Nelson, 1997), p. xiii.

8. H. Jackson Brown, Jr., *P.S. I Love You* (Nashville, TN: Rutledge Hill, A Thomas Nelson Company, 1990), p.13.

Epilogue

CPSIA information can be obtained
at www.ICGtesting.com
Printed in the USA
BVOW08s1952050417
480434BV00001B/1/P